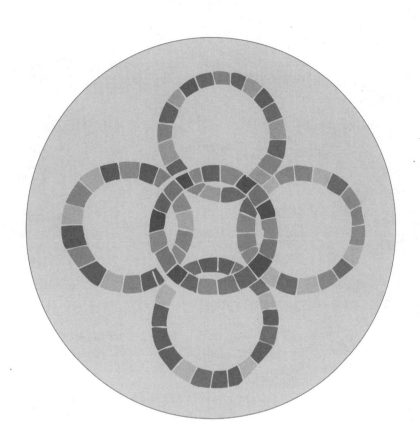

Quick-Guides to Inclusion

Quick-Guides to Inclusion

Ideas for Educating Students with Disabilities

SECOND EDITION

edited by

Michael F. Giangreco, Ph.D.   &   Mary Beth Doyle, Ph.D.

University of Vermont   St. Michael's College

with contributions by

Alfredo J. Artiles, Ph.D.
Barbara J. Ayres, Ph.D.
Donarae Cook, C.A.G.S.
Lia Cravedi, M.Ed.
Bridget Dalton, Ph.D.
Linda A. Davern, Ph.D.
Ruth E. Dennis, Ed.D., OTR/L
June E. Downing, Ph.D.
Janet M. Duncan, Ph.D.
Susan W. Edelman, Ed.D., PT
Karen A. Erickson, Ph.D.
Douglas Fisher, Ph.D.
Timothy Fox, M.Ed.

David Gordon, M.F.A.
Beth Harry, Ph.D.
Deborah L. Hedeen, Ph.D.
Cheryl M. Jorgensen, Ph.D.
David A. Koppenhaver, Ph.D.
Robi M. Kronberg, Ph.D.
Patricia A. Lee, Ph.D.
Deborah Lisi-Baker
Marie MacLeod, M.Ed., PT, CLT
John McDonnell, Ph.D.
Irene McEwen, PT, Ph.D.
Jayne McGuire, M.Ed.
Patricia McGonegal, M.A.

Marie-Christine Potvin, M.H.S., OTR
Patricia A. Prelock, Ph.D
Zach Rossetti, M.Ed.
George B. Salembier, Ed.D.
Richard Schattman, Ed.D.
Mary Schuh, Ph.D.
Katharine Shepherd, Ed.D.
Frank Sgambati, M.Ed.
Nancy Talbott, C.A.G.S.
Carol Tashie, M.Ed.
Alice Udvari-Solner, Ph.D.
Michael L. Wehmeyer, Ph.D.
Timothy J. Whiteford, Ph.D.

·P A U L·H·
BROOKES
PUBLISHING CO®

Baltimore · London · Sydney

Paul H. Brookes Publishing Co.
Post Office Box 10624
Baltimore, Maryland 21285-0624
www.brookespublishing.com

Typeset by Integrated Publishing Solutions, Grand Rapids, Michigan.
Manufactured in the United States of America by
Versa Press, Inc., East Peoria, Illinois.

All royalties from the sale of this book are donated to nonprofit groups or agencies that meet human needs.

All examples in this book are fictional based on composites of various people and circumstances or pseudonyms have been used. Any similarity to actual individuals or circumstances is coincidental and no implications should be inferred.

Gender specifications alternate throughout the text.

All cartoons are reprinted by permission. The cartoons appear in the following books by Michael F. Giangreco, all published by Peytral Publications, Minnetonka, Minnesota:
Ants in His Pants: Absurdities and Realities of Special Education (1998).
Flying by the Seat of Your Pants: More Absurdities and Realities of Special Education (1999).
Teaching Old Log News Tricks: More Absurdities and Realities of Education (2000).

Library of Congress Cataloging-in-Publication Data

Quick-guides to inclusion: Ideas for educating students with disabilities / edited by Michael F. Giangreco, Mary Beth Doyle; with contributions by Alfredo Artiles . . . [et al.].—2nd ed.
 p. cm.
ISBN-13: 978-1-55766-897-4
ISBN-10: 1-55766-897-3
1. Inclusive education—United States. 2. Students with disabilities—Education—United States.
I. Giangreco, Michael F., 1956– II. Doyle, Mary Beth. III. Title.
LC1201.Q53 2007
371.9′046—dc22   2007001319

British Library Cataloguing in Publication data are available from the British Library.

Contents

Section I: Foundational Ideas

Section II: Relationships & Self-Determination

Section III: Communication & Behavior

Section IV: Curriculum & Instruction

Section V: Literacy & Numeracy

Section VI: High School & Transition

Section VII: Personnel & Administration

Quick-Guide Extras

About the Editors

Michael F. Giangreco, Ph.D., Professor, College of Education and Social Services, University of Vermont, 208 Colchester Avenue, Mann Hall 301A, Burlington, VT 05405

Michael F. Giangreco has spent over 30 years working in a variety of capacities with children and adults with disabilities, their families, and service providers. Prior to joining the faculty at University of Vermont in 1988, he spent 13 years serving a variety of capacities (e.g., community residence counselor with adults with disabilities, special education teacher, special education administrator). His work focuses on various aspects of education for students with disabilities within general education classrooms, such as curriculum planning and adaptation, related services decision-making and coordination, and, most recently, paraprofessional issues. Dr. Giangreco is the author of numerous professional publications (e.g., books, research studies, journal articles) on a variety of special education topics and has published over 300 cartoons depicting educational issues and research findings.

Mary Beth Doyle, Ph.D., Associate Professor, Department of Education, St. Michael's College, 1 Winooski Park, Colchester, VT 05439

Mary Beth Doyle's primary work is in teacher preparation. She supports undergraduate and graduate students who are seeking initial teacher licensure at the secondary education level. In this capacity she has the opportunity to influence students who will ultimately be general education classroom teachers, who have the attitude and skills to support the inclusion of students with disabilities. Her additional areas of interest include paraprofessional support and training, as well as curriculum adaptations and accommodations to meet the needs of students with moderate and severe disabilities. Ultimately, Mary Beth Doyle's intention is to support teachers in creating welcoming classroom communities where children and youth are supported by a variety of adults.

Contributors

Alfredo J. Artiles, Ph.D.
Professor
Division of Curriculum and Instruction
Arizona State University
Farmer Education Building ED 244B
Post Office Box 2011
Tempe, AZ 85287
alfredo.artiles@asu.edu

Barbara J. Ayres, Ph.D.
Kindergarten Teacher
Raymore-Peculiar School District
Stonegate Elementary School
900 South Foxridge Drive
Raymore, MO 64083
bayres1@earthlink.net

Donarae Cook, C.A.G.S.
Director of Special Education
Washington West Supervisory Union
1673 Main Street, Suite A
Waitsfield, VT 05673
dcookwwsu@gmavt.net

Lia Cravedi, M.Ed.
Senior Lecturer
College of Education and Social Services
University of Vermont
406 Waterman Building
Burlington, VT 05405
lcravedi@uvm.edu

Bridget Dalton, Ph.D.
Chief Officer
Literacy and Technology
CAST Universal Design for Learning
40 Harvard Mills Square, Suite 3
Wakefield, MA 01880
bdalton@cast.org

Linda A. Davern, Ph.D.
Associate Professor
School of Education
The Sage Colleges
45 Ferry Street
Troy, NY 12180
daverL@sage.edu

Ruth E. Dennis, Ed.D., OTR/L
Research Assistant Professor
College of Education and Social
    Services
University of Vermont
Center on Disability and Community
    Inclusion
208 Colchester Avenue
Mann Hall 302A
Burlington, VT 05405
Ruth.Dennis@uvm.edu

June E. Downing, Ph.D.
Professor
College of Education
California State University, Northridge
18111 Nordhoff Street
Northridge, CA 91330
june.downing@csun.edu

Mary Beth Doyle, Ph.D.
Associate Professor
Department of Education
St. Michael's College
1 Winooski Park
Colchester, VT 05439
mdoyle@smcvt.edu

Janet M. Duncan, Ph.D.
Associate Professor and Department
    Chair
Foundations and Social Advocacy
State University of New York
College at Cortland
Cornish Hall D-226
Post Office Box 2000
Cortland, NY 13045
duncanj@cortland.edu

Susan W. Edelman, Ed.D., PT
Research Associate Professor
College of Education and Social
    Services
University of Vermont
Center on Disability and Community
    Inclusion
208 Colchester Avenue
Mann Hall 302A
Burlington, VT 05405
susan.edelman@uvm.edu

Karen A. Erickson, Ph.D.
Associate Professor and Director
Center for Literacy and Disability Studies
University of North Carolina at Chapel Hill
CB# 7335
Chapel Hill, NC 27599
Karen_Erickson@med.unc.edu

Douglas Fisher, Ph.D.
Professor
College of Teacher Education
San Diego State University
San Diego, CA 92182
dfisher@mail.sdsu.edu

Timothy Fox, M.Ed.
I-Team Coordinator
College of Education and Social Services
University of Vermont
Center on Disability and Community
    Inclusion
208 Colchester Avenue
Mann Hall 302A
Burlington, VT 05405
timothy.fox@uvm.edu

Michael F. Giangreco, Ph.D.
Professor
College of Education and Social
  Services
University of Vermont
Center on Disability and Community
  Inclusion
208 Colchester Avenue
Mann Hall 301A
Burlington, VT 05405
Michael.Giangreco@uvm.edu

David Gordon, M.F.A.
Director of Communications
CAST Universal Design for Learning
40 Harvard Mills Square, Suite 3
Wakefield, MA 01880
dgordon@cast.org

Beth Harry, Ph.D.
Professor
Department of Teaching and Learning
University of Miami
222 Merrick Building
Post Office Box 248065
Coral Gables, FL 33124
bharry@miami.edu

Deborah L. Hedeen, Ph.D.
Interim Dean
Professor
College of Education
Idaho State University
1550 East Terry Street
Pocatello, ID 83201
hededebo@isu.edu

Cheryl M. Jorgensen, Ph.D.
Research Assistant Professor
Institute on Disability
University of New Hampshire
10 West Edge Drive, Suite 101
Durham, NH 03824
cherylj@cisunix.unh.edu

David A. Koppenhaver, Ph.D.
Associate Professor
College of Education
Appalachian State University
124 Edwin Duncan Hall
Boone, NC 28608
koppenhaverd@appstate.edu

Robi M. Kronberg, Ph.D.
Consultant
4573 East Lake Circle North
Littleton, CO 80121
RMKronberg@aol.com

Patricia A. Lee, Ph.D.
Associate Professor Emeritus
University of Northern Colorado
10 Quedo Road
Santa Fe, NM 87508
pleesf@comcast.net

Deborah Lisi-Baker
Executive Director
Vermont Center for Independent Living
11 East State Street
Montpelier, VT 05602
deborah2@vcil.org

Marie MacLeod, M.Ed., PT, CLT
Research Associate
College of Education and Social Services
University of Vermont
Center on Disability and Community Inclusion
208 Colchester Avenue
Mann Hall 302A
Burlington, VT 05405
Marie.MacLeod@uvm.edu

John McDonnell, Ph.D.
Professor
College of Education
Department of Special Education
1705 East Campus Center Drive
221 MBH
Salt Lake City, UT 84112
mcdonnell@ed.utah.edu

Irene McEwen, PT, Ph.D.
George Lynn Cross Research Professor
Department of Rehabilitation Sciences
University of Oklahoma Health Sciences
  Center
Post Office Box 26901
Oklahoma City, OK 73190
irene-mcewen@ouhsc.edu

Jayne McGuire, M.Ed.
Doctoral Candidate
College of Education
Department of Special Education
1705 East Campus Center Drive
221 MBH
Salt Lake City, UT 84112
jayne.mcguire@utah.edu

Patricia McGonegal, M.A.
Director
National Writing Project in Vermont
University of Vermont
208 Colchester Avenue
Mann Hall 201
Burlington, VT 05405-1757
Patricia.McGonegal@uvm.edu

Marie-Christine Potvin, M.H.S., OTR
Research Associate
College of Education and Social Services
University of Vermont
Center on Disability and Community
  Inclusion
208 Colchester Avenue
Mann Hall 302A
Burlington, VT 05405
marie.potvin@uvm.edu

Patricia A. Prelock, Ph.D.
Professor and Chair
Department of Communication Sciences
University of Vermont
489 Main Street
407 Pomeroy Hall
Burlington, VT 05405
Patricia.prelock@uvm.edu

Zach Rossetti, M.Ed.
Doctoral Candidate
School of Education
Syracuse University
370 Huntington Hall
Syracuse, NY 13244
zsrosset@syr.edu

George B. Salembier, Ed.D.
Associate Professor
College of Education and Social Services
University of Vermont
499B Waterman Building
Burlington, VT 05405
george.salembier@uvm.edu

Richard Schattman, Ed.D.
Principal
Waitsfield Elementary School
3951 Main Street
Waitsfield, VT 05673
rschattman@madriver.com

Mary Schuh, Ph.D.
Associate Director
Institute on Disability
University of New Hampshire
10 Ferry Street, Box 14
Concord, NH 03301
mcschuh@cisunix.unh.edu

Katharine Shepherd, Ed.D.
Assistant Professor
College of Education and Social Services
University of Vermont
499B Waterman Building
Burlington, Vermont 05405
katharine.shepherd@uvm.edu

Frank Sgambati, M.Ed.
Research Associate
Institute on Disability
University of New Hampshire
10 Ferry Street, Box 14
Concord, NH 03301
fs@cisunix.unh.edu

Nancy Talbott, C.A.G.S.
Teacher Consultant
National Writing Project in Vermont
Co-Coordinator of Special Education
Addison Northeast Supervisory Union
10 Orchard Terrace Park
Bristol, VT 05443
nztalbott@aol.com

Carol Tashie, M.Ed.
Consultant
74 Baxter Street
Rutland, VT 05701
cztashie@yahoo.com

Alice Udvari-Solner, Ph.D.
Faculty Associate
Department of Curriculum and
   Instruction
University of Wisconsin–Madison
225 North Mills Street, Room 224A
Madison, WI 53706
alice@education.wisc.edu

Michael L. Wehmeyer, Ph.D.
Professor
Department of Special Education
Director
Kansas University Center on Developmental
   Disabilities
University of Kansas
1200 Sunnyside Avenue, Room 3136
Lawrence, KS 66045
wehmeyer@ku.edu

Timothy J. Whiteford, Ph.D.
Associate Professor
Department of Education
St. Michael's College
1 Winooski Park
Colchester, VT 05439
twhiteford@smcvt.edu

What Are Quick-Guides
and How Are They Used?

The *Quick-Guides* contained in this book are meant to provide relevant information that can be read in a short amount of time. So many of the teachers we encounter are anxious to get relevant information, but find that they don't have enough time to read long articles and books.

Each of the 20 *Quick-Guides* contained in this volume follows a similar format. Therefore, you may consider each of the 20 *Quick-Guides* as individual documents that can stand alone, even though they are interrelated.

Each *Quick-Guide* has

- A letter to the teacher that introduces the content
- A list of 10 *Guidelines-at-a-Glance* (the 10 most important points)
- A page of text discussing each of the 10 guidelines
- A short list of *Selected References*

There are also three *Quick-Guide Extras* that provide the same kind of practical information but don't follow the same format. The *Quick-Guides* and *Quick-Guide Extras* are written primarily for general education teachers, although they can helpful to a variety of team members. You have permission to photocopy the contents in this book to share with your colleagues. We thought this might be especially helpful for special educators, administrators, and related services personnel who are working with general education teachers to facilitate the supported education of students with disabilities. In the first edition, the *Quick-Guides* were frequently shared with general educators by special education colleagues, were passed out to faculty members by their principal, and were used by staff development specialists and trainers as part of information packets. Some people used them to share information with parents, therapists, community members, school board members, student teachers, and college students. We encourage you to share them with whomever you'd like—that's the whole idea!

Good luck!
Michael & Mary Beth

What's New in This Edition?

Between 1997 and 2002, three separate volumes of the *Quick-Guides to Inclusion* were published. Each volume contained five different topics, for a total of 15 different topics, plus one *Quick-Guide Extra*. In this second edition, we have combined all 16 of these previously published pieces into a single, revised, and expanded volume.

We are pleased that all of the past *Quick-Guide* authors have returned to update their chapters and share their wealth of knowledge and experience with us. Each *Quick-Guide* has been updated and, in some cases, extensively rewritten. We are also pleased to tell you that we have added five new *Quick-Guides* and two new *Quick-Guide Extras*. The topics we have added include:

- QG 3: Considerations About the Cultural Nature of Inclusion, Teaching, and Learning
  Beth Harry and Alfredo J. Artiles
- QG 6: Listen to Me: What Students Want Teachers to Know
  Mary Schuh, Frank Sgambati, and Carol Tashie
- QG 9: Universal Design for Learning
  Bridget Dalton and David Gordon
- QG 14: Writing Matters
  Patricia McGonegal and Nancy Talbott
- QG 15: Making Math Meaningful for Students with Special Needs
  Timothy J. Whiteford
- QGE 2: Community-Based Instruction
  John McDonnell and Jayne McGuire
- QGE 3: Simple Technology to Encourage Participation
  June E. Downing

Mary Beth Doyle has graciously agreed to join me in editing this second edition. We hope you like the new content that has been added as well as the revised and updated sections. Most of all, we hope you are able to put this information to good use on behalf of the students in your schools!

Section I

Foundational Ideas

INSPIRED BY A PUBLIC SCHOOL STUDENT WITH DISABILITIES

CLEARING A PATH
FOR PEOPLE WITH SPECIAL NEEDS
CLEARS THE PATH FOR EVERYONE!

Including Students with Disabilities in the Classroom

Michael F. Giangreco

Quick-Guides to Inclusion
Ideas for Educating Students with Disabilities, Second Edition

Michael F. Giangreco & Mary Beth Doyle
Editors

Dear Teacher,

You just found out that a student with disabilities is being placed in your classroom. For some of you, this is an experience you've had before—although maybe this new student presents unique challenges and opportunities. For others, this may be a first-time experience. Regardless, I understand that you have lots of questions about what is expected of you, what to do, and how to do it. Hopefully, some of your questions will be answered in the following pages.

As you already know, there are countless resources to choose from to learn more about teaching a student with disabilities, but rumor has it you simply don't have time to read them all. Don't worry! My guess is that you probably already know much of what you need to for this to be a successful experience for you and your class. A big part of successful inclusion is a matter of applying the knowledge and skills you already possess to a new situation. Other teachers have done this successfully, and you can do it too! Most of what you need to do requires common sense—this isn't rocket science, but it is important!

This Quick-Guide is designed to give you succinct information about some of the most important guidelines for successfully including students with disabilities in your classroom. These guidelines are, of course, most effective when individualized in a thoughtful manner to match your own situation. I've listed 10 guidelines, each of which is followed by a brief explanation. Obviously, there is much more to learn than is presented in this short resource, so at the end of the Quick-Guide you'll find a list of "Selected References." In the meantime, this Quick-Guide will help get you started.

Good Luck!
Michael

GUIDELINES-AT-A-GLANCE

1. Get a Little Help from Your Friends

2. Welcome the Student in Your Classroom

3. Be the Teacher for All Your Students

4. Establish a Classroom Community

5. Develop Shared Educational Program Expectations

6. Have Options for Including Students

7. Make Learning Active and Participatory

8. Adapt Classroom Strategies and Materials

9. Make Sure Support Services Are Really Helping

10. Evaluate the Effectiveness of Your Teaching

Get a Little Help from Your Friends

There's lots to do, but no one expects you to do it all by yourself. Similarly, no one expects you to know all the specialized information that might accompany a student with disabilities. Luckily, you're not alone. Schools where students with disabilities are taught in general education classes develop teams to help plan and implement students' individualized education programs. Members always include you as the teacher, along with the student's parents, special education teacher, and the student when appropriate.

Depending upon a student's needs, teams sometimes include other members, such as a speech/language pathologist, physical therapist, occupational therapist, school psychologist, counselor, or possibly a paraprofessional. But make no mistake about it, general education teachers have much to contribute to the educational team for a student with a disability! Your knowledge of the general education curriculum and instructional methods, along with your teaching experiences, are critical team resources.

Although collaborative teamwork is a crucial element of quality education for students with disabilities, be on the lookout for good ideas run amuck. Just because a group of adults is assigned to the same student doesn't mean they are a team. Groups sometimes become unnecessarily large and unwieldy or have too many meetings without a clear purpose and outcome. These problems can complicate communication and decision making among team members, overwhelm families, and inhibit constructive action. For example, it's problematic if team members agree that each of the professional disciplines will have their own separate goals corresponding with their respective disciplines. Although members may reach consensus, a desirable action, the positive aspects are canceled out when the consensus is reached to pursue different goals—this is pseudo-teamwork. In contrast, a real team shares a single set of educational goals that belong to the student rather than any particular discipline. Members collectively pursue the student's goals in a coordinated manner based on a shared vision of the student's future.

The adult members of your team won't necessarily be present all the time to help you. So don't overlook the energetic people who are in your room all the time. Your students offer a ready supply of ideas, inspiration, and assistance—they can be your greatest resource if you create an environment that welcomes their contributions.

2 Welcome the Student in Your Classroom

Welcoming a student with disabilities in your classroom may seem like a simple thing to do—and it is—but you might be surprised how frequently it doesn't happen. A common, yet devastating, experience for students with disabilities and their families is getting a message that the student is not welcome in the school or must "earn" the right to belong.

It can be a difficult and unpleasant experience for students with disabilities and families to be actively or passively rejected by school personnel. We know such exclusion wouldn't be acceptable based on other diversity characteristics (e.g., race, ethnicity, gender, socioeconomic status), yet for some reason people still feel justified excluding students based on disability. Invariably, arbitrary standards and criteria for inclusion differ from school to school and state to state. You can find two students with nearly identical characteristics, but in one school the student is placed in a regular class full time, and in another school the student is placed in a special class. This tells me that placement can be more about the characteristics of the school and its personnel than it is about the characteristics of students with disabilities.

Beyond the effects on the student and family, what kind of message does your reaction to a student with disabilities send to students and colleagues? As the classroom teacher, the students in your class look to you as their primary adult model during the school day. What do you want to model for your students about similarities and differences, change, diversity, individuality, and caring? Whatever actions you choose to take or not take in terms of welcoming all your students can have powerful implications concerning their school experience and learning.

There is no avoiding the fact that your colleagues at school will be watching too. My own experience is that, more often than not, it is the adults who have difficulties accepting students with disabilities more so than the students. By providing a welcoming and accepting environment for all the students who live in our communities, a new generation is emerging who are more likely to have friends with disabilities in their classrooms and neighborhoods as a typical part of daily life.

So when a child with a disability comes to your classroom, welcome her as you would any other student. Talk to her, walk with her, encourage her, joke with her, involve her, and teach her. Let her know through your ongoing actions that she is an important member of your class.

Be the Teacher for All Your Students

When a student with disabilities is placed in a general education class, a common misunderstanding is that you, as the classroom teacher, are primarily a host rather than a teacher. Many teachers welcome this notion with open arms. It means someone else is responsible for actually teaching the student with disabilities. This makes sense to many teachers who already feel they have too much to do and wonder if they have the skills to be successful with their students who have disabilities. There's just one catch: merely hosting doesn't work very well.

When the teacher serves as host, it's someone else, such as a paraprofessional, special educator, or another support person, who takes turns working with the student who has a disability in the back of the classroom or in a different room. The teacher ends up having minimal or superficial interactions with this student and not having a good handle on what is going on with him or her educationally. This does not sit well with many teachers because they want to, and should, be in charge of activities and people in their classroom.

Yet some teachers say they don't really think of the student with disabilities as one of *their* students. I've heard teachers say, "I have 26 students plus John [a student with disabilities]. My job is to teach my 26 students and Karen's job [paraprofessional] is to teach John." This "hosting" approach perpetuates a lack of ownership and responsibility for the student's education, and too often it leaves major curricular and instructional decisions to hard-working but potentially underqualified paraprofessionals.

Although your student with disabilities should expect to receive individually determined special education supports, I strongly encourage you to really be the teacher for all the students who are placed in your class. That means knowing what all your students are learning and personally spending time teaching each of them, including your students with disabilities.

Be flexible, but don't allow yourself to be relegated to being an outsider in your own classroom. You are successful teaching students without disabilities; that means you have the core set of knowledge and skills to be successful teaching students with disabilities. Teachers who have embraced the challenge of teaching their students with disabilities often report that they have learned approaches that benefit their entire class and that they keep using after the student with a disability has moved on to the next grade.

Establish a Classroom Community

In conjunction with welcoming the student with disability in your classroom and establishing yourself as the teacher, it's important to have the student be a valued member of the classroom community. Where students spend time, what they do, when, and with whom, play major roles in defining affiliation and status within the classroom. Too many students with disabilities are "placed" in the general education class, but are not included much of the time or in ways that are perceived as important by their classmates. Some students with disabilities spend a significant amount of time separated from their classmates, do different activities, and have a different daily schedule than their peers. These experiences inhibit learning with and from peers, contribute to social isolation, and result in missing out on valuable peer-to-peer learning. When teachers create favorable environments for learning together, it's amazing how much students can learn from their classmates, regardless of disability or other labels.

It is all too common to find the student with a disability seated on the fringe of the class. Make sure this student has the same kind of desk as classmates (or as similar as possible) and is seated with them rather than apart from them. Students with disabilities have to be physically present to be part of what's happening. If the desks are arranged in groups of four, make sure the student with a disability is in a group with three other students who do not have disabilities. In other words, don't group all the students who have special needs together. Of course, location and presence in the classroom is just a starting point.

Make sure that the student with disabilities participates in the same activities as his classmates as much as possible, even though the student's goals may different than those of other classmates. If everyone in the class writes in a journal, so should this student, even if it requires adaptation to a non-written form. If all the students do homework, so should this student, at an appropriate level in terms of amount and difficulty. If the class is doing a science experiment, the student with a disability should be involved, even though in some cases the student's targeted learning outcomes within the science experiment activity may be different than those of classmates (e.g., literacy, following directions, taking turns). Although individualization may be necessary, the student's daily schedule should allow ample opportunities to learn, socialize, play, hang out, and work with the rest of the class.

5 Develop Shared Educational Program Expectations

One of the most common sources of anxiety for classroom teachers is understanding what others, such as parents, administrators, and special educators, expect them to teach: "Do you expect me to teach this student most or all of what the other students without disabilities are learning?" Sometimes the answer will be "Yes," sometimes "No." A crucial step is to make sure that team members share common expectations about what the student should learn in the class and who will be doing the teaching.

Start by having the team identify a small set of the student's highest priority learning outcomes. Next, have the team agree on a larger set of additional learning outcomes that reflect a broad-based educational program. These additional learning outcomes should clarify what parts of the general education curriculum the student will be expected to pursue and may include learning outcomes that are not typically part of the general program. For example, some students with more severe disabilities may need to learn skills, such as early communication, social, or self-care skills, that most students are assumed to have mastered before entering school. These foundational skills may not be part of the general education curriculum at any level, but still may be appropriate for some students with disabilities to pursue.

Many students with disabilities also need to be provided with supports that allow for their active participation in class. These supports should be identified and distinguished from learning outcomes. When supports (e.g., repositioning a student with physical disabilities, providing tactile materials for a child who is blind) are inadvertently confused with learning outcomes (e.g., goals, objectives) it can lead to an unnecessarily passive educational program for the student with disabilities and will interfere with tapping his/her learning potential.

It can be helpful to summarize the educational program: 1) priority learning outcomes, 2) additional learning outcomes, and 3) supports, on a one- or two-page "Program-at-a-Glance." This type of concise listing of learning outcomes and supports can assist in planning and scheduling, serve as a helpful reminder of the student's individualized needs, and provide an effective way to communicate student needs to special area teachers such as art, music, and physical education teachers. By clarifying what the team expects the student to learn, the stage is set for a productive school year.

6 Have Options for Including Students

When the educational needs (e.g., goals and objectives) of a student with disabilities differ from those of the majority of the class, it is not uncommon for teachers to question the appropriateness of the placement. "Why is the student being placed in my sixth-grade class when she is functioning at a much earlier level?" A student with a disability doesn't have to be at grade level to have a successful educational experience in any particular grade. The Individuals with Disabilities Education Improvement Act (IDEA) of 2004 doesn't require that students with disabilities function at the same level as their age peers in order to be included. Rather, IDEA 2004 allows for students to be included in regular education classes as long as their educational needs can be met, given supplemental supports and aids, regardless of their disability labels, severity of disability, or functioning level. Some schools are intentionally utilizing multi-grade classrooms where teachers successfully accommodate students with a wide range of abilities in the same class.

It is important to have options for including a student with disabilities in class activities when some or many of the student's educational needs differ from those of other class members. The easiest option exists when the learning outcomes for the student with disabilities are the same as those for the rest of the class. In such cases, the student may or may not require instructional accommodations or other supports to successfully participate in class activities.

A second option exists when the student participates in class activities while pursuing learning outcomes in the same curriculum area as the rest of the class but at a different level, such as different vocabulary words, math problems, or science concepts. These differences can be in content or amount.

A third option exists when the student with disabilities participates in class activities while pursuing individually determined learning outcomes from different curriculum areas than the rest of the class. For example, the student could be learning communication, literacy, or social skills in a science activity where the rest of the students have science learning outcomes. There also may be rare occasions when the student with a disability requires an alternative learning experience that is not part of a class activity. However, when the classroom teacher differentiates instruction according to content, process, or product, it increases the likelihood that all students can meaningfully participate in class activities.

7 Make Learning Active and Participatory

I've heard teachers say, "A student with disabilities wouldn't get a lot out of being in that class, because the teacher does a lot of large-group lectures, worksheets, and paper-and-pencil tests." My first reaction is, "You're right, it doesn't sound like that situation matches the needs of the student with disabilities." This leaves me wondering how many students who don't have disability labels would find this kind of educational situation a mismatch. Given the diversity of learning styles among students, educators are increasingly questioning whether class lessons that are too frequently large-group, passive, and didactic really meet the needs of very many students.

Activity-based learning is well suited to including learners with a wide range of educational needs and learning styles. One of the gifts that students with disabilities can bring to the classroom is to highlight the need to use more active, participatory, creative approaches to learning. In the process of increasing the amount of activity and participation to accommodate the needs of a student with disabilities, teachers often realize that these approaches are motivating, preferred, and effective for many other students in the class who don't have disability labels.

Although active and participatory approaches typically require a bit more preparation time, they are more enjoyable for students and teachers alike. I've spoken to several teachers who have told me that their teaching has been invigorated because of what they have learned from having a student with a disability in their class.

Increasing activity and participation can include a wide range of options, such as individual or cooperative projects, drama, experiments, field study, art media, computers, research, educational games, multimedia, various forms of choral responding, and many others. Exemplary practices in general education are often highly compatible with the inclusion of students with disabilities, because such approaches stress active engagement and individualization.

Making sure students have a lot of interesting and motivating work to do can have side benefits, such as decreasing behavior problems and encouraging positive social behaviors. Problems often arise when students are bored or otherwise disinterested or disengaged. Your students can be very creative and helpful in designing active learning experiences, so don't hesitate to include them in the planning process.

Adapt Classroom Strategies and Materials

8

When placing students with disabilities in general education classes, it is important to ensure that the instruction they receive is effective in meeting their individual needs. Often, when teaching students with disabilities, we need to be more precise and deliberate in how we teach. Even if the content of instruction is meaningful and at an appropriate level of difficulty, it's not enough; we still have to provide effective instruction.

Providing effective instruction to students with disabilities, within large groups, in small groups, or individually, often requires that instruction be adapted. This can mean adapting the instructional arrangement to facilitate learning opportunities, proximity to peers, or access to competent modeling. Sometimes the adaptation can be as basic as considering a different way for a student to respond if he has difficulty using typical modes like speaking or writing. Sometimes it means adjusting the length of the activity or the amount of content the student is expected to complete.

Adapting teaching methods should also be considered. For example, if group lecture doesn't seem to be working, consider alternatives (e.g., smaller cooperative groups, computer-assisted instruction, guided practice, peer-assisted instruction). More specific instructional procedures may also need to be used, such as extending wait time, using both positive and negative examples to illustrate a concept, or offering memory aids.

Materials can also be adapted to match the student's characteristics or interests. For example, adding tactile or auditory cues for a student with visual impairments, making something bigger or easier to manipulate for a student with physical disabilities, or accounting for a student's interests when adapting materials may increase the motivation of a student who is easily bored or distracted.

Rely on the whole team and class to assist with adaptation ideas; this provides opportunities for teachers and students to put their creativity into action. Don't forget to ask the most important person: the student in need of support. Sometimes we learn that supports designed to help a student may be stigmatizing or unwanted (e.g., individual paraprofessional support in the classroom). Students with disabilities often can provide keen insight into their instructional needs if we ask and then listen.

9

Make Sure Support Services Are Really Helping

It is important to find out what types of support personnel are available to assist students with disabilities in your class. While you are undoubtedly familiar with how to access many commonly available support services (e.g., your school's educational support team, speech-language pathologist, school counselor, school psychologist), the special education teacher in your school may be knowledgeable about other, individually determined support personnel (e.g., occupational therapist, physical therapist, teacher of the blind and visually impaired, teacher of the deaf and hearing impaired, assistive technology specialist, augmentative communication specialist, orientation and mobility specialist, vocational rehabilitation specialist).

Having support service personnel involved in your classroom should be helpful, though it can inadvertently be a hindrance. Often it comes down to how individuals work with you to support the class. In the best-case scenarios, you will work with support personnel who are collaborative and understand the context of your classroom. These folks will ensure that what they do helps you teach your students more effectively, by getting to know your students and the routines of your classroom. They will seek to understand your ideas and concerns.

In other words, effective support personnel won't have a separate agenda. Their collaboration with you will be designed to: 1) account for components of the student's educational program your team previously determined, 2) favorably influence students' social relationships, and 3) minimize potential disruptions to your classroom and the student's schedule. Refer to Quick-Guide 18 for more information about getting the most out of support services.

You can advocate for yourself and your students by becoming an informed consumer of support services. Learn to ask good questions. Be assertive if you feel you are being asked to do something that doesn't make sense to you. Be as explicit as you can about what type of support you need. Sometimes you may need specific information or materials, or someone to demonstrate a technique. At other times, the need may be for someone with whom you can exchange ideas or just get some validation that you are headed in the right direction. When you are on the receiving end of appropriately provided support services, you will feel like you have been helped, because you have been.

Evaluate the Effectiveness of Your Teaching

Evaluating the effectiveness of our own teaching is important for adjusting and improving future instruction and to determine whether the outcomes of our collective efforts have made a difference for the student. To determine the extent and quality of learning, the team initially must have done a good job of determining important learning outcomes and stating them as observable, measurable, goals and objectives at appropriate levels of difficulty. Although evaluation for students with disabilities may take some of the same forms as it does for other students (e.g., written tests, reports, projects), some students with disabilities will need alternative testing accommodations (e.g., more time to complete a test or assignment, having directions read, use of a computer or scribe).

In other cases, data collection must be individualized and precise, such as counting the frequency with which a certain behavior occurs, recording the number of correct steps in a task sequence, or applying gradations in the prompting levels required for a student to respond successfully. Additionally, portfolio assessments can be adapted for use with students with disabilities. For example, some portfolios may include digital photos or videos of a student demonstrating newly acquired skills or the application of skills under new circumstances (e.g., across settings, people).

Often we assume that if students without disabilities get good grades or score well on whatever measures we have created, this will translate into future life success in education, employment, and opportunities. Unfortunately, we have far too many graduates with disabilities whose postschool lives are marked by unemployment, health problems, loneliness, inadequate recreational opportunities, and isolation from community life—despite the fact that their school progress reports were glowing.

Therefore, we need to continually evaluate whether a student's achievement is being applied to real life, as evidenced by outcomes such as physical and emotional health; positive social relationships; and the ability to communicate, self-advocate, make informed choices, demonstrate personal growth, and increasingly access places and activities that are personally meaningful. In so doing, we can strive to ensure that our teaching will really make a positive difference in our students' lives. We need to keep asking ourselves whether our teaching is making a real difference in student's lives.

Selected References

Bauer, A.M., & Brown, G.M. (2001). *Adolescents and inclusion: Transforming secondary schools.* Baltimore: Paul H. Brookes Publishing Co.

Downing, J. (2002). *Including students with severe and multiple disabilities in typical classrooms: Practical strategies for teachers (2nd ed.).* Baltimore: Paul H. Brookes Publishing Co.

Giangreco, M.F., Dennis, R., Cloninger, C., Edelman, S., & Schattman, R. (1993). "I've counted Jon:" Transformational experiences of teachers educating students with disabilities. *Exceptional Children, 59,* 359–372.

Harmin, M. (1994). *Inspiring active learning: A handbook for teachers.* Alexandria, VA: Association for Supervision and Curriculum Development.

Individuals with Disabilities Education Improvement Act of 2004, PL 108-446, 20 U.S.C. §§ 1400 *et seq.*

Jorgensen, C.M., Schuh, M.C., & Nisbet, J. (2006). *The inclusion facilitator's guide.* Baltimore: Paul H. Brookes Publishing Co.

Kennedy, C.H., & Fisher, D. (2001). *Inclusive middle schools.* Baltimore: Paul H. Brookes Publishing Co.

Kennedy, C.H., & Horn, E.M. (2004). *Including students with severe disabilities.* Needham Heights, MA: Allyn & Bacon/Pearson Education.

McGregor, G., & Volgelsberg, R.T. (1998). *Inclusive schooling practices: Pedagogical and research foundations: A synthesis of the literature that informs best practices about inclusive schooling.* Baltimore: Paul H. Brookes Publishing Co.

Ryndak, D.L., & Fisher, D. (Eds.). (2003). *The foundations of inclusive education: A compendium of articles on effective strategies to achieve inclusive education.* Baltimore: TASH.

Snell, M.E., & Janney, R. (2005). *Collaborative teaming: Teachers' guides to inclusive practices (2nd ed.).* Baltimore: Paul H. Brookes Publishing Co.

Thousand, J.S., Villa, R.A., & Nevin, A.I. (2002). *Creativity and collaborative learning: The practical guide to empowering students, teachers, and families* (2nd ed.). Baltimore: Paul H. Brookes Publishing Co.

Villa, R.A., & Thousand, J.S. (Eds.). (2005). *Creating an inclusive school* (2nd ed.). Alexandria, VA: Association for Supervision and Curriculum Development.

Quick-Guide #2

Building Partnerships
with Parents and Caregivers

Linda A. Davern

Quick-Guides to Inclusion
Ideas for Educating Students with Disabilities, Second Edition

Michael F. Giangreco & Mary Beth Doyle

Editors

Dear Teacher,

Successful partnerships with your students' parents and caregivers create the foundation for high-quality inclusive experiences. Making a substantial investment in creating strong and positive relationships with families can pay huge dividends for teachers. These relationships can provide invaluable information and ideas for enhancing the educational outcome for students. Parents' roles as team members need your support to be fully realized.

In working with parents over many years as well as conducting formal interviews (see Selected References), I have had the privilege of listening to them talk about what teachers can do to create productive connections between home and school. Parents are often very generous in sharing their experiences and ideas. They do this with the wish that sharing their perspectives may be helpful to others.

The parents I have spoken with identify several steps that school personnel can take to build productive alliances (or strengthen existing relationships) with parents or caregivers of students with disabilities. They suggest that school personnel show interest in the uniqueness and value of the child, teen, or young adult, and communicate this clearly and consistently—particularly when the relationship is just getting started. From this foundation, real planning and information sharing can occur. Attempting to understand the family's frame of reference will increase the likelihood that interactions with parents will be positive and productive. Establishing ways of communicating and planning that are workable for parents, and respectful of a range of ways that we may differ (e.g., culture, language, socio-economic factors, educational background), is absolutely necessary. Finally, embracing the principle of being an ally with families will ensure that you persevere in creating the best possible partnership. Through this partnership, teachers can be more successful with their goal of creating excellent educational experiences for all students.

Good Luck!

Linda

GUIDELINES-AT-A-GLANCE

1. Send a Clear Message of Regard and Value

2. Put Yourself in the Shoes of the Parents

3. Demonstrate Genuine Interest in Parents' Goals

4. Use Everyday Language

5. Talk with Parents About How They Want to Share Information

6. Expand Your Awareness of Cultural Diversity

7. See Individuals—Challenge Stereotypes

8. Create Effective Forums for Planning and Problem Solving

9. Support Full Membership for All Students

10. Persevere in Building Partnerships with Parents

Send a Clear Message of Regard and Value

The ways in which school personnel talk about students early in the school year, in both formal and informal interactions, have a significant impact on the development of relationships with families. As school personnel, we may assume that parents know we value their child. But parents have had years of experiences with a range of medical and educational personnel before meeting us. At times, their experience may include listening to a litany of ways that professionals think their child is deficient. Parents cannot always trust that we see the value in their child. We have to express that we do.

The ability to see appealing aspects of a student's personality, aside from the arena of academic achievement, is important to many parents. As one mother, Gail, put it,

> . . . for teachers to say to me, "I really like your kid," or "You know, he really has a great sense of humor" . . . that really lets me know a couple of things . . . that they really care about him as a person and see him as a person.

Conveying excitement and optimism about the child are teacher characteristics that are greatly valued by many parents. Parents appreciate personnel who are able to focus on their individual child's progress, as opposed to constantly using other children as a point of reference for comparison.

Additional characteristics that indicate to some parents that school personnel value and accept their children include 1) a willingness to listen to the child, 2) not engaging in interactions that are demeaning to the child (e.g., talking about the child in his or her presence), and 3) talking respectfully to the child. As Anna, another parent, put it, "Just take her for who she is . . . so she's not going to be the top of her class in gym. We understand that. Just take her for who she is. Find space for her."

Building a foundation of good feeling starts with staff conveying consistent messages that they see the child as an interesting individual, are happy to have the child in class, and hold high expectations for what the child will achieve. Once parents can see that the child is viewed as important and fully valued, parents are much more likely to be open and interested in exploring a range of topics with professionals. A spirit of teamwork toward the education of the child is now possible and probable.

Put Yourself in the Shoes of the Parents

Parents are unlikely to ever completely understand the life of the teacher, and, likewise, most teachers will not fully appreciate the day-to-day experiences of the parent who has a child with a disability. Parents have communicated that they recognize and appreciate the effort put forth by school personnel to understand what it is like to have a child with a disability—what it is like to negotiate with both the general and special education bureaucracies in order to gain access to classes, accommodations, and support services for their child.

For many of the parents, advocacy was necessary to achieve what they viewed as a decent education for their children. They felt there was no alternative to fighting. Parents felt they were often viewed as impatient, and they wanted staff to better understand their frustrations with the slow pace of change. Whether the change was in the areas of building friendships, developing adaptations, or developing effective planning teams, some parents felt they couldn't afford to accept a slow rate of progress. As one parent put it, "You gotta understand; we don't have time. . . . My daughter is getting older every year. . . . I haven't got a lot of time." Understanding and respecting this sense of urgency, and the history behind it, can be very helpful in building a home–school partnership.

Some parents may differ from school personnel in significant ways—such as struggling with homelessness or speaking a language that is shared by very few, if anyone, in the school community. At times, teachers can attempt to imagine the experience of the parent. How does one avoid feelings of despair when struggling with a basic need such as housing? What must it be like to navigate the complexities of a school system while in the initial stages of learning a second language?

It *is* possible to build empathy for human experiences we have not shared. School staff who attempt to understand the parents' frame of reference are less likely to develop judgmental attitudes that could be damaging to the home–school relationship. Teachers often are wise to assume that parents are trying their best and that they love their children. The role of the teacher is to create a team that provides and encourages active roles for parents in the education of their child, while realizing that a particular parent's ability to be active at any given time will vary.

3 Demonstrate Genuine Interest in Parents' Goals

School personnel need to demonstrate an interest in what the parents see as meaningful goals for their child. A first step in creating this dialogue is establishing rapport with individual parents. Angela spoke repeatedly about a teacher her son had the previous year.

> She's just the type of person . . . big smile . . . very warm and very assertive. . . . Maybe I might be a little bit nervous the first meeting. And she answered questions I would have [asked] before I could even ask them. She makes me feel comfortable. Her first priority is not only with the child, but with the parent.

Parents view some staff as very skilled in lessening the psychological distance between parents and professionals. These teachers are able to create an atmosphere where parents do not feel that they have to "watch their P's and Q's," as one parent put it. School staff do this through their choice of language as well as their interaction styles.

Parents also discussed a considerable number of interactions as evidence of an "expert kind of syndrome." Some parents got the feeling that the attitude coming from staff was, "You couldn't possibly know what you're talking about." One parent described a critical distinction between those personnel who talk **with** parents and those who talk **at** them. This type of tone is sometimes more likely to occur during formal meetings. Professionals who are conscious of this will do what they can to support parents' comments and perspectives as much as possible at these times.

Teachers can inquire about what a parent's highest priorities are for their child. For some families, it may be a particular area of academic achievement (e.g., literacy, math). For others, it may be a social area (e.g., developing friendships) or a behavioral issue.

Assessing parents' priorities, discussing instructional strategies with parents, making sure all team members are apprised of these priorities, and regularly reporting progress are keys to the home–school partnership. When this type of pattern is evident early in the school year, a foundation is established for true teamwork. Teachers can maintain their expertise as educators while fully acknowledging the information and insights held by parents. The interplay of these complementary roles can greatly enrich the outcome for students.

Use Everyday Language

4

Parents can feel excluded from the planning process when professionals use educational terms that are unclear to the parents. One parent referred to this practice as "blowing all that smoke." Jargon is frequently used in relation to test results, staffing patterns, and ways of organizing or identifying services. For example, it would not be unusual to hear a statement like this one during a planning team meeting: "He's currently in a 12–1–1 and could move to consult if the one-to-one follows along. Could the O.T. do push-in in that setting? His fine motor skills need a lot of work." Although a person who is a member of the school community may be able to make sense of these statements, a parent is often left guessing. As another parent put it,

> You know, that's a riot when they start talking "parallel curriculum." When you do that stuff you just close out the parent—as soon as you use the language that's exclusive of the parent, they're gone. You have to get rid of the jargon.

It is an unfortunate irony that in order to graduate from many teacher preparation programs, preservice teachers must master a professional language that ultimately creates significant barriers in being effective in their interactions with the families they are meant to serve. Perceptive teachers recognize the distance that is created by the use of professional jargon and minimize its use. These teachers maintain this awareness in both speaking and writing.

Teachers also take leadership actions in the presence of other professionals who may not have the same level of awareness. When speaking in a meeting, they may interject on behalf of the parents by saying, "Could you define that phrase for us?" While some parents may make this type of request themselves, it is not reasonable to assume that all parents are comfortable doing so. This type of action is helpful not only for family and other community members, but also for school personnel who may not have the same area of expertise as the speaker. When writing, if a technical term or phrase is needed for purposes of clear communication with another professional, the teacher can use a common word or phase and place the technical term or phrase in parentheses. These seemingly minor decisions can have a cumulative result of strengthening the partnership between home and school.

Talk with Parents About How They Want to Share Information

5

Successful collaboration requires effective ongoing communication between home and school. Some parents I spoke with thought that having one person as the primary contact would be helpful, yet several parents did not want to have a person affiliated with special education as their primary connection for fear that this would lessen the feelings of ownership on the part of the general education classroom teacher for the child's progress. This dilemma results from the interplay between two systems.

Many of these parents have struggled over a period of years to create a place for their child within the "general" education structure. When the primary contact with school is a representative of the separate structure, the child's membership can feel tenuous. Parents want their child to be viewed as "just one of the kids." Any practice that places more ownership and responsibility for the child's success on the special educator (or sometimes a related services provider) for the most part may be unsettling for some parents. However, consistent communication with a person who really knows the child is important!

School personnel need to discuss with parents how they would like to communicate, with whom they would like to communicate, and what frequency of communication can be feasibly arranged with specific members of the team. For some parents, phone contact is an optimal and easy way to share information. For others, e-mail may be an option.

Given the complexity of some students' characteristics, there may be a need for daily contact through a notebook that goes back and forth between school and home. For example, if a child has a very significant communication disability, a parent may want information on the child's participation in activities. If a child has nutritional problems, a report on whether the child ate lunch may be needed. Topics for sharing information are determined in conversation with parents (Davern, 2004).

In addition to the form and frequency of communication, personnel need to understand that parents' preferences for involvement may change over time given a variety of factors, such as the child's age and the family's circumstances. So it is important to revisit patterns and processes of communication with parents during the year.

Expand Your Awareness of Cultural Diversity

6

Building on awareness of cultural diversity will strengthen school personnel's ability to teach their students as well as interact successfully with families. Marguerite, a parent, shared her observations:

> I think a lot of the teachers have never been in contact with minority children, or had any training in multiculturalism or diversity, or know anything about these children or their cultural backgrounds and their lives, and then they are making assessments of these children based on their values and I think it's wrong.

Schools that are working toward multiculturalism provide diversity-related learning experiences for staff, and also ensure that children see representation of their ethnicity in personnel as well as curriculum and materials. In addition, the emphasis on varied styles of learning that accompanies a multicultural approach can lessen the likelihood of special education referral for some children.

Through effective staff development, schools can assist personnel in examining "the cultural base of their own belief system" (Harry, 1992, p. 23) in relation to children and families and how these beliefs have an impact on relationships. Culture must be addressed in all its complexity by emphasizing that "cultures are fluid and are greatly influenced by acculturation, generational status, gender, social class, education, occupational group and numerous other variables" (Harry et al., 1995, p. 106). Such an approach will ensure that personnel are aware of the cultural lenses through which they make judgments.

Ignorance of cultural differences can create significant barriers to the home–school partnership. For example, Harry (1992) noted that some non–European American groups are not comfortable with the informal approach often used by many European Americans—who are the majority of teachers. Harry recommends a more formal, yet personalized approach with some ethnic minority cultures. What may feel "natural" within a teacher's own cultural framework is not a good match for all parents. In addition, it is important to be sensitive to cultural issues that may affect parents' thoughts on their role in their child's education. School personnel may have one set of beliefs, and parents may have another (Kalyanpur & Harry, 1999). Asking parents what their preferences are is viewed as a sign of respect (Zionts, Zionts, Harrison, & Bellinger, 2003). Above all else, it is the demonstration of respect that is the first step in teaming with families.

7 See Individuals–Challenge Stereotypes

Some parents express concerns about assumptions they feel are made about them and their parenting skills simply because their child has a disability. One mother, Doria, saw some of these attitudes arising from a lack of understanding of some types of disabilities, such as emotional disturbance:

> I didn't think [teachers have] had enough training to realize that this child had a particular problem . . . they just see it as a child coming from a home that wasn't properly fit or something . . . they were trying to blame it on the parent.

Another parent, Marguerite, felt that school personnel frequently "lumped parents together"—working from inaccurate assumptions about single parents and parents who were not of European heritage: "All single parents are dysfunctional, all minority parents are . . . that's a crock."

These comments were parents' perceptions. We can't know whether these reflect the reality of personnel perspectives. But it is clear from such comments that these parents did not feel an overall sense of support and positive regard from school personnel. Under these conditions, comments can be open to misinterpretation.

It is not that difficult to assess a team's attitude toward parents. When challenges or frustrations arise in teaching, consider whether team members make comments about the family such as, "The apple doesn't fall far from the tree," "Well, when you consider the family . . . ," or "At home he's expected to do nothing." Watch for school personnel saying things like, "How can they expect us to make that adaptation? Don't they realize there are other children that need some attention too?" or "They are calling constantly!"

Teachers who are committed to home–school partnerships do not engage in these types of exchanges, but rather, place focus on productive actions such as the following: 1) supporting staff development efforts that focus on the power of partnership with parents and diversity in families (e.g., sexual orientation, social class, culture, language), 2) promoting disability awareness information-sharing sessions, and 3) being thoughtful in their comments so as to break down stereotypes, such as offering examples from their own experiences that contradict the stereotypes expressed by others.

Create Effective Forums for Planning and Problem Solving

8

Yearly meetings, mandated by law, are held for each child with an individualized education program. During these meetings, assessments are reviewed, individual goals are identified, placement decisions are made, and support services are determined. Some of the most difficult interactions parents experience occur at these meetings. It is not unusual for parents to describe these meetings as "very, very intimidating." Parents often report feeling that their ideas were rarely being sought in a meaningful way.

In contrast, some teams hold meetings not just yearly, but on an ongoing basis. The key people involved with a student (e.g., teachers, parents, related services providers, classroom assistants) meet regularly throughout the year. These meetings provide a context and opportunity for coherent planning for a student. This includes sharing successful teaching strategies, discussing student progress, identifying the next year's teacher early in the current school year, and ensuring that important information is shared year to year.

Although problems may be discussed at these meetings, they are not the sole focus. Opportunities exist to discuss achievement, friendships, interesting stories, or humorous anecdotes. As one mother put it, "When we go to team meetings, a lot of times it is a celebration; that's how it feels. By George, we're doing something right here—it's working!"

Districts need to develop willingness and expertise in the area of team planning for individual children (Giangreco, Cloninger, & Iverson, 1998). At least one parent who had initiated such meetings could see how a similar model had utility for a number of children throughout the school whose situations required key adults to do some intensive planning on a short- or long-term basis. While time is always a challenge for school personnel, the benefit of such meetings can be significant, including broader access to priorities and information about necessary supports and greater ability to be responsive to students as they encounter obstacles to social development and academic achievement.

9 Support Full Membership for All Students

Parents often have to advocate extensively in order to gain a general class placement for their child. Too often, such placements are the result of their efforts as opposed to a policy or initiative by the school. Year after year, some parents must once more make a case for an inclusive setting for their child. As children get older, if a system is not designed for inclusive teaching, their work becomes much more difficult, and some simply accept a special class placement because they are tired of fighting.

Schools will not become proficient in building alliances with families until general class membership, with adequate supports, is the norm for students with disabilities. Teachers can actively support such restructuring by taking the following leadership actions.

1. Support staff development efforts that are aligned with building expertise with diversity. Initiatives such as *Universal Design for Learning* (see Quick-Guide 9 or go to www.cast.org) and *differentiated instruction* (Tomlinson & McTighe, 2006) have been helpful in assisting teachers in building a vision and repertoire for teaching all students.

2. As an IEP team member, challenge plans to refer children to more restrictive settings. Sometimes all it takes is the voice of one strong advocate to assist a team in developing a program of full membership for a child who is on the verge of placement in a different setting. Reframe the discussion to address the question: "What do we need to do to accommodate this student?" In this way, teachers can shift the focus to finding solutions as opposed to placements. Help your colleagues to see that, as a faculty, you have the talent and commitment to make that happen.

3. Join community organizations whose goals are related to building inclusive schools; unite with other staff and parents who have similar goals and interests related to inclusive practices; and initiate and serve on school restructuring work groups.

When teachers decide to take leadership on this issue, inclusive settings become available to those children and teenagers whose parents are not in a position, for various reasons, to undertake extensive advocacy on behalf of their children.

Persevere in Building Partnerships with Parents

Although school teams are required by federal law to invite parents into the planning process for their children with disabilities, the collaborative outcome envisioned by legislation does not always materialize. Perseverance in attempting to form partnerships with parents is a posture that many parents feel is critical.

Many parents with whom I spoke thought that schools gave up too quickly and that some personnel were quick to dismiss parents who didn't attend meetings. These parents felt that building partnerships took commitment and vision over the long term and that the degree of parent participation, for many families, was a direct result of school practices. They suggested looking at how schools share information with parents, how schools can demonstrate more flexibility in setting up meeting times with parents, and ways to assist parents in connecting with each other in order to provide assistance, such as alternating child care to free each other to attend planning meetings. As one parent put it, school personnel need to "make it happen"; that is, to extend themselves and do what needs to be done to build partnerships with parents.

As stated by a father, once a district begins to work in a different way with families, it might take time, but the word gets around:

> Once you make that decision to team [with parents]—the first year that you do it, maybe you're not going to get all the parents. But parents know each other, and give it a little time, nurture it along, and you get a parent saying, "This new thing—there's a lot more sharing there—it's better."

Welcome families to your school and classroom. Attempt to make them as comfortable as possible. Express a sincere interest in their role in the student's education.

When teachers bring these attitudes to talking and planning with parents, they increase the likelihood that the parent who is shy, unsettled in school meetings, or unhappy with previous teachers will be willing to start anew. The home–school partnership is the foundation to achieving a quality education.

Selected References

CAST: Center for Applied Special Technology. http://www.cast.org/

Davern, L. (1994). Parents' perspectives on relationships with professionals in inclusive educational settings. *Dissertation Abstracts International, 56,* 9522518.

Davern, L. (2004). School-to-home notebooks: Guidance from parents. *Teaching Exceptional Children, 36*(5), 22–27.

Giangreco, M.F., Cloninger, C.J., & Iverson, V.S. (1998). *Choosing outcomes and accommodations for children (COACH): A guide to educational planning for students with disabilities* (2nd ed.). Baltimore: Paul H. Brookes Publishing Co.

Harry, B. (1992). *Cultural diversity, families, and the special education system.* New York: Teachers College Press.

Harry, B., Grenot-Scheyer, M., Smith-Lewis, M., Park, H., Xin, F., & Schwartz, I. (1995). Developing culturally inclusive services for individuals with severe disabilities. *Journal of The Association for Persons with Severe Handicaps, 20,* 99–109.

Kalyanpur, M., & Harry, B. (1999). *Culture in special education: Building reciprocal family–professional relationships.* Baltimore: Paul H. Brookes Publishing Co.

Soodak, L.C., & Erwin, E.J. (2000). Valued member or tolerated participant: Parents' experiences in inclusive early childhood settings. *Journal of The Association for Persons with Severe Handicaps, 25,* 29–41.

Tomlinson, C., & McTighe, J. (2006). *Integrating differentiated instruction and understanding by design: Connecting content and kids.* Alexandria, VA: Association for Supervision and Curriculum Development.

Turnbull, A.P., & Turnbull, H.R. (2001). *Families, professionals, and exceptionality: Collaborating for empowerment (4th ed.).* Upper Saddle River, NJ: Prentice Hall.

Zionts, L.T., Zionts, P., Harrison, S., & Bellinger, O. (2003). Urban African American families' perceptions of cultural sensitivity within the special education system. *Focus on Autism and Other Developmental Disabilities, 18*(1), 41–50.

Quick-Guide #3

Considerations about the Cultural Nature of Inclusion, Teaching, and Learning

Beth Harry and Alfredo J. Artiles

Quick-Guides to Inclusion
Ideas for Educating Students with Disabilities, Second Edition
Michael F. Giangreco & Mary Beth Doyle

Editors

Quick-Guides to Inclusion: Ideas for Educating Students with Disabilities (2nd ed.) © Michael F. Giangreco, 2007
Available through Paul H. Brookes Publishing Co., Baltimore, 1-800-638-3775

Dear Teacher,

Culture is all around us. It encompasses all aspects of human affairs, such as inclusive education practices, student and teacher learning, and teaching approaches. In this Quick-Guide, we invite you to challenge the common assumption that culture pertains only to members of ethnic and linguistic minority communities. Remember that our teaching is usually culturally appropriate to mainstream students; the challenge is to learn how to reach all students. We will focus on the experiences of culturally and linguistically diverse students because 1) these groups have suffered high rates of poverty and school failure, 2) in some higher-incidence disability categories (e.g., learning disabilities, intellectual disabilities, emotional/behavioral disorders), such students are identified and labeled at disproportionately high rates and disproportionately placed in segregated settings, and 3) children in the lower-incidence disability categories (e.g., multiple disabilities, deafblindness) are often viewed only in terms of their disability, ignoring the importance of their home cultures and languages.

There are crucial questions we must ask regarding parents' empowerment for advocacy. For example, are parents well informed of their rights? Is their consent truly informed? Have they been included as fully as possible in educational interventions prior to referral? Does the evaluation process take into account the family's cultural practices? When a child is placed in a special education setting, has the family's input been sought regarding inclusive placement? Are the individualized education program (IEP) goals culturally appropriate?

To become culturally responsive in our interactions with all families, we must be aware of our own cultural assumptions. Questions to ask ourselves include: What are our assumptions about what makes a "good" family structure or a "good" pattern of family authority? Do our assumptions implicitly favor the cultural practices of certain groups of families (e.g., white middle class families)? Do we assume that when parents disagree with a diagnosis they are "in denial"? Do these beliefs affect the way we interact with families or the decisions we make about their children?

Good luck in your efforts to become culturally responsive!
Beth and Alfredo

GUIDELINES-AT-A-GLANCE

1. Become Aware of Your Own Cultural Assumptions

2. Study Both the Cultures In Your Classroom and the Classroom Cultures

3. Learn About the Cultural Nature of Learning

4. Collaborate to Create Authentic Parent Engagement

5. Foster Respectful and Reciprocal Interactions

6. Be Aware of Patterns of Minority Disproportionality

7. Develop Equitable Prereferral and Referral Processes

8. Communicate Effectively with Families

9. Arrange Informational Opportunities for Parents

10. Stand Firm Against "I'm Tired of Culture" Rhetoric

Become Aware of Your Own Cultural Assumptions

In becoming *culturally responsive* educators, we must attend to three dimensions, namely those that are *personal*, *technical* (e.g., strategies, methods, models, and approaches), and *institutional* (e.g., regulations, rules, procedures, and policies that enable implementation) (Richards, Brown, & Forde, 2004). We focus in this section on the *personal* dimension, though we note that *culturally responsive* education only exists when the three dimensions are addressed simultaneously.

Culture is like the air we breathe—it is mostly invisible to us but permeates all human activities. Culture includes a wide range of beliefs and practices, from our deepest values about family, religion, or interpersonal behavior, to the simple routines we do everyday. Because these beliefs and practices are so much part of us, we take them for granted and assume that they represent what is "normal."

Beliefs about disabilities are deeply embedded within cultures. Our laws on disability represent key Western assumptions, such as the belief that conditions that differ significantly from our established norms are signs of pathology and should be treated by scientific or educational methods. We assume that parents who mean well will agree with our diagnoses and recommendations. However, many families may interpret a physical condition as a sign of a spiritual condition or may disagree that a child's difficulties in learning are important enough to be labeled as a disability. Some families may appear to agree with our opinions or recommendations but only because their cultural values regarding teachers' status and knowledge compel them to withhold their disagreement.

When we work with families, we should begin by noting that the recommendations we make are shaped by our own cultural values rather than universal truths. If we remember this, then we will find it easier to respect families who hold different values. Even when we do not agree with different cultural beliefs, we need to learn about differing views and develop a respectful dialogue that allows families and service providers to learn from each other.

Study Both the Cultures in your Classroom and the Classroom Cultures

Educators must be aware of both the *cultures in the classroom* (e.g., students' cultural communities) and the *classroom cultures* (e.g., the values, assumptions, practices that are routine in the classroom but that also have a cultural nature). Examples of cultural practices of classrooms include the participation frameworks teachers set up for classroom discourse (e.g., "the rights and obligations of participants with respect to who can say what, when, and to whom") and the criteria used to assess what counts as a good narrative or answer.

In our multicultural society, it is not possible to be competent in all the students' cultures represented in our classrooms. However, if teachers build on what Gonzalez and Moll (2002) called children's "funds of knowledge" (prior learning in their own communities) they can engage children's attention while also showing respect for their family and community backgrounds.

The first step in developing cultural awareness is to acknowledge our own ignorance. How wonderful it would be for a teacher to say to children, "I don't know much about your experiences or your language, but I'd love to learn." This approach can include visits to the home, projects in which students collect information from their individual cultural communities, or classroom visits by local role models. In Gloria Ladson-Billing's (1994) study of effective teachers of African American students, one teacher invited a child's mother, who was known in the neighborhood for her excellent sweet potato pies, to demonstrate her baking to the class. Teachers can link such activities to curriculum concepts and skills.

The same approach is important for language differences. The building of shared classroom communities can be encouraged by opportunities for English language learners and speakers of English dialects to share information about their language with their peers. Finally, assessing children in their native languages is essential so that language difference is not mistaken for a learning deficit.

Learn About the Cultural Nature of Learning

How often have you visited a place of worship or spiritual development other than your own? Have you eaten in a small restaurant in an ethnically diverse neighborhood where your school is located? Have you attended a neighborhood activity frequented by your students? These experiences enable teachers to understand the cultural practices and resources of students' communities, and to appreciate that those cultural communities might have different goals for their children's development and might use alternative means of participation and supports in everyday life (Rogoff, 2003).

If schools are to become truly part of their communities, interactions have to be two-way. For example, school personnel often assume that letters sent home are enough to explain school policies and intentions. Often, however, these communications are not only inadequate, but are misunderstood because they do not take account of the community's cultural beliefs, goals, and practices. For example, Harry's (1992) research with Puerto Rican families indicated that parents had no idea of the real meaning of the IEP document developed at the meetings they attended. Harry and Klingner's (2006) study also revealed that school personnel based many of their beliefs about African American and Haitian American children's circumstances on unfounded stereotypes about families. Similarly, Arzubiaga, Ceja, and Artiles (2000) showed that parenting styles (e.g., control, discipline) in Latino communities in Los Angeles were not the direct result of ethnic beliefs, but rather, were shaped by the interaction of cultural beliefs and the social ecologies of communities (e.g., perceptions of risk and violence).

Professional development can be a powerful means to deepen your understanding of the cultural nature of learning. Examples include outreach activities such as presentations by key community leaders and providers of local services. They should also include opportunities for school personnel to participate in their students' cultures, rather than knowing the children only by their school identities. Professional development could also include teacher study groups that engage teachers in critical examination of their daily practices.

Collaborate to Create Authentic Parent Engagement

Family and community members can be wonderful sources of culturally responsive support and practical help in schools. This is particularly so in urban neighborhoods, which are populated by a sizable proportion of people from ethnic and linguistic minority backgrounds. Unfortunately, schools tend to use a form of parent involvement that privileges families from middle class backgrounds. How can schools nurture parent engagement beyond "official school tasks" that privilege only those families who have important advantages, such as higher education levels and economic or sociocultural capital?

Answering this question doesn't mean educators shouldn't engage parents in traditional school tasks. For instance, school personnel could develop a list of specific activities in which family members can regularly help; these could include 1) office tasks such as photocopying or distributing written information, 2) classroom tasks such as setting up display boards or decorating for traditional holidays, and 3) communication tasks such as making phone calls home in languages other than English or taking a note to a family who does not have a phone. As is appropriate for all volunteer arrangements, the administration should ensure that due respect is accorded the volunteers and that gratitude is expressed through small, but thoughtful gestures of acknowledgement.

Some schools, such as those qualifying for Title I supports, have funding available for school liaison personnel. Employing family and community members in these roles can be a way to build a bridge between diverse communities and schools. For many immigrant communities, issues of immigration status or lack of experience with the school system in the U.S. can keep parents away. For native minorities, such as American Indians and African Americans, the history of exclusion and discrimination may be a continuing contributor to mistrust. Educators need to gather information about parents' views on how they should engage in their children's education and also on parents' cultural resources (e.g., funds of knowledge) that might be used to enrich the school curriculum.

Foster Respectful and Reciprocal Interactions

5

All teachers know that respect for others is one of the central tenets of the American belief in individual rights and equality. However, there are many school-based situations in which school personnel, imbued with a "we/they" mindset regarding parents, treat parents as if they are less important than professionals.

Respect goes way beyond "good morning" and "have a nice day." In fact, the notion of respect is shaped largely by cultural models that mediate (not determine) people's everyday actions. For example, how should a teacher behave when a parent drops in unexpectedly to the classroom? Does the parent understand the school cultural practices about visits? What are the parent's beliefs about such matters? Is there a clear school policy regarding such visits and, if so, does the teacher politely explain this policy and quickly arrange another opportunity for a conversation with the parent? When a teacher has to phone home regarding a student's learning or behavioral problem, is this attempt to contact the parent the first one, or has the teacher previously contacted the parent with a positive message? Is there someone available to make the phone call if it is known that the parents do not yet speak English? In parent–teacher conferences, is the parent accorded a title equivalent to those used for professionals, such as Mr. or Ms., rather than being addressed as "Mom" or "Dad" or by a first name? When an interpreter is mediating a teacher–parent conversation, does the teacher make eye contact with the parent or does she keep looking at the interpreter while purportedly addressing the parent?

Reciprocity is an even more challenging concept for professionals. Steeped in the belief that our expert knowledge is the main source of understanding children's difficulties, we seldom embrace the idea of learning from parents. We often assume that our diagnoses about children are correct and parents who disagree are "in denial." Based on this belief, school personnel's idea of communication is often a one-way process in which we give information to the parent. We recommend to all teachers the "cultural reciprocity" process designed by Harry, Kalyanpur, and Day (1999).

Be Aware of Patterns of Minority Disproportionality

6

Ethnic minority students have continued, for over three decades, to be disproportionately placed in special education programs for students with higher-incidence disabilities (Artiles, Trent, & Palmer, 2004). The patterns vary widely across disability categories and across states and school districts (Donovan & Cross, 2002). Nationwide statistics show consistent overrepresentation of African American students in the mental retardation and emotional/behavior disorders categories, while American Indian students tend to be overrepresented in the specific learning disability (SLD) category. For Hispanic students, while nationwide averages do not show overrepresentation, there is much variability across states, with disproportionality often evident in the category SLD or speech and language impairments. Conversely, these three minority groups are consistently underrepresented in programs for the gifted and talented, while Asian American students are consistently underrepresented in the disability categories and overrepresented in programs for those labeled gifted.

The fact that disproportionality appears only in the higher incidence categories suggests that the pattern is problematic. The diagnoses of these categories are based on clinical judgment rather than on objectively identifiable biological causes. By contrast, minority student placement in the low-incidence categories (which is usually based on identifiable physical or sensory causes), do not reflect ethnic disproportionality. Thus, it is very likely that biased judgments affect placement decisions in the higher-incidence groups.

The variability of the higher-incidence placement rates over time and place have resulted in federal government mandates that require both the Office for Special Education Programs and the Office for Civil Rights to collect annual or biannual data on ethnic representation in special education programs. We recommend Artiles and Rueda's (2002) guidelines to assessing these patterns, and a school self-assessment tool developed by the National Center for Culturally Responsive Educational Systems, which is available at http://www.nccrest.org/publications/tools/assessment.html.

Develop Equitable Prereferral and Referral Processes

7

By what process does a child come to be found eligible for special education services? Based on three years of research in a large urban school district, Harry and Klingner (2006) identified numerous risk factors in schooling and recommended 1) careful attention to the provision of adequate opportunities to learn, especially for students who enter school without the advantage of typical middle class cognitive and linguistic preparation and 2) observation of the classroom environment, since poor instruction and classroom management or detrimental peer interactions could be contributing to the difficulties. Referral committees should strive to include professionals with expertise on cultural and linguistic diversity issues (Ortiz, 2002).

The referral process should focus on identifying the student's specific areas of need and should outline the instructional or behavioral interventions to be implemented, by whom, and in what time frame. Review of the referral should be timely and thorough in order to determine whether further assessment is needed.

The assessment itself must include cross-cultural considerations regarding the identity and interaction style of the assessor as well as the cultural content of the testing. In the case of English language learners, referrals are appropriate (Ortiz, 2002) when 1) the student has good native language communication skills, yet his performance lags behind his native language peers after instructional adaptations have been implemented; 2) the student has good English academic proficiency, received effective academic instruction, and still has significant academic difficulties; and/or 3) the academic language skills don't improve after effective English as a Second Language or bilingual interventions.

In the case of students with specific learning disabilities, referrals should be informed by current research on the *response to intervention* approach with attention to cultural issues (Klingner & Edwards, 2006). Regarding students with emotional and behavioral disabilities, all schools should be aware of models of *positive behavior support* (Turnbull et al., 2002).

8 Communicate Effectively with Families

The term "communication structure" highlights the idea that communication does not occur in a vacuum. School cultures include the rules and the circumstances for communication with family members, and also determine, sometimes inadvertently, what the nature of that communication will be.

Many cultural assumptions, which are often hidden or unacknowledged, set the stage for the type of communication that will occur between service providers and family members. For example, when conducting face-to-face conferences, the structures provided for communication reflect assumptions about which participants are more important and what kinds of information will be valued. Communication structures include:

1. Physical settings, such as arrangements for seating of family members and professionals

2. The order in which reports are given at conferences

3. Whether the announcement of the conference requested information on parents' availability

4. Whether family members' input is integral to the meeting or requested as an add-on

For example, parents' comments should be an explicit part of an IEP conference agenda. Communication structures also include whether needed translation services are provided and whether reports are delivered in understandable language, with true opportunities for questioning and reflection.

Many parents, particularly those from nonmainstream cultures, who may not be in synch with school assumptions and practices, need a more personalized interaction approach. This approach is sometimes referred to as "high context" as opposed to "low context" communication. In *high context communication*, adequate respect is given to personal identity, and opportunities are provided for the exchange of a broader range of cultural and contextual information, such as current or past family situations or concerns. Remember that all cultural communities develop proficiency in particular ways to communicate and to tell stories. Educators need to understand parents' communication practices and explore with them structures to communicate formally or informally, in ways that may be different from the structures traditionally used by schools.

Arrange Informational Opportunities for Parents

Many parents from particular cultural communities are unaware of the meaning and process of the special education system or of the rights that the law affords them. Even the written materials provided for parents in a variety of languages may be difficult for some parents to understand, either because of the level of the language, the use of educational jargon, or the cultural assumptions embedded in key concepts. For example, parents from certain cultural communities may not understand that relatively mild learning difficulties might be assessed as "disabilities" and, like some of the parents in Harry's (1992) study with Puerto Rican parents, may believe that school personnel are saying that their children are "loco" ("crazy"). On the other hand, immigrant parents from countries where there is no educational provision for students with significant disabilities may not fully understand the meaning and purpose of inclusive programs.

The 2004 reauthorization of the Individuals with Disabilities Education Improvement Act of 2004 calls for school districts to make every effort to ensure that parents understand the proceedings of meetings and the meaning and process of the IEP. True understanding often requires face-to-face opportunities for parents to engage in explanatory conversations with knowledgeable others. Schools, perhaps through the parent–teacher association, can form committees whose purpose is to explain to parents the provisions and services of special education or the inclusion process. Including family or community members on such committees could provide effective peer support to parents who may find the special education system overwhelming or may be intimidated by the school's cultural or linguistic practices. It can also be helpful to hear information from other families with similar challenges.

Schools should nurture productive partnerships with parents who can bring an insider's understanding of particular cultural communities. At the same time, educators should remember that parents who might be considered "insiders" in their own communities with regard to certain activities could also be perceived by their communities as "outsiders" in other contexts.

Stand Firm Against
"I'm Tired of Culture" Rhetoric

Have you heard any of your colleagues sighing, "I'm tired of culture! Why do I have to deal with all this? These minorities just need to assimilate!"? Although minorities have to adapt to the mainstream environment, the process of adaptation in the U.S. is more like a "cultural dialogue" than a one-way assimilation. This is more true today than ever, for at least two reasons. First, the vast majority of immigrants now come from non-white and non-European cultures that differ in deep-rooted ways from traditional Anglo-Saxon culture. Second, the Civil Rights movement of the mid-twentieth century radically changed the status of native minorities, particularly African Americans and Native Americans. The old vision of a "melting pot" that included a mixture of primarily European groups, while excluding people of color, is now history. However, we remain with the challenge of remedying the legacy of exclusion and discrimination that was inherent in that history.

A dialogue is emerging as U.S. culture takes account of people of different colors, religions, cultures, and languages; it promises truly rich, previously unknown *pluralistic national identities*. Our challenge is to confront and resolve what Artiles, Trent, and Palmer (2004) have called the "dilemma of difference," a human tendency to resist and mistrust "the other" and to assume that one's own heritage is superior to those of others. After all, definitions of difference are always based on a comparison— "different from what?" The challenge for educators is to be clear about why we feel threatened by "difference."

Special education, with its foundational value on the inherent dignity of all human beings, should be an ideal forum for celebration of the cultural nature of inclusion, teaching, and learning. As special educators, we believe in valuing and supporting, not excluding or changing, people's differences. When your colleagues seem to be losing heart, remind them that the core of special education is its celebration of diversity. This is as true regarding culture and language as it is regarding differences in abilities. It is part of our identity to be leaders in welcoming cultural diversity.

Selected References

Artiles, A.J., & Rueda, R. (2002, March–April). General guidelines for monitoring minority overrepresentation in special education. *CASE Newsletter, 43*(5), 5–6.

Artiles, A.J., Trent, S.C., & Palmer, J. (2004). Culturally diverse students in special education. In J.A. Banks & C.M. Banks (Eds.), *Handbook of research on multicultural education* (2nd ed.) (pp. 716–735). San Francisco: Jossey Bass.

Arzubiaga, A., Ceja, M., & Artiles, A.J. (2000). Transcending deficit thinking about Latinos' parenting styles. In C. Tejeda, C. Martinez, & Z. Leonardo (Eds.), *Charting new terrains of Chicana(o)/Latina(o) education* (pp. 93–106). Cresskill, NY: Hampton.

Donovan, S., & Cross, C. (2002). *Minority students in gifted and special education.* Washington, DC: National Academy Press.

González, N., & Moll, L. (2002). Cruzando El Puente: Building bridges to funds of knowledge. *Journal of Educational Policy, 16*, 623–641.

Harry, B. (1992). *Cultural diversity, families, and the special education system.* New York: Teachers College Press.

Harry, B., Kalyanpur, M., & Day, M. (1999). *Building cultural reciprocity with families: Case studies in special education.* Baltimore: Paul H. Brookes Publishing Co.

Harry, B., & Klingner, J.K. (2006). *Why are so many minority students in special education?* New York: Teachers College Press.

Individuals with Disabilities Education Improvement Act of 2004, PL 108-446, 20 U.S.C. §§ 1400 *et seq.*

Klingner, J.K., & Edwards, P.A. (2006). Cultural considerations with response to intervention models. *Reading Research Quarterly, 41*(1), 107–117.

Ladson-Billings, G. (1994). *The dream-keepers.* San Francisco: Jossey Bass.

Ortiz, A.A. (2002). Prevention of school failure and early intervention for English language learners. In A.J. Artiles, & A.A. Ortiz (Eds.), *English language learners with special needs* (pp. 31–48). Washington, DC: Center for Applied Linguistics.

Richards, H.V., Brown, A.F., & Forde, T.B. (2004). *Addressing diversity in schools: Culturally responsive education.* Practitioner Brief Series. NCCREST.

Rogoff, B. (2003). *The cultural nature of human development.* New York: Oxford University.

Turnbull, A., Edmonson, E., Griggs, P., Wickham, D., Sailor, W., Freeman, R., et al. (2002). A blueprint for school-wide positive behavior support: Implementation of three components. *Exceptional Children, 68,* 377–358.

Section II

Relationships &
Self-Determination

JUDY'S BRAND OF "IN-YOUR-FACE"
SELF-ADVOCACY FIRST SHOWED
ITSELF AT AN EARLY AGE.

Quick-Guide #4

Supporting Friendships
for All Students

Carol Tashie and Zach Rossetti

Quick-Guides to Inclusion
Ideas for Educating Students with Disabilities, Second Edition

Michael F. Giangreco & Mary Beth Doyle

Editors

Dear Teacher,

So much of school is about memorable experiences with people: inspirational teachers, best friends, boyfriends, girlfriends, "just friends," and ex-friends. Sure, students learn about history, math, and English, but even more so, students learn about friendship, diversity, and loyalty. Students develop relationships through their participation in classes, clubs, teams, and committees. Through these relationships, students learn a great deal about getting along with other people—now and in the future.

All students need a wide variety of relationships with their classmates. Not everyone will have an honor roll grade-point average, be the captain of the team, or have the lead in the school play. But everyone can make friends. Unfortunately, many students with disabilities do not have friends. Far too often, they spend the bulk of their school days surrounded by adults. Many parents of students with disabilities report that their children are lonely, with only the television, other family members, or paid adults to keep them company after school. The phone never rings; no one comes to visit.

As a teacher, you may encounter students who face the world pretty much alone. You may wonder what you can do to respect the need for belonging that all students feel. In many ways you can act as a bridge between students with and without disabilities who may not naturally connect in the ways that they might want to. You can also work to overcome the barriers that prevent students with and without disabilities from seeing each other as potential friends. What follows are suggestions on how to support students to develop meaningful and reciprocal relationships with others in their lives. We encourage you to view these connections as important and crucial parts of every student's education.

Peace,
Carol and Zach

GUIDELINES-AT-A-GLANCE

1. Everyone Can and Should Have Friends

2. Model High Expectations for All Students

3. Make Sure All Students Share Time, Space, and Activities

4. Even if Students Don't Speak, They Still Have Things to Say

5. Create Classes that Celebrate, Not Simply Tolerate, Diversity

6. Respect the Space that Friendships Require—Don't Get in the Way

7. Seek the Perspectives and Involvement of Classmates

8. Families Are Essential—You Can't Do it Alone

9. Pay Attention to What Friendship Is and Isn't

10. Provide Intentional Facilitation

Everyone Can and Should Have Friends

Over the last few years we have discovered a great deal about friendships between students with and without disabilities. From talking to students and listening to their stories, we have learned that friendship can be a reality for all students. We also have learned that friendships are more likely to occur when all of the people in a student's life truly believe that she is someone who would make a great friend. In school, this awareness begins with the classroom teacher, paraprofessional, and any other adults who will teach a student.

As a classroom teacher, you have the opportunity to create environments and conditions that foster relationships between all students. Classroom lists and activities should include all students. You can begin the school year having all students participate in "get acquainted" activities. These activities give students the opportunities to get to know their classmates in fun and memorable ways.

You can utilize cooperative learning lessons in which all students participate, affirming the notions of interdependence and the power of students working together. Learning centers and other small group situations develop social bonds as students teach and learn from one another.

Develop a sense of your students' individual strengths so you can structure learning situations in which all students both give and receive help. This helps to avoid students without disabilities taking on caregiving roles with their classmates with disabilities, which can become a barrier to the development of friendships. Even when students are working independently, teachers can encourage student connections by allowing them to ask each other for help, proofread first drafts, and brainstorm ideas with each other. These kinds of classroom strategies can provide the foundation for the development of meaningful and reciprocal friendships.

This foundation may be solid enough to support relationships for many students. For some students, teachers will need to work closely with team members to develop and implement individual plans for the active facilitation of friendships. The following pages offer further guidelines to assist in developing these plans.

Model High Expectations for All Students

2

The ways in which students are regarded by their classmates are strongly influenced by how they are perceived and treated by their teachers. Therefore, the likelihood that friendships will develop increases when you consider and treat all of your students as valued, capable, and interesting individuals.

When students with disabilities are consistently characterized by their labels (e.g., "the student with Down syndrome"), spoken to as if they don't understand, or spoken about as if they aren't present, it is less likely that classmates will take the time to look past the label and get to know the person. Since children observe and internalize much of what we do, these messages can convey to classmates that the student is "not worth knowing" or is unable to develop a relationship. This can build formidable barriers to friendship before students ever have a chance to get to know each other.

To avoid or overcome these barriers, you can be a role model for your students and the other adults in your school. Through respectful language, you can model for others that the student with disabilities is a person first (e.g., "Shaffer, who loves lacrosse and the Grateful Dead . . . "). You can show your students, through your actions and words, that you believe they all possess the potential to be successful and to live the lives they wish to lead. One way to do this is to ensure that all students receive all handouts and worksheets during classwork time. By talking to and about the student in ways consistent with his age, you model age-appropriate expectations. When you make modifications to curriculum only when necessary, and are always respectful of the student's gifts, learning style, and grade level, other students will be able to view him as a contributing and integral member of the class.

When you demonstrate your belief that the student with disabilities is not deficient, but simply moves through the world in different ways, you teach your students that the student with disabilities is not "broken," does not need to be "fixed," and has much to contribute as a student and as a friend. Maintaining and modeling high expectations for all students sends the message to your class that everyone can and will make friends.

Make Sure All Students Share Time, Space, and Activities

3

Students need to be together to develop respect, mutual interests, and real friendships. Classrooms provide all students with the opportunities to share experiences and appreciate each other's company. Great classrooms offer students planned and spontaneous chances to learn together as well as to connect socially. However, for too many students with disabilities, even those who are in general education classes, their school day still consists of separate places and lessons. Far too many students with disabilities continue to be "pulled out" of their classrooms to receive services from special educators and therapists. Not only has the educational value of using pull-out approaches been questioned, it significantly affects students' abilities to make friends. Students who leave the classroom miss important opportunities to connect with classmates around content, knowledge, and activities. They may eventually be viewed as part-time members of the class, or as too unlike their classmates to be potential friends.

As a teacher, you can reject the notion that some students must leave the classroom in order to learn. You can encourage push-in therapies and multimodal lessons in which various supports can be incorporated. You have the power to embrace and develop a classroom environment that allows each student to participate in, and learn from, all lessons. For example, when teaching a history lesson on World War II, you can provide students different ways to develop and demonstrate their knowledge. Some students may write a journal in the style of Anne Frank; others can create a mural representing the treaty at Yalta; while still others may develop a game of *Jeopardy* in which all students can participate as hosts, card turners, or contestants.

You can utilize an array of direct instruction, paired reading, small-group activities, and class projects in all of your lessons. Teaching with this emphasis on different avenues of involvement recognizes that all students can learn and that we value the ways in which they do. By supporting meaningful learning outcomes for all students, teachers can send the clear message that a disability need not be a "handicap" to learning, ability, or friendship.

Even if Students Don't Speak, They Still Have Things to Say

4

For too long, people believed that students who did not speak, or did not speak easily, did not have very much to say. Assumptions about students' abilities, comprehension, and even interests were made based on archaic views of intelligence and capability. However, the advent of various forms of augmentative and alternative communication (AAC) has allowed so many people, once labeled "mentally retarded" because they could not fully express themselves, to now communicate their intelligence, wit, and personality.

We also know that even when students are not yet able to express all they know, they are still communicating. Whether through body language, facial expressions, behaviors, or gestures, everyone communicates. It is up to us to pay attention and to learn to listen to what they are saying. When we believe that every student has something to say, we can tap into the resources of AAC to augment a student's ability to communicate knowledge, thoughts, and desires.

Supporting a student's ability to communicate is critical to developing social relationships. Though having a sophisticated means of communication is not a prerequisite for friendship, it does assist students to interact and get to know each other more easily.

An effective starting point is to ask families and classmates about the ways in which a student currently communicates and what other things she may want to say. Try to avoid restricting the student's communication to a limited number of word or symbol choices. If a student uses a communication device, classmates can suggest words to include, based on what students her age talk about.

As the teacher, you are key to making sure a student's communication device is always within her reach and that all other students understand how and why it is used. You can also practice role modeling to show students how to have conversations and how to look for nonverbal communication with a classmate who does not speak or use a communication device. It is important to let students know about *all* of the ways a student communicates, for when students know how to communicate with each other, they usually do.

Create Classes that Celebrate, Not Simply Tolerate, Diversity

It is not enough for schools to simply tolerate the differences among us, for tolerance implies a hierarchy of value. One prizes good health, but tolerates a cold. When schools promote tolerance, they send the message to students that, "You are welcome only if you act, look, sound, think, and talk like us." This reinforces the prejudice of a social hierarchy, decreasing the likelihood that students will become friends. On the other hand, when schools strive to celebrate diversity, they send the message to all students, "You are welcome as you are and we need you as you are."

To create a classroom that celebrates diversity, many teachers have found it useful to embed the contributions of people with disabilities into their lessons. When studying inventors, teachers highlight Temple Grandin, a woman with autism and a Ph.D. who is an inventor of livestock management equipment and techniques. When choosing literature, teachers can introduce *Stuck in Neutral* (Trueman, 2000), a book about a teenager who has cerebral palsy. When teaching about civil rights, teachers can include the contributions of Ed Roberts to the independent living movement, and the 1988 student protest at Gallaudet University.

Teachers can infuse in the curriculum the fact that many influential people in history have had disabilities. For example, U.S. President Franklin Delano Roosevelt and famed artist Frida Kahlo both had physical disabilities. By teaching about the contributions of former NBA basketball player Mahmoud Abdul-Rauf, who has Tourette syndrome; Albert Einstein and Hans Christian Andersen, who had dyslexia; and Stephen Hawking, who has amyotrophic lateral sclerosis; teachers can stress that disability is a natural part of all of our lives.

By including people with disabilities as an integral part of the curriculum, teachers create classrooms that celebrate the contributions of everyone. When the abilities of each student are equally celebrated, students learn to appreciate their own and other's gifts. This celebration of diversity often results in friendships, because students want to be friends with classmates they perceive as popular, skilled, or valued by the teacher.

6 Respect the Space that Friendships Require—Don't Get in the Way

When students were asked why no one ate lunch with Esther, her teachers expected to hear complaints of personal eating habits or difficulty with communication. Instead they got an earful: no one eats with Esther because no one wants to sit with the adult who is always by Esther's side. For too many students with disabilities, their independence is inadvertently stifled by the presence of a paraprofessional.

Imagine for a moment what it would be like to be Esther, having the ever-constant presence of an adult nearby. How difficult would it be to connect with classmates, try new things, or even just relax, knowing an adult was always by your side? While a paraprofessional's role can be extremely useful in providing educational support, it can also act as a barrier, literally, to students developing relationships with classmates.

As a classroom teacher, you can ensure that the adults working in your classroom (e.g., paraprofessionals, special educators, related services providers, volunteers) understand their roles in supporting students both educationally and socially. You can help team members understand the importance and potential of social relationships and developing friendships. You can model and teach other adults in the classroom to fade back so that other students can fill the spaces formerly occupied by adults. You can encourage social relationships by helping students take advantage of naturally occurring opportunities to interact, without providing excessive or unnecessary adult involvement. Based upon your knowledge of your students, you can encourage them to recognize their common interests, hobbies, and activities.

An important role of the other team members in your classroom is to support you to be an effective teacher for all students in your class. You can let the team know that you see the student with disabilities as one of your students and you do not want an adult (e.g., special educator, therapist, or paraprofessional) sitting too close to the student, talking for her, or standing in the way of "kids being kids." Together, you can set the stage for friendship; then step back as the magic unfolds.

Seek the Perspectives and Involvement of Classmates

As every teacher knows, students are not just learners; they are valuable teachers of everything from helping classmates learn new skills to creating classroom rules. Similarly, students can be incredible resources to help teams understand ways to support a student to become more connected with his classmates. Following these two basic guidelines will serve you well: 1) ask students to tell you what you need to know, and 2) tell the students what they need to know.

Students can give you information about what friendship is like for kids their age. They can tell you how they meet, where they go, and why they like to hang out together. They can inform you about opportunities for social connections and let you know what students with particular interests do to get together. They can let you know about school functions, sleepovers, study sessions, parties, and general times when they just hang out.

Students can advise you on who a student may want to spend time with and can serve as inside connectors to introduce one student to another or to a group. They can tell you when adults should step in and when they should bow out. Many teams believe so strongly in the value of the information that students can supply that they regularly and intentionally seek their input throughout the school day and at team meetings.

In addition to asking students' advice, it is also important to provide students with the information they require to better connect with their classmates. In order for students to become friends, they need to understand everything from how an individual communicates and the ways in which he requires support, to what his interests are and what he finds irritating. Students may want to know about their classmate's disability, but may be too shy or scared to ask. Talk to the student and his family to be sure it is okay, and then provide the information they need to truly get to know one another.

While we encourage you to draw upon your own memories as a student, no adult can truly know what it is like to be a student in today's classroom. Luckily, teachers have easy access to the real experts—students.

Families Are Essential— You Can't Do it Alone

8

Open and honest communication between families and schools is key to the collaboration that is required to support all students to have meaningful relationships. It may be helpful to follow two basic guidelines with families, including 1) *asking* families to tell you what they believe, desire, and require, and 2) *informing* families what you know, need to learn, and hope to accomplish.

Families know their children best and are invaluable resources when trying to understand a student's interests and gifts. They know that their child would make a great friend and can help you achieve this. Families can provide information about the things their children do at home, which may translate into how a student can get involved at school. Families can also provide a historical perspective, such as which classmates a student has known for years, what they like to do after school, and ways in which relationships were developed in earlier grades.

It is crucial to recognize and respect that the risk-taking friendships involve can be difficult for some families. A useful strategy is to ask families about their "nonnegotiables." What are the things that they cannot ignore, compromise, or alter, no matter what the cost? For example, one family did not want their daughter to eat out with friends. When it was understood that their nonnegotiable limit was the student's macrobiotic diet, the issue was resolved by providing her friends with a list of foods she could and could not eat. Once nonnegotiable concerns are on the table, collaboration becomes more effective and less stressful for all involved.

It is also helpful to give families information about friendship. Teachers can give families ideas of which students share their child's interests, schedules of school and non-school sponsored activities, and ideas for car pools. Schools can help families connect with other students who can offer valuable information about the ins and outs of friendship. Just saying that you are open to collaboration on issues of friendship will be a helpful and hopeful start to the school year. Open these lines of communication between teacher and family, and take advantage of all that you can do together.

9

Pay Attention to What Friendship Is and Isn't

In third grade, Kevin's team developed a buddy list so that he would always have someone to play with at recess. The team was surprised that Kevin was not happy at recess, except every tenth day when Trey was his assigned buddy. The teacher quickly realized that Kevin did not want a rotation of classmates; he wanted a friend. She took down the buddy list and began supporting the budding relationship between Kevin and Trey while also extending the network of relationships.

In the quest to help students develop authentic relationships with others their age, many teachers implement strategies such as buddy lists for lunch and recess. Although done with good intentions, these strategies often perpetuate the notion that students with disabilities cannot have true friends and that being with an assigned buddy is the best they can do. Just as important, you may be fooled into thinking that your work is done when you see two students sitting together at lunch and think that they are friends.

As a teacher you are in the unique position to support the development of true friendships. You can see which students have a natural affinity to each other and can encourage ways for those students to get to know each other better. You can group these students together for cooperative learning lessons, to work on the class bulletin board, and to play on the same dodge ball team at recess.

If you do not see these relationships extending beyond the classroom, you can have conversations with students to find out what questions they have and what supports and information they need. You can also pay attention to the natural places and ways that your students interact. If for example, in primary grades students play in the sand box at recess, you can encourage the student with a disability to join them. If middle school students play card games at lunchtime, you can make sure the student with a disability is in the middle of the action. If high school students meet at their lockers during the few minutes before class, you can support the student with a disability to be there. The key is to pay attention to what friendship really is for all kids and not be fooled by what it isn't.

Provide Intentional Facilitation

10

Hopefully, the nine guidelines you have read so far have given you ideas on how to create classroom and school environments that provide fertile ground for friendships to grow. However, for some students, it may be necessary to provide *intentional facilitation* of friendship. Although it sounds formal, *intentional facilitation* is simply the process of getting to know the student and then supporting her to become better connected. It is an active process that requires intentional planning, but it will be different for each student, based on individual interests and environments.

The person who provides intentional facilitation should be well versed with the nine guidelines previously described and be able to confidently convey these values to others. This person should be someone with whom the student is comfortable and who strongly respects her gifts. For older students, the facilitator can be someone close to the student's own age. While this person will lead the process, he must recognize that it is a cooperative effort, involving the student, family, school, and classmates. In fact, he can be the team motivator or instigator of the process.

The process begins by getting to know the student and others her age. Ways to gather this information include conversations with and observations of the student, conversations with classmates, families, and teachers, as well as the use of a formal process such as MAPs (Falvey, Forest, Pearpoint, & Rosenberg, 1994). It is essential to gather information on what friendships look like for students of the same age, as well as an understanding of what is typically available in the school and neighborhood for students with similar interests. Once this information is all gathered, the facilitator can begin to connect the student with people, clubs, and events that match the student's desires. Not every effort will be successful, so we want to stress that *intentional facilitation* is an ongoing process.

Intentional facilitation is not magic—it is the deliberate connection of one student with others who may share her interests and activities. However, when done right, it can unleash the real magic of friendship.

Selected References

Biklen, D. (Ed). (2005). *Autism and the myth of the person alone.* New York: New York University Press.

Bogdan, R., & Taylor, S. (1989). Relationships with severely disabled people: The social construction of humanness. *Social Problems, 36*, 135–148.

Causton-Theoharis, J.N., & Malmgren, K.W. (2005). Building bridges: Strategies to help paraprofessionals promote peer interactions. *Teaching Exceptional Children, 37*(6), 18–24.

Giangreco, M.F., Luiselli, T.E., & MacFarland, S.Z.C. (1997). Helping or hovering? Effects of instructional assistant proximity on students with disabilities. *Exceptional Children, 64,* 7–18.

Lovett, H. (1996). *Learning to listen: Positive approaches and people with difficult behavior.* Baltimore: Paul H. Brookes Publishing Co.

Falvey, M.A., Forest, M., Pearpoint, J., & Rosenberg, R. (1994). *All my life's a circle. Using the tools: Circles, MAPs and PATH.* Toronto: Inclusion Press.

Meyer, L.H. (2001). The impact of inclusion on children's lives: Multiple outcomes, and friendship in particular. *International Journal of Disability, Development and Education, 48,* 9–31.

Schnorr, R.F. (1990). "Peter? He comes and goes . . . ": First graders' perspectives on a part-time mainstream student. *Journal of the Association for Persons with Severe Disabilities, 15,* 231–240.

Snell, M., & Janney, R. (2006). *Teachers' guides to inclusive practices: Social relationships and peer support* (2nd ed.). Baltimore: Paul H. Brookes Publishing Co.

Strully, J., & Strully, C. (1992). That which binds us: Friendship as a safe harbor in a storm. In A.N. Amado (Ed.), *Friendships and community connections between people with and without developmental disabilities* (pp. 213–225). Baltimore: Paul H. Brookes Publishing Co.

Trueman, T. (2000). *Stuck in neutral.* New York: HarperCollins.

Van der Klift, E., & Kunc, N. (2002). Beyond benevolence: Supporting genuine friendships in inclusive schools. In J.S. Thousand, R.A. Villa, & A.I. Nevin (Eds.), *Creativity and collaborative learning: The practical guide to empowering students, teachers, and families.* Baltimore: Paul H. Brookes Publishing Co.

Quick-Guide #5

Self-Determination

Michael L. Wehmeyer

Quick-Guides to Inclusion
Ideas for Educating Students with Disabilities, Second Edition

Michael F. Giangreco & Mary Beth Doyle

Editors

Dear Teacher,

In the course of your teaching career, have you met students who you knew would make it in life? These students have goals and the plans to achieve them. They can identify barriers to success and solve problems to remove them. They know what they are good at and capitalize on their strengths. These students are self-determined. They take charge of their own learning, work toward self-set goals, and are ready when opportunity comes knocking! Ever wish you could bottle whatever it is that the self-determined student has and use it to inoculate all your students? Of course, nothing in education is ever as easy as just giving a shot, but you can ensure that your students have the opportunity to become more self-determined.

Promoting self-determination is important for all students. It is never too early or too late to teach students the skills that will enable them to become more self-determined. In fact, the odds are good that there are content standards in your school district for all students to achieve that reflect self-determination skills like problem solving, decision making, or goal setting. Too often, students with disabilities have not had the opportunity to learn the skills they need to become self-determined as a part of their curriculum, often because others don't think they can become self-determined. There is, however, quite a bit of research showing that students with all types of disabilities can become more self-determined. That's what this Quick-Guide is about. When students learn skills leading to greater self-determination, they can take more responsibility for directing their own learning and become less dependent on others. Promoting self-determination provides a useful strategy to enhance inclusion in the general education classroom and curriculum and helps students with disabilities lead more personally fulfilling lives.

Good Luck!
Mike

GUIDELINES-AT-A-GLANCE

1. It Starts with Your Example: Model Problem Solving

2. Tell Each Student You Believe He or She Is Capable

3. Emphasize Student Strengths and Uniqueness

4. Create a Learning Community that Promotes Risk Taking

5. Structure Your Classroom to Promote Choice Making

6. Empower Students to Make Decisions and Set Goals

7. Teach Students Self-Determination Skills

8. Encourage Student-Directed Learning

9. Involve Peers to Provide Supports

10. Explore Technology to Support Student Self-Direction

It Starts with Your Example: Model Problem Solving

A problem is an event or task for which a solution is not known or readily apparent. Problem solving is a process of identifying one or more solutions to a problem and selecting the best solution. If you think about it, life is full of problems that one must solve and keep solving. Not only big problems, like how to pay the rent or put food on the table, but everyday problems, like what to do when your child is sick and can't go to school but both parents have work deadlines, or how to get gum out of the carpet! Many problems are social in nature, involving problems in relationships and peer interactions, which may be particularly important to students who have difficulty with interpersonal interactions.

How can you teach problem solving? The general education curriculum in most states includes standards in multiple grades and content areas addressing problem-solving skills. Students can be taught how to identify and generate solutions to a problem. Most problem-solving processes have only a few steps: 1) identifying and defining the problem, 2) listing possible solutions, 3) identifying the impact of each solution, 4) making a judgment about a preferred solution, and 5) evaluating the efficacy of the judgment.

Older students should be given chances to solve increasingly complex problems and apply their emerging problem-solving skills in making decisions about their lives. Students with disabilities, like all students, need such instruction and can acquire better problem-solving skills.

Perhaps as importantly, however, you need to model the problem-solving process you apply to solve the problems that confront you every day. Most adults apply problem-solving approaches to situations, but don't usually verbalize them. What do you do when you turn on the overhead projector and the light bulb goes out? Instead of just solving the problem, you can verbalize the steps you are using to solve your problem and communicate to students what it takes to solve the myriad of problems they will confront day-to-day. Believe it or not, they really do watch what you do and learn from you!

2

Tell Each Student
You Believe He or She Is Capable

It is important to focus on skill development and knowledge attainment to promote self-determination. Certainly, teaching students skills like problem solving, decision making, goal setting, self-advocacy, or self-regulation are critical components of your role in enhancing self-determination. However, it is not enough *just* to teach these skills. "Ability is of little value without opportunity," Napoleon Bonaparte is alleged to have said. Opportunity is important because you not only get the chance to practice new skills and refine longer-held skills, but you also begin to believe you are capable and can make things happen in your life.

At its core, self-determination is about making things happen in your life. Even people with limited decision-making or problem-solving skills can make things happen in their lives. We can almost always find ways to get around skill or knowledge limitations—we do it all the time in our own lives! People who aren't good at math can use an accountant to do their taxes.

It's equally important for students with disabilities to find ways around any limitations. Just because a student cannot read does not mean, for example, that he or she cannot learn some of the content being taught if there is access to a text reader. Learning skills is important, but we can accommodate for situations when students don't acquire important skills.

When, however, students believe they are not capable or that they cannot overcome barriers in their way to achievement, we can't just accommodate with technology or pedagogical strategies. Too often students with disabilities have "learned" that they are not capable, either because they have failed in school frequently, or because others have communicated this to them.

Students with disabilities can come to believe they are capable, however, and can overcome barriers through opportunities to learn and practice skills related to self-determination, by succeeding in tasks, and by being told by adults in their lives that they are capable, competent, valued individuals. Saying "I believe in you" might be more important than anything else you do. Do it often and with conviction!

Emphasize Student Strengths and Uniqueness

3

Historically, special education has had a deficit focus. That is, the emphasis in special education services has been on identifying student deficits and providing instruction to, in some sense, "fix" that deficit. It is not unusual for students with disabilities to have a broad and expansive knowledge about what they do not do well and about their problems, yet not be able to tell you a single thing about what they do well.

Students with disabilities have, almost universally, experienced failure in the school system. The very process that students go through to be eligible to receive special education services begins with student failure in one or more academic areas, as eligibility for special education services is based upon the negative impact of the student's disability on his or her educational performance. Educational meetings that set goals about the student's individualized education all too often begin with a litany of what the student cannot do, the goals the student has not met, and the tests documenting the student's disability. Not a fun experience!

It goes without saying that this focus on deficits and disability does not make it easy to convince students they are capable, competent learners. When the education process focuses solely upon what the student cannot do, it increases the likelihood that the student will perform up to, or down to, expectations—low expectations, that is.

One consistent finding in the education literature is that students achieve what teachers expect them to achieve. As you plan your lessons and units and implement instruction for your students, it is important to think about each student's abilities and uniqueness and to build on those. There are a host of strategies that enable you to individualize instruction to take advantage of student strengths, like differentiated instruction. Students need to learn that everyone is unique and learns differently. Students with disabilities need to learn that they may have unique learning needs, but that those learning needs can be met and that those needs are balanced by their abilities. Further, students need to learn how to maximize their capacities and abilities, and learn strategies that will enable them to overcome their limitations.

Create a Learning Community that Promotes Risk Taking

One way to meet the needs of students with diverse learning, language, cultural, and economic characteristics is to create *learning communities* that respect, indeed celebrate, this diversity. Learning communities are intentionally created environments where students 1) learn to respect and value individual differences, 2) work in a self-directed manner, 3) apply problem-solving and decision-making strategies to educational problems, and 4) participate in setting classroom rules. This latter element, student involvement in rule making, can be a particularly powerful way to teach students that they have a voice in their lives.

Teachers who create learning communities do so by 1) gaining knowledge about the capacities and abilities of all their students, 2) developing systematic ways to collect meaningful information on student progress to modify existing lessons and plan future lessons, 3) using strategies such as collaborative teaming, cooperative learning, and differentiated instruction to individualize student educational experiences, and 4) taking on the roles of coach and facilitator as well as instructor.

Creating learning communities is critical to promoting self-determination. In such settings, students learn that they have a voice in the educational process by their participation in rule setting. They learn about other students and their unique abilities and needs and to solve social problems through conflict resolution processes.

Perhaps most importantly, they learn they can take risks. It is essential that students feel comfortable to take risks if they are to learn skills such as problem solving, decision making, goal setting and attainment, and self-advocacy, all of which require students to "risk" failure by brainstorming answers, trying different solutions, and setting potentially unattainable goals (which can, of course, be revised!). When students feel that they will be ridiculed or punished for failing, they don't take such risks and, as a consequence, do not learn these essential skills. Intentional learning communities support and even value risk taking and, in turn, teach students that failure is not an end, but a means to success and, in the end, self-determination!

Structure Your Classroom to Promote Choice Making

One of the better ways to teach students that they can make things happen in their lives is to provide them with multiple opportunities to make choices and to infuse those choice opportunities across the curriculum and throughout the school day. Making a choice is simply communicating a preference between two or more equally available options.

Unlike goal-setting, decision-making, or problem-solving skills, we rarely have to teach students how to make a choice. True, some students with more severe learning impairments may need to be taught how to more effectively communicate their preferences and interests, or will have to learn that there are only particular times during which the choice can be made, but for the most part students come to school with a bundle of preferences and they are perfectly willing and able to tell you about them or to communicate them to you in some manner!

Believe it or not, this works to your advantage in promoting self-determination. If you structure your classroom to maximize the opportunity for students of all ages to make choices, you are creating an environment in which students will learn that their opinions and preferences are valued and that they can influence their own learning outcomes. Moreover, many younger children (and for that matter older students) need to learn that not every option is available to them, even if they prefer that option!

There are many ways to infuse choice into instruction, such as letting students choose where or with whom they perform an activity, when they work on a task, when they begin or end a task, and so forth. Even when what the student must learn is dictated to the student, as is the case with much of the content in the general education curriculum, you can create choice opportunities by offering different ways to learn the same information or material. In addition, students can choose what outcome they work toward and, in essence, begin to learn how to set their own goals. Goal setting is, after all, simply choosing a particular outcome one would like to achieve. In the end, providing students with frequent opportunities to make choices teaches them that they can have a "voice" in their lives.

Empower Students to Make Decisions and Set Goals

6

Empowerment is a term usually associated with social movements and used in reference to actions that enable people to control their own lives. To empower students is to enable them to exert some influence over their lives and to make things happen for themselves. The verb *enable* is used purposefully, for usually we do things "to" or "for" students, particularly students with disabilities. Instead, we need to serve as a catalyst to ensure that students have the chance to have a voice in their lives, to provide support to students who are unsure about their capacity to make something happen, and to create the circumstances under which students can exert control.

The educational process is goal oriented, and there is no better way to empower students to influence their lives than to actively involve them in setting goals about their instruction. Goals specify what a person wishes to achieve and act as regulators of human behavior. If a person sets a goal, it increases the probability that he or she will perform behaviors related to that goal. The process of promoting goal-setting and attainment skills involves teaching students to 1) identify and define a goal clearly and concretely, 2) develop a series of objectives or tasks to achieve the goal, and 3) specify the actions necessary to achieve the desired outcome.

At each step, students must make choices and decisions about what goals they wish to pursue and what actions they wish to take to achieve their goals. The word *involve* comes from the Latin word *involvere,* which means to enwrap or entwine. We need to get students enwrapped in their education by enabling them to set goals and by supporting them in making decisions about their education and their lives.

Students with disabilities are particularly likely to have others make decisions about them and to have goals set for them by others, including teachers or their family members. In many ways, the special education process creates dependency. Involve all students in the educational decision-making process. Enable them to set goals that are meaningful to them. In so doing, you enable them to regulate their own learning and empower them for life.

7 Teach Students Self-Determination Skills

Learning skills to become more self-determined helps students to be more self-reliant. There is a wide array of skills and knowledge related to self-determination that students need to learn. Problem-solving, decision-making, and goal-setting skills have already been mentioned in previous guidelines. Additionally, students need to learn to self-regulate learning and self-manage their lives, a focus discussed in a subsequent guideline.

There are still other important areas, however. Students need to learn how to become self-advocates—how to stand up for their rights and advocate on their own behalf. To do so, they will need to learn some effective communication skills, how to negotiate and compromise, or how to use persuasion to get what they want. They will need to learn to listen as well as speak, or to communicate through nonverbal means.

There are ample opportunities for students to practice and learn self-advocacy skills within the context of the educational planning process. Students need to be provided real-world opportunities to practice these skills. This can be done by embedding opportunities for self-advocacy within the school day by allowing students to 1) set up a class schedule, 2) work out their supports with a resource room teacher or other support provider, or 3) participate in IEP and transition planning meetings.

Another important area is in the domain of self- and disability awareness. The importance of emphasizing capacity and uniqueness has already been discussed, and this is particularly important in promoting self- and disability awareness. The purpose of such activities is not to get the student to simply accept the label the school has determined for that student, but to explore his or her areas of strengths and what unique needs will enable the student to succeed.

Like all students, young people with disabilities need friends, and the importance of peer relationships is stressed elsewhere. In addition, however, students with a disability can learn and grow from relationships with adult mentors who have a similar disability and whose life stories inform the students and encourage them to work toward self-reliance and self-sufficiency.

8 Encourage Student-Directed Learning

School has been described (only slightly tongue-in-cheek) as a place students have to go to do something someone else tells them they must do. Most of what happens in schools is teacher-directed or dictated by the curriculum. Traditional models of instruction have teachers setting instructional goals, identifying resources, providing instruction, evaluating student progress, and assigning grades. Models like direct instruction, which are frequently used with students with disabilities, are particularly other-directed. While these teacher-directed activities are, in some cases, necessary, you can often teach students to do for themselves what you might otherwise do to or for them.

Take tracking progress on student goals as an example. Typically, that is a responsibility exercised exclusively by the teacher. You record grades in a grade book, score papers, collect data on task completion, and engage in a myriad of other activities that enable you to determine student progress. However, it is really quite easy to set up systems where students are responsible for tracking their own progress on goals. They can do so in a variety of ways, like keeping a graph of their progress, maintaining a log, or self-monitoring time on a task. Students with more significant cognitive disabilities may need highly individualized ways to track progress, but there is almost certainly a way that can be developed that would enable them to do that, even if it is as simple as placing a marker of some sort (e.g., poker chip, token) when an activity has been completed successfully.

There are many ways we can enable students to self-direct learning. Teaching students problem-solving and goal-setting steps enables them to more effectively self-direct educational goal setting. Students can be provided pictures of a task they are to perform in the correct sequence that enables them to proceed without an adult prompting them. With digital cameras that process is very simple! Materials can be available where all students can access them. The key is for you to look at what you do for students that they could do for themselves.

9 Involve Peers to Provide Supports

Another excellent way to promote self-determination is to link students with their same-age peers without disabilities in cooperative or collaborative learning groups. Same-age peers don't tend to do as much for or to students with disabilities and, instead, focus on support. It is likely that many teachers have learned how to "let go" and let students with disabilities do things for themselves by watching how classmates interact with the student!

You should, of course, be cautious not to place peers without disabilities in roles that simply make them "mini-teachers," and you also need to ensure that peers have ample opportunities to interact with the student as a classmate, potential friend, and fellow student. However, having a peer who is seated next to a student with a disability assist the student on academic and other tasks serves to both provide support to the student needing assistance and to create an interaction and an opportunity to develop a friendship. Research is clear, by the way, that these types of peer-mediated learning situations do not negatively affect the academic performance of peers without disabilities and, in fact, provide an opportunity to teach students about living in a diverse world.

To say that peers are important for all children is to state the obvious, but perhaps it cannot be overstated that students with disabilities need to have opportunities to build friendships with peers who do not have a disability. Too many children and adolescents with disabilities do not have frequent "play" or "get-together dates" with friends or get invited to birthday parties or other social events.

The participation by students with disabilities in the general education classroom is a first step to promoting relationships with peers and encouraging friendships, but it is *only* a first step. Teachers have to be intentional and design the classroom environment and schedule so that peers without disabilities have the opportunity to get to know the student with a disability as a person first, and not just as a "disabled" person. Peers who begin providing supports and assistance may graduate to becoming the student's ally and advocate, employer, and, hopefully, friend.

Explore Technology to Support Student Self-Direction

10

Technology has the capacity to enable students with disabilities to become more self-determined. For example, one area of dependence for many students with disabilities involves financial planning and budget management. Many students with cognitive disabilities could not do the math required to prepare a budget and maintain a checking account. With the availability of budget-management software programs, however, the requirements for maintaining a checkbook register and budgeting change, from having to possess math skills to being able to input data and use the software. Moreover, with the capacity to download one's monthly bank statement directly from a bank web site into such software, even data entry becomes unnecessary.

In this area, and in many areas pertaining to transition outcomes, technology can enable students with disabilities to become more independent and, perhaps more importantly, enable them to exert greater control in their lives and thus become more self-determined. Therefore, you can promote self-determination by exploring (with students) how technology, from computers to digital assistants, can enable students to be less dependent on other people. For example, there are now quite a few prompting systems that operate from a handheld computer platform and enable students to, in essence, prompt themselves as they perform tasks. These programs use digital photographs and recorded sound to provide students with audio and video prompts, thus cueing the student to start and complete the task.

Not only can the use of technology decrease a student's dependence, but the student also may begin to believe he or she is more capable of being independent and, as such, the technology may lead the student to take greater risks. It doesn't hurt that technology like iPods™, computers, or palmtop PCs are socially desirable, and that their use may increase the student's social status among his or her peers. Technology changes rapidly, so you need to stay up with what is new to the market, but there are many off-the-shelf devices that can provide the support that enables a student to be less dependent and, thus, more self-determined.

Selected References

Agran, M., King-Sears, M., Wehmeyer, M.L., & Copeland, S.R. (2003). *Student-directed learning: Teachers' guides to inclusive practices.* Baltimore: Paul H. Brookes Publishing Co.

Field, S., & Hoffman, A. (2005). *Steps to self-determination (2nd ed.).* Austin, TX: PRO-ED.

Halpern, A.S., Herr, C.M., Doren, B., & Wolf, N.K. (2000). *NEXT S.T.E.P.: Student transition and educational planning (2nd ed.).* Austin, TX: PRO-ED.

Van Reusen, A.K., Bos, C.S., Schumaker, J.B., & Deshler, D.D. (2002). *The self-advocacy strategy for enhancing student motivation and self-determination.* Lawrence, KS: Edge Enterprises.

Wehmeyer, M.L., Agran, M., Hughes, C., Martin, J., Mithaug, D.E., & Palmer, S. (2007). *Promoting self-determination and self-determined learning for students with intellectual and developmental disabilities.* New York: Guilford Press.

Wehmeyer, M.L., & Field, S. (2007). *Self-determination: Instructional and assessment strategies.* Thousand Oaks, CA: Corwin Press.

Quick-Guide #6

Listen to Me

What Students Want Teachers to Know

Mary Schuh, Frank Sgambati, and Carol Tashie
Based on conversations with students (see following page)

Quick-Guides to Inclusion
Ideas for Educating Students with Disabilities, Second Edition
Michael F. Giangreco & Mary Beth Doyle

Editors

Quick-Guides to Inclusion: Ideas for Educating Students with Disabilities (2nd ed.) © Michael F. Giangreco, 2007
Available through Paul H. Brookes Publishing Co., Baltimore, 1-800-638-3775

Based on Conversations with

Katie Basford, a college student at Southern State Community College in Ohio, who loves dance, music, Ping Pong, and hanging out with friends in her new apartment.

Byron Holmes, a fifth grader at Kimball Elementary School, New Hampshire, who is committed to ridding the school yard of bullies and snitches, and plans on being a paleontologist when he grows up.

Jill Libby, a junior at Merrimack Valley High School, New Hampshire, who is on the field hockey and track teams and loves hanging out with friends.

Rebecca Madore, an 8th grader at Bow Middle School, New Hampshire, who is in the drama club and loves swimming and basketball.

Michael McCray Nowak, a junior at Portsmouth High School, New Hampshire, who plays basketball, performs in community theatre, and is active in local and national politics.

Michael Sgambati, a graduate of Winnisquam High School, New Hampshire, who now works at the Whole Child Center and volunteers at the Veterans Home, while attending New Hampshire Technical Institute.

Marika Steir, a recent graduate of Timberlane High School, New Hampshire, who is currently collaborating on writing a book about her life and has plans to open her own business.

Shawnee Stevens, a fourth grader at Colebrook Elementary School, New Hampshire, who loves soccer, football, basketball, swimming, and dancing.

Dylan Stewart, a fifth grader at Broken Ground Elementary School in Concord, New Hampshire, who loves music, books, swimming, and horseback riding.

Ryan Trinkley, a recent graduate of Concord High School, who works part time at the New Hampshire Division of Mental Health and Developmental Services and loves the ocean, seafood, and politics.

Dear Teacher,

   We know that teachers get lots of advice from lots of people. While we don't want to make your job any harder, we have a lot to say that could help you become an even better teacher than you already are, and will help us too. We are the students in your classes who have disabilities. We have all sorts of labels, like: learning disabilities, autism, blind, deaf, Down syndrome, attention-deficit hyperactivity disorder, emotional disabilities, and others.

   Some of us get around walking like most of the other kids in class. Some of us get around using crutches, walkers, or wheelchairs. Some of us learn very quickly. For some of us, learning new things can be difficult and take more time. We all communicate in different ways. Some of us talk like most of the other kids in our class. Some of us use sign language, point to symbols or pictures on a communication board, or use a computerized device. A few of us communicate using sounds, gestures, body movements, and facial expressions. Regardless of how we say things, all of us communicate, and we really want people to listen (sometimes it doesn't seem to us like they do).

   Have you ever thought about what it is like to be in our shoes? I know you are a teacher because you care about kids. I hope this means you care about us too. Even though some things about us are different than some of our classmates, we have more in common with the rest of the kids in the class than you might think. We want to tell you some things that will help us to feel more respected and valued as students, so we can get the most out of our school years. We hope you hear us and consider what we have to say, so we can learn and grow to our greatest potential. Not all of the ideas we share in this Quick-Guide apply to all of us—so you'll have to decide which ones apply to you.

   Our thoughts and suggestions are being shared with you in this Quick-Guide through our friends, Mary, Frank, and Carol, who spent time asking us questions and listening to us talk about our experiences and needs.

   Now for our first piece of advice—something all students will agree on: ASSIGN LESS HOMEWORK!

From,
Your Students (with help from Mary, Frank, & Carol)

GUIDELINES-AT-A-GLANCE

1. Be My Teacher

2. Treat Me Like Other Kids My Age

3. Notice What I Am Good at

4. Treat Me Like I Am Capable

5. Ask (and Listen to) Me and My Family if You Have Questions

6. Understand that Some Things Are Really Hard for Me

7. Teach Me Interesting Stuff in Ways I Can Understand

8. Listen to What My Behavior Is Saying

9. Help Me Make Friends

10. Believe I Can Be Something Great When I Grow Up

Be My Teacher

I want the teacher to be my teacher. The assistant should just help the teacher make this happen.

The aide is always sitting next to me and it's kind of getting on my nerves.

I wish she would sit somewhere else.

We are not really that much different than other kids in your class. We want the same things as everyone else. We want to learn, have friends, and feel important. One thing that makes us feel very different is when a teaching assistant acts as our teacher instead of you; we do not want this. It makes us feel different and not as important as the other kids in our class. We want you, the teacher, to be our teacher. We want you to take time and explain things to us and to give us the same attention you give to other students. We really like it when you get to know us, take a special interest in us, and like having us in your classes. These things let us know that we really matter.

Like everyone else, we learn by watching the other kids in our class and working with them. But sometimes it seems like everyone expects that we will only learn from a teacher assistant and she is expected to teach us everything. This makes us feel like the teacher has no time for us.

Sometimes we have to sit in the front or back of the room, with the assistant sitting right next to us or very close by. What kid wants to sit with an adult? When you were a kid, how would you have felt if you went through school sitting next to an adult instead of with the other kids? It is almost like being punished. Just because we might need some help from a teaching assistant doesn't mean she has to sit right next to us. It makes us feel like we can't do things on our own. Whenever the teaching assistant is out sick, we feel more independent. Our aides are very nice and we really don't want them to be sick, but when they are absent it is a nice break and makes us feel more like all the other kids. If the teaching assistant worked with all the kids and not just us, it would be better. Sitting in the middle is good for a lot us. Sitting with friends makes it even better. But instead of guessing or assuming what we want, you can just ask us. Every year, Jennifer Parrot (a great teacher in Ohio), asks each of her students to tell her what they need from her. It all starts by asking your students to tell you what they want and need you to know.

Treat Me Like Other Kids My Age

I don't want to be seen as different. Don't treat me different. Treat me like everyone else.

Teachers who have a sense of humor help me get through the hard times.

Talking to us like we are babies doesn't help—it only embarrasses us.

Can you remember what it was like when you were a student? Imagine how you would have felt if everyone treated you like a baby? Some people talk to us as if we are little kids, with a sing-song tone in their voice and using babyish words. We want people to talk to us like they do other people our own age. We know that sometimes we have tough times learning, and that means sometimes the work we need to do is a little different than our classmates; but that does not mean we should get baby work!

We want to do the same kinds of schoolwork as other students. If everyone is doing a report, we want to do a report. If everyone is doing a lab experiment and has their own materials or is sharing with a partner, we want to do the same. When you give us materials that look like they are for students a lot younger than our age, or don't give us the materials at all, it makes our classmates look at us and treat us differently, like we are younger than we really are or like we can't learn. When the other kids notice this, sometimes it makes them feel sorry for us or think we do not really belong in the class. Sometimes they do not want to get to know us, be our friends, or be our partners in class activities. When you plan lessons, please remember that even though we may learn differently and stuff we work on may need to be a little different, we should still have the same types of materials as the rest of the class.

It's funny; sometimes we are babied, but sometimes we are expected to act perfect. All we want is to do the same things as other students in the class, not only important stuff like schoolwork but also things like passing notes, breaking the rules, or going to the bathroom even when we don't really need to. Because there is usually an adult watching us, or because we have behavior plans and individualized education programs (IEPs) it feels like we are expected to be perfect all of the time. We just want to be treated like other kids our age.

Like everyone else, we have good and bad days. Sometime we get really tired in school. Sometimes we get upset, excited, or act in confusing ways. Please help us through these hard times and let us know you care and will be there to help us through the good and the bad times. We really do want you to be proud of us.

Notice What I Am Good at

I'm just the low guy on the totem pole.

Actually the chair is the lowest; and then me.

Everyone has things they are really good at. For some of us, those may not be so obvious, so you may have to look a little harder to find them. But they are there if only you take the time to notice. When you do, it means so much to us; it makes us feel as if we matter to you and that you think we are cool kids. Too often, it feels as if our teachers just think we are problems and they don't act as if they are very happy to have us in class. Can you imagine what that feels like to us? Sometimes we hear what teachers say about us to the teaching assistant or even to our parents. When we hear only bad things said about us, it makes us feel like we are lower than low. Then we wonder if we should even try any more. If no one appreciates what you can do, why bother to work hard?

Just like all of our classmates, we need to feel loved and liked and appreciated for who we are. We need our teachers to recognize our talents and the things we are good at. We work hard at learning new subjects in school, like social studies, music, geology, art, math, and independent reading. These are all things we enjoy and want to learn more about—like all students. Maybe we have some trouble learning everything you try to teach us; but just because we don't always learn everything doesn't mean we are not learning anything. Pay attention to what we are learning and get excited about this! That makes us feel like you think we are important students in your class.

We want to be included and noticed for our interests and talents in all different areas. We like to be recognized for being a good friend, being a helper in your class, and being a partner that other students can count on. Sometimes it feels like the class is arranged like a totem pole. The students who don't learn as easily are on the bottom and don't get the same attention as the students on the top; they always get recognized for their good grades and sometimes even for "snitching" behavior. We think most kids want to be in the middle of the totem pole and have it turned sideways, so they are happy with friends on either side, and able to be recognized for being right and sometimes wrong.

4 Treat Me Like I Am Capable

Why do specialists ask me to leave the class all the time, but when I want to leave the class like other kids to get a drink or something I always have to ask and they don't?

I always have a grown-up taking me around.

So many of us are forced to leave your class to get things like speech therapy or help with reading or physical therapy. We know people are trying to help us—sometimes it does help, sometimes it doesn't. Some of us have to leave for just a little while, but some of us are out of class for large chunks of the day. Do you think that what is going on outside of your class is more important than what is happening in your classroom? Well, we can tell from experience, it isn't! We think that what you are teaching and what all of the students are learning by being together is "where it's at."

Because we don't want to leave, sometimes we end up fighting the teacher who comes to take us. We act up and try to get her to let us stay; but that hardly ever works and it just gets us in trouble. Can't you understand why we fight? We don't want to leave your class. Rather than thinking we are bad, can't you take it as a compliment? We want to stay in your class and learn the things that everyone else is learning. Leaving just makes us feel dumb and unwanted—kids make fun of us.

When we leave class, we miss a lot. We try to catch up with what we missed, but it never seems to work out; then we feel lost. Sometimes we have to bring our classwork to the resource room to do it. Why? Why can't we do our schoolwork with the class like everyone else? For some of us, the resource room is a place where we feel comfortable. But that's not right. Can't you figure out a way for us to feel comfortable in your classroom, so that we can stay with our friends and learn the same stuff? Sometimes we get candy and stickers and other rewards when we leave the class. We all like candy, but why do we get different rewards than our friends? We aren't sure why that happens.

It's a funny thing: we have to leave our classroom more often than our classmates, but when we want to leave the classroom to get a drink of water or go to the bathroom, we have to ask for special permission and then an adult comes with us. All we want is to have the same opportunities for coming and going as the other students in your class.

Ask (and Listen to) Me and My Family if You Have Questions

One of my favorite teachers always started class by checking in with everyone. You see, he thought of the class as a family, and family members help each other out. He was the best.

Since we probably can't convince you to give us less homework, you should know that the people who help us the most with our homework are our Moms and Dads and brothers and sisters. They are the ones who know what we are good at and what kind of help we need. We tell them what we like in school (being with friends, learning new things) and what we don't (feeling unappreciated, having to leave class). They understand how hard we work and encourage us to do our best.

As with all kids, our parents want what's best for us. Sometimes that means that our parents spend more time at school than maybe they'd like to and they (and you) probably have to go to a lot of meetings about us. Do you wish you didn't have to go to so many meetings? Do you sometimes feel like you are auditioning for the part of our teacher? We do not want you to feel this way, and neither do our parents. It's not that they don't trust you; in most situations they do. They just want you to really understand how we learn, what is important to us, and what they know works for us.

When you are not sure about the best way to teach us, why we are doing something, or if you don't understand something about us, ask *us*! That is one of the best ways to get your questions answered. We like to speak for ourselves. You can help us practice speaking for ourselves by holding class meetings where everyone has a chance to talk. Please invite us to any meetings you have about us. At those meetings, please talk about interesting things that are important to us; don't make the meeting only about things you do not like about us. Let us invite friends to these meetings so they can help give the kids' perspective. You will hear that kids just want to learn together, have fun, and feel like they belong.

We have something very important to tell you. Sometimes teachers talk about us outside the classroom door or in the back of the room. When this happens, it makes us feel terrible, like we are dumb, bad, or losers. We think that if someone did it to you, it would make you feel terrible too. So *please* remind people not to do it anymore.

Ultimately, when you have questions we can't answer, ask our parents. Usually, this is better than asking the specialists who typically don't spend much time with us, or trying to find the answer in our files. Just call or e-mail our Moms and Dads—they will have lots of great ideas.

Understand that Some Things Are Really Hard for Me

I would like to tell the teacher she is fired if she doesn't understand why it is hard for me to sit down like other kids.

There are all sorts of rules in school, and we know that they are important. But for some of us, our disabilities make it hard—and sometimes impossible—to follow them all. And so while it may look like we don't understand the rules or we are just misbehaving, that's not always true. For some of us, our disability makes it really hard to sit still, concentrate on lots of things at the same time, or keep our hands quiet. We are not trying to be bad; this is just who we are.

For example, sometimes it may look like we are not paying attention or that we don't care about what is happening around us. But honestly, most of the time we do. If you think what you are teaching is important and the rest of the class does too, we can guarantee that 99% of the time we think the same thing. We just may show it in different ways. So if our bodies are behaving differently, like walking around the room, or twirling objects, or fidgeting, it doesn't necessarily mean that we are not paying attention. In fact, for some of us it may mean that we are paying so much attention to the lesson that we can't really pay attention to keeping our bodies still. Keeping our bodies still is very hard work for some of us.

Also, for some of us, it is not always easy for us to look at people's faces to show that we are listening. For some of us, especially those of us who have autism, looking someone in the eyes is difficult. And if you ask us to make eye contact with you, it just makes it that much harder to concentrate on what you are saying. So for us, please let us look away from your face, and know that this actually helps us pay more attention.

We know that understanding some of our differences can be confusing to teachers. And that is why we think you should ask our parents to help you figure these things out. Our parents have known us for a long time (our whole lives!) and they have a good idea of the things that are in our control and the things that are a part of our disability. And they can help you figure out which rules we can follow just like everyone else, and which ones have to be bent just a little bit to make it possible for us to learn.

You wouldn't get mad at someone who is blind for not being able to follow the rule of red means stop, so please don't get mad at us when we are not able to follow every single rule because of the things that are really hard for us.

Teach Me Interesting Stuff in Ways I Can Understand

Mr. Porter was a great teacher. One time he split the table down the middle and we debated as Republicans and Democrats. Another time we held court. I sat on the plaintiff's side and helped cross examine the witness. I learned so much and had fun.

No one wants to be bored in school. We know that learning is work, but work doesn't always have to be boring does it? No! We all have had teachers who knew how to make learning fun and interesting. These are our best teachers, those we remember with happiness in our hearts. Of course, we have also had teachers who were just the opposite. Teachers who don't enjoy teaching make it impossible for us to enjoy learning. We don't mean to be disrespectful, but those teachers should retire and find different jobs. They would be happier, and we would be happier too.

Probably the most boring lessons are when teachers stand in front of the room and lecture to us. We know you have a lot of good information to teach us, but most kids don't learn by just sitting and listening. Have you ever noticed how most of your students have trouble paying attention when you lecture? And using a computer slide show only makes it a little better. Instead, we love it when classes are interactive and when we get to work in small groups. Working in small groups lets us learn together and teach each other, and that is really great. We appreciate guest experts, mini field trips, playing learning games, and doing research using the computer and the library. We especially love it when you let us use our personal interests and experiences to learn a new subject. That helps us relate what we are learning to our everyday life. And using technology not only makes learning fun, but for some of us it is the best way to learn.

Every student is unique, and we all learn in different ways. Some of us can listen and learn while sitting at a desk, others of us have to move around the room or look out the window to concentrate best. Some of us can show you what we know by writing on paper, others of us do better by typing on a keyboard or dictating our thoughts through words and pictures. If you believe there is not just one way to learn, then we hope you will believe that there is not just one way to demonstrate our learning. Let us show you what we know in many different ways.

In the end, the best teachers are those who love teaching and love all of their students. These creative teachers show us how much they care, and we respond by doing our best. We hope that all of our teachers can be like that!

8 Listen to What My Behavior Is Saying

If no one listens to me, then I have to get even louder and louder.

Everyone has different ways of telling the world what they like and dislike. Even people who talk use other behaviors to get their points across. Teachers do this—when they are angry, they use their bodies and faces, not just their voices, to show us what they are feeling.

For some of us, especially those of us who do not talk, or for whom talking is not easy, we use our behavior to let the world know what we are thinking and feeling and wanting. Sometimes this is easy and people love it, like when we smile or laugh to show we are happy. But sometimes, it is not so appreciated. In fact, when we use our behavior to tell you that we are upset, scared, angry, or bored, we usually end up in trouble. But how else can we tell you these things? If you only tried to understand what we are trying to tell you, then everything would be much better. We are not trying to be bad; we are just trying to get our points across.

We also sometimes get in trouble when we use our behavior to get someone's attention. Sometimes when we reach out to someone we like, everyone gets all upset. We think they get upset because they think we are going to hurt that person, but really, all we are trying to do is say hi. Remember, we want to make friends just like everyone else does.

Because our behaviors can sometimes be confusing, we think that you should do a few things. You should always believe that we are using our behavior to communicate. If you don't understand what we are trying to say, please ask us, our parents, and even our classmates. Together we can help you figure this out. But if you are thinking we are just trying to be annoying or bad, then you will probably never figure it out and it will only get worse for all of us.

Please pay attention and make us feel wanted. Don't just let the aide take over. Ask us if we are okay. Give us a smile to show that you understand us. Talk to us; don't just tell us to be quiet. Help us calm down by being calm and allowing us to participate in different ways.

And don't send us to a separate room and think we are going to learn how to behave there. Remember, we are not being bad—we are just trying to say something. And your room is the best place for us to communicate and learn.

Help Me Make Friends

My favorite time of the school day is talking with my friend Derrick in between classes.

Do you remember what it was like to be a kid in school? What do you remember the best? We bet you would say it was your friends and all of the fun times you had with them. And you know what? We are just like you were—we think making friends is the most important part about being a kid.

For some of us, making friends is not so easy. There are lots of reasons: for example, some of us have a tough time letting kids know we want to be friends, and some of us have adult aides with us all of the time, which makes the other kids stay away. Some of us hardly get to spend any time at all in class; we are always getting pulled out of class. Some of us are treated like babies by our teachers, which makes the other kids think we are not cool. All of these reasons make it hard for us to make and keep friends.

And so we really need your help. Teachers can help us make friends by sticking up for us. When other kids see us doing something they think is different or wrong, our teachers can help by explaining why we do things the way we do. If the other kids in our class understand us better (our gifts and our talents, what we like and don't like) it might be easier for us to make friends.

Teachers can and should prevent bullying. Bullying happens all the time in our schools, and lots of times teachers just ignore it. We don't think this is right. Grown-ups should not look the other way or tell us to just ignore it. Maybe if teachers stepped in, there would be more chances for kids to get to know one another and become friends. We think that would help.

We don't need to be friends with the whole class. Not everyone needs to be our friend. Having one or two *real* friends would be enough. We don't want special treatment: unless all kids have a "buddy club" or sign-up lists to eat lunch together or play at recess, we don't want that either. We don't want other students to get credit by being our "friend." Those things just make us feel and look like losers. We just want the chance to get to know other kids in the same ways that all kids learn about each other, being part of classroom learning groups, and participating in after-school clubs and activities like other kids our age. Don't rule out an opportunity for us to join an activity that we might think is fun. This is where new friendships are made and old ones have a chance to grow stronger and better.

Believe I Can Be
Something Great When I Grow Up

I want to be a paleontologist. I want to be a heart doctor. I want to be a gym teacher.

I want to be a cosmetologist or a massage therapist. I want to be a football player.

I want to be a good person. I want to be a licensed nursing assistant.

I want to run my own daycare. I want to go to college.

As you can see, we all have dreams for our futures. Our dreams are not any different because we have disabilities. Like all kids, when we are little we dream of being astronauts, and soccer stars, and firefighters. As we get older, our dreams mature and we start to think about what we love, what we are good at, and what we want to do when we are adults. We all dream about our futures.

We need our teachers to believe that we can have big dreams and hopes just like all kids. Don't think that just because we have disabilities we cannot do great things. The only things that will hold us back are people who try to step on our dreams or hold us back from participating and learning.

We need you to support our dreams to come true. There are lots of ways you can do this. You can encourage us in our studies to learn about the things that interest us. You can make sure that we have ways to demonstrate what we are passionate about in our lives. You can tell us that you believe in us and that you will help us learn everything we can to achieve our dreams.

But how are we to know what we are passionate about if we don't get exposed to all the possibilities life has to offer? If you never took a science class, how would you know if you loved science? So we need teachers to make sure that we have the same chances as everyone else to figure out what we enjoy and what we are good at. Make sure we take all of the subjects and classes that are available to other students. Support us to join extracurricular activities and to participate in clubs and sports. Don't make us miss a field trip or a guest lecturer because we need to go to therapy. If we are in high school, make sure we take all of the required classes and attend college fairs and have internships and mentors who can help us achieve our dreams. The only way we can learn about what is possible is to participate in everything that schools have to offer.

And don't think that college is not for us. People with disabilities can go to college, and if we say we want to go, please help us make that dream come true. Just imagine that we didn't have disabilities. How would you help us to create and achieve our dreams? This is what we want you to do for us.

Selected References

Armstrong, T. (1994). *Multiple intelligences in the classroom.* Alexandria, VA: Association for Supervision and Curriculum Development.

Biklen, D. (2005). *Autism and the myth of the person alone.* New York: New York University Press.

Biklen, D., & Burke, J. (2006). Presuming competence. *Equity and Excellence in Education, 39,* 1–10.

Brendtro, L., Brokenleg, M., & Van Bockern, S. (1990). *Reclaiming youth at risk: Our hope for the future.* Bloomington, IN: National Educational Service.

Falvey, M.A., Forest, M., Pearpoint, J., & Rosenberg, R. (1994). *All my life's a circle. Using the tools: Circles, MAP's and PATH.* Toronto: Inclusion Press.

Jackson, L. (2002). *Freaks, geeks, and Asperger syndrome.* London: Jessica Kingsley Publishers.

Kasa-Hendrickson, C. (2005). "There's no way this kid's retarded": Teachers' optimistic constructions of students' ability. *International Journal of Inclusive Education, 9,* 55–69.

Lovett, H. (1996). *Learning to listen: Positive approaches and people with difficult behavior.* Baltimore: Paul H. Brookes Publishing Co.

Mooney, J., & Cole, D. (2000). *Learning outside the lines: Two Ivy League students with learning disabilities and ADD give you the tools for academic success and educational revolution.* New York: Simon & Schuster.

Prince-Hughes, D. (2002). *Aquamarine blue 5: Personal stories of college students with autism.* Athens: Swallow Press.

Sienkiewicz-Mercer, R., & Kaplan, S.B. (1989). *I raise my eyes to say yes: A memoir.* West Hartford, CT: Whole Health Books.

Tashie, C., Shapiro-Barnard, S. & Rossetti, Z. (2006). *Seeing the charade: What to do and undo to make friendships happen.* Nottingham UK: Inclusive Solutions.

Tomlinson, C.A. (1999). *The differentiated classroom: Responding to the needs of all learners.* Alexandria, VA: Association for Supervision and Curriculum Development.

Trueman, T. (2000). *Stuck in neutral.* New York: HarperCollins.

Section III

Communication & Behavior

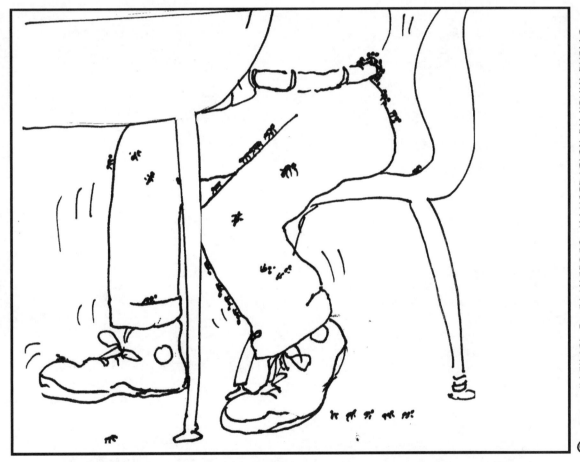

AFTER A HASTY SPECIAL EDUCATION
PLACEMENT FOR BEHAVIOR PROBLEMS,
SCHOOL OFFICIALS WERE EMBARRASSED
TO LEARN THAT MARTY REALLY DID HAVE
ANTS IN HIS PANTS.

Quick-Guide #7

Communication Systems in the Classroom

Janet M. Duncan and Patricia A. Prelock

Quick-Guides to Inclusion
Ideas for Educating Students with Disabilities, Second Edition
Michael F. Giangreco & Mary Beth Doyle

Editors

Dear Teacher,

You are undoubtedly aware of the many ways that your students communicate with you and with each other throughout the school day. They communicate about their classwork, the lunch menu, and activities that are happening before, during, or after school. Some students do not communicate in a traditional manner (i.e., spoken language). Be careful not to assume that just because some people with disabilities do not speak, they don't have something to say. Instead, assume that they understand part or all of what is said and have plenty to say.

Some students with disabilities require specialized systems or devices to communicate. These ways of communicating are called augmentative and alternative communication (AAC). AAC includes pointing, gesturing, and eye gazing, as well as using sign language, letterboards, picture symbols, drawings, photographs, keyboards, computer-generated speech, and other forms of computer assistance. Some students use AAC to augment their speech; others use it as an alternative to speech. Some students use more than one type of augmentative system, depending on the situation and their communication partners.

Whatever system a student uses, it is important for you as the classroom teacher to become comfortable with it and to know how to communicate with the student. This will require getting to know the student and the unique aspects of the student's communication system. These guidelines will help you think about strategies for including students who use AAC in class routines so that they will always have opportunities for communication, both receptively and expressively. As you become more knowledgeable about your students' communication, you can share what you have learned with the other students in the class so they can become skillful communication partners in both academic and social situations. It is important to remember that using AAC is simply another way for a student to communicate.

Good Luck!
Janet and Patty

GUIDELINES-AT-A-GLANCE

1. Learn About Each Student's Preferred Communication

2. Provide Each Student with Necessary Supports

3. Create a Communication-Friendly Environment

4. Make Sure Each Student Has a Way to Communicate at All Times

5. Involve Classmates as Communication Partners

6. Respect Each Student's Communication

7. Use Natural Experiences and Direct Teaching

8. Create and Maintain a Back-Up System

9. Update Communication Systems Frequently

10. Evaluate Communication Progress

Learn About Each Student's Preferred Communication

Verbal communication is not the only way that individuals let us know what they want to say. You should assume that individuals are able and want to communicate, even though they may be using a different means than you expect. All behaviors, including body language, gestures, and glances, communicate messages; often we use these modes of communication to enhance our verbal messages. A student who does not use speech as a primary means of communication may point, look, gesture, sign, or use a variety of symbols to convey a message. It is important to learn your student's communication strengths and preferences, because the specific system selected should capitalize on strengths and increase the student's potential for becoming an independent communicator.

When selecting a student's communication system, initial steps include identifying the student's current ways of expressing and receiving communication and determining the level of understanding of the communicative intent. You need to know: 1) if the student attempts to communicate, and 2) if the resulting message is what was intended. Finally, it is important to be attuned to changes in the student's expressive communication and receptive comprehension as it grows over time.

When selecting a communication system, you and the other team members should look for a device that is portable and that has symbols with a high degree of *iconicity*. *Iconicity* refers to how much a symbol looks like what it represents (Lloyd & Blischak, 1992); a highly iconic symbol resembles its referent closely. Portability and iconicity will assist the student to participate, with little delay, in communicative interactions because these characteristics help make the communication more accessible to a variety of communication partners, including both peers and adults. The team should also consider the motor competence required and the ease of access and use for both the nonspeaking student and the student's communication partners.

Once a communication system is selected, it requires timely set-up or programming so that vocabulary can be expanded and curricular themes can be incorporated. Effective implementation of any communication system requires the thoughtful reflection of each team member.

Provide Each Student with Necessary Supports

To use a communication system effectively, a student may need various forms of assistance, such as physical or sensory support and another person's guidance. This assistance can be provided in a very unobtrusive, but deliberate manner.

Physical and sensory supports are particularly important for a student who has coordination, mobility, hearing, or vision impairments. First, be certain that the student is positioned in a way that allows for effective access to and use of the communication system. Sometimes parents, special educators, or related services staff can recommend warm-up exercises to improve mobility or tips to maximize sensory capabilities. They can also determine seating arrangements that are most conducive to the student's use of AAC.

Next, various team members may be especially helpful in determining appropriate physical or sensory supports or equipment. They may notice small but important factors that can make a difference in a student's ability to communicate, including seat height, lighting, and position of materials.

Consider using the support of others; after all, communication requires reciprocity. A classmate or adult may need to assist the student in using the AAC system. For example, the student may need help to turn on a computer or to access the software. To locate accessible software check out http://www.closingthegap.com/rd/. For information on Internet accessibility, see http://www.cast.org/bobby.

Classmates may need to be taught how to use and respond to the communication system (e.g., picture exchange, American Sign Language). It is particularly important that all communication partners know how to use the AAC system so they can interact with the student using the system and their speech.

The use of an AAC system has the best chance for a positive impact in an atmosphere of encouragement, in which the students' classmates constantly acknowledge and respect communication and approach each student. This encouragement is especially important in situations in which it is unclear whether the student understands the entire exchange. By respecting the communication, you and other communication partners are making the "least dangerous assumption" (Donnellan, 1984, p.141).

Create a
Communication-Friendly Environment

Developing awareness among other students and school personnel of AAC systems used by your students is the first step you can take to create a communication-friendly environment. In other words, helping all students and school staff achieve a level of familiarity with the AAC systems used by students in the school makes the use of AAC systems ordinary and typical. Initial training for all school personnel and teams in AAC use is necessary and one of the most important factors in supporting the communication success of students (King, 1999; Parette, 1997).

Classrooms are naturally language-rich environments. Elementary classrooms have language experience charts, visual schedules with pictures and the printed word, interactive bulletin boards, predictable stories, big books, and so forth. Secondary classrooms have agendas posted, homework listed, and systems for individual accountability (e.g., signing in/out, dropping off homework). The use of AAC systems should be built into those naturally occurring opportunities. Students who use AAC systems will benefit from exposure to print and spoken language, whereas students without disabilities will learn valuable communication and social skills by interacting with a classmate using AAC (e.g., active listening, turn taking). Teachers can model these skills for students through their daily interactions.

Teachers can show all students ways to augment their ability to communicate with peers who have limited communicative abilities, including but not limited to use of the student's AAC system. You might ask students, "How can you communicate your ideas other than by speaking or by writing?" All students can be encouraged to use aids such as the computer, gestures, or dramatic presentation to augment their spoken and written communication. You can also teach your students American Sign Language or other ways to communicate like exchanging pictures with peers to express an idea or respond. When situations arise that require another person to interpret the student's communicative intent, you can ask a classmate to do so.

Modeling the value and use of a student's AAC system sets a powerful example for your students. As students develop an understanding of the AAC system, their sense of community will grow along with their acceptance of the students who use AAC systems.

Make Sure Each Student Has a Way to Communicate at All Times

Imagine how frustrating it would be if you were not able to communicate in a manner that others understood or to which they responded. Imagine that this situation lasted for an hour or a day. How about years?! Now imagine how you might feel or act. This is why it is imperative that students who rely on AAC systems have access to their own system or a back-up system at all times. It is equally important that the team has a plan in place to address any breakdowns or technological glitches that will interfere with the students' ability to use a preferred AAC system (see Guideline #8).

Although speech, gestures, and sign language are examples of communication systems that do not require special equipment, some students who use AAC need devices to communicate. Sometimes this equipment can be as small and simple as a *communication wallet* with photographs or drawings. At other times it can be as sophisticated and technologically advanced as an individualized, speech-output computer-based system. Portability is always a concern when selecting a communication system, because a highly portable system allows the student to have access to a means of communication at all times. The less portable the system, the greater the likelihood that it will be left behind when the student leaves the classroom to go to the cafeteria, playground, gymnasium, or on field trips.

Even when a student effectively uses a communication device, it is crucial to develop back-up systems for times when the device is forgotten, misplaced, or broken. To prevent gaps in communication, it is valuable to encourage the student to use multiple communication methods. For example, a student who uses a voice-output keyboard may opt to carry a small laminated letter board in a pocket folder. Other back-up systems may involve hand signs, pointing, vocalizations, picture symbols, gestures, or eye movements. Using multiple ways to communicate encourages students to use speech when possible or in situations in which it is appropriate. For example, a student may first try to communicate by using speech. If the communication partner does not understand what is being said, an augmentative or alternative approach can be used to communicate the message more clearly (e.g., pointing to an object or picture, miming an action, drawing a picture). Regardless of the specific AAC system, the student should have access to it at all times. That access should be shared across environments so that the student knows how and what can be used at home, at school, and in the community.

Involve Classmates as Communication Partners

5

If a student is to communicate successfully using an AAC system, it is important to have as many communication partners as possible. Classmates are invaluable and often willing communication partners.

Sometimes, when a student is learning to use an AAC system, teachers tend to think of the process as something very specialized to be addressed only by a speech-language pathologist or special educator. This need not be the case. Students want and need to communicate with other students, and these interactions are essential for developing social relationships and for enhancing self-image. By communicating with one another, students learn so much from each other.

Many students today regularly use a variety of forms of communicating with each other including, e-mail, text messaging, PDAs, and personal web pages. These same communication strategies can be useful learning tools for students with disabilities as well (Peters-Walters, 1998; Trollinger & Slavkin, 1999). For information about accessible web pages, check out http://trace.wisc.edu/world/computer_access.

You can support students who use AAC by helping their classmates learn the communication system. You can share information about the AAC system early in the school year. A detailed explanation of AAC is not necessary; rather, explain to the class how the student with limited verbal skills communicates best. The student and parents can help by demonstrating for classmates how the AAC system works. Throughout this process, maintain a respectful attitude of both the student and the AAC system. While you want classmates to be comfortable with the student's AAC system, you also want them to understand that this is a very personal and important piece of equipment.

The student may choose one or two classmates to whom they will teach their system first and expand from there. You can help by modeling effective communication interactions on several occasions (e.g., one-to-one conversations, small- and large-group activities, discussions). Don't forget to give the student the privacy and space to interact without always being shadowed by adults. In a very short time you may find that peers become quite knowledgeable about the student and the AAC system.

Ultimately, students who are AAC users and their classmates are involved in giving and receiving language input. The speaking communication partners provide valuable language stimulation and should be encouraged to acknowledge and respond to their nonspeaking partners.

6 Respect Each Student's Communication

Regardless of how simple or sophisticated the AAC system is, it is important to respect the communication expressed by the student who uses the system. At its most basic level, this means responding to the student's communication. For example, if the student requests a drink by pointing to a cup on the communication board, the strongest response would be to provide a drink immediately. At the early stages of learning, you want the student to understand that using the AAC system has a direct and immediate impact on his or her personal world. Regardless of whether or not you always like or agree with what a student has to say, it is crucial for students to know that you hear and respect their communication.

Sometimes circumstances will not permit you to address every request in such an immediate manner. In these cases, you should acknowledge the student's request and address it as soon as possible, at which time you should use the AAC system again to teach the connection between system use and the response to the request.

Honoring communication also requires you to make sure the student has communication partners. Sometimes students who have communication boards on their lap trays make silent selections that no one notices, and their communication is not acknowledged. If people are not always present to notice these types of expressions, the student may need a signaling device to get the attention of a communication partner. Voice output communication devices that record messages using the voice of an adult or a same-age and same-gender classmate may ensure the "voice" of the AAC user is heard. For information about voice-activated software, go to http://www.ibm.com/software/speech/ or http://www.dragonsys.com.

Finally, provide privacy for communication. Many forms of AAC are highly visible and can be seen and understood without the AAC user's intent, approval, or knowledge. It is also important for communication partners to assist the student in selecting privacy if needed. Be aware of the orientation of the communication display in relation to other people. Allow privacy of written communication, such as by deleting messages from computer screens, shredding printouts, or putting printed communication in a folder marked "Confidential." Use the general consideration: *if the student didn't use an AAC system, what level of privacy would be afforded?*

Use Natural Experiences and Direct Teaching

To learn to use a communication system effectively, students and their classmates need naturally occurring opportunities to communicate (e.g., classroom, hallway, cafeteria, playground), as well as direct teaching and practice. You can initiate this with the team by listing those opportunities that happen throughout the school day. If you have difficulty, then an AAC specialist can help you as well as provide support regarding direct instructional approaches. An AAC specialist's help is appropriate at certain times because merely providing a student with an AAC device or system does not ensure that the student or adults will know how to use the system.

Typically, students need direct and repeated instruction to learn the system, and real opportunities to use their communication skills. This instruction and application can occur concurrently. Too often students are required to learn skills in isolation before they can apply these skills in more natural contexts. Learning in isolation is undesirable, because more natural settings can provide students with important motivations and feedback for learning. Further, the direct modeling by a speaking communication partner, whether it is an adult or a peer, can be the most effective way to teach the use of an AAC system in the natural environment (Cafiero, 2005).

You can expand and adapt a student's communication system to the natural environment in several ways. You could show a student how to use her system in a new context or activity. You could introduce a new communication partner. You could add new content to the system so that a student participates more frequently in a variety of school activities.

The level of assistance provided to the student might also be reduced. Ultimately, the goal is for a student to independently access an augmentative communication device or communication system of choice and utilize the power of the device or system to establish communication with as many communication partners as possible. Once a student is comfortable with a system, the team can decide whether it is time to introduce a greater level of complexity. When complexity is added to the system it will be important for the student, as well as the adults and peers who are that student's communication partners, to receive clear instruction and support as they learn the nuances of the device. Further, the team will need to decide which learning contexts make the most sense to introduce added complexity.

8 Create and Maintain a Back-Up System

High-technology devices have many positive features that make them attractive options for certain students. Some of these notable features include: 1) voice, print, or Braille output; 2) reprogramming capability; 3) portability; 4) expandability; 5) large capacity; and 6) switch activation, such as pressing or touching the switch with any controllable body part, coming close to a magnetic or temperature-sensitive switch, sipping or puffing on a pneumatic switch, or moving a light beam on a head switch. In today's computer-saturated society, it is important to remember that although high-technology AAC systems offer highly desirable features and are getting easier to use all the time, they may not be right for every student who uses AAC.

With high-technology equipment come high-technology problems. Team members must become well versed in troubleshooting in case something goes wrong—and it will. We don't want to discourage you from getting involved with high-technology AAC systems, but you should understand that there are limitations for which advance planning is essential. Often replacement parts can be costly, and the time needed to repair a broken device can be extensive. Many AAC users cannot afford a second high-technology back-up system. When their primary systems fail, however, they still need to communicate.

Overreliance on technology for communication can thus leave high-technology AAC users without a viable means of communication, so it is essential to have inexpensive alternatives (such as low-technology AAC systems) that can be put in place quickly as a temporary measure. Back-up systems should be ready for use before a high-technology breakdown occurs. If your student uses a high-technology AAC device, ask the speech-language pathologist, occupational therapist, or special educator to create and maintain a back-up system.

All team members, including parents, should be familiar and comfortable with the primary uses and workings of both high- and low-technology AAC systems to ensure the student's successful communication across home and school. Training will be an important part of the AAC system and services that the IEP team defines for an individual student requiring an augmentative communication system.

Update Communication Systems Frequently

9

Communication systems are dynamic in nature and need to be expanded and modified over time. The needs and interests of students continually change (e.g., topics of interest, classes, friends, current events, hopes, dreams, experiences). Therefore, the AAC system must change accordingly. AAC systems can be expanded so a student can engage in a variety of communicative functions such as greeting people, making requests, making choices, answering or asking questions, saying "Yes" or "No," describing objects, commenting, relating experiences, offering opinions, expressing emotions, and conversing.

As a student gets older, the symbol choices and styles should match the student's chronological age and incorporate local slang or popular phrases. Also, the symbols should reflect the personality, cultural traditions, and perspective of the student. If the student's team does not attend to these concerns, there is the danger that the symbol system will more closely reflect the communication preferences of adult members of the team rather than those of the student. It may also influence the student's motivation to use the symbol system.

You and other adults may have to offer support during the process of updating the AAC system. Your school speech-language pathologist, an occupational therapist, or a consulting augmentative specialist can help, as they usually have specific expertise in developing, evaluating, and updating communication systems for students with limited verbal skills. Updating may also require the student to learn new skills (e.g., expand symbol repertoire).

If a student makes extremely good progress with one type of symbol system, he may need to switch to a more sophisticated system. For example, systems that use pictures or drawings offer a limited number of possible messages, depending on the availability and quantity of the symbols, whereas systems based on the alphabet provide the greatest degree of communicative freedom. With an alphabet-based AAC system, the possible message combinations are limitless. Often updates and expansion include the alphabet plus commonly used words. Whatever the decision, as the classroom teacher you are in a good position to observe and determine whether or not the AAC system has the vocabulary needed for kids to be kids.

10   Evaluate Communication Progress

Whichever communication system is selected for a student, it is important that you and other team members systematically evaluate the impact of the AAC intervention program and the student's communication progress across a variety of situations. Following are 10 questions to ask when evaluating an AAC system.

1. How often does the student access the communication system?

2. In what contexts does the student use the communication system?

3. When does the student experience the most successful communication attempts?

4. What are students' and peers' frequency and use of the communication system in academic and social contexts?

5. What other systems of communication does the student use, and how effective are these systems?

6. What is the classroom teacher's level of involvement in helping the student improve her communication abilities?

7. How is the curriculum adapted for and integrated into the student's augmentative communication system?

8. In which situations has communication failed between the student and her peers when using the communication system?

9. What are the most effective supports currently being used to ensure communication success?

10. What are the perceptions of teachers, peers, and the student regarding the effectiveness of the communication progress?

Assessment of a student's AAC system is conducted in the actual environments in which the system will be used to support the student's communication (Cafiero, 2005). You can use ongoing evaluation to monitor student progress and teaching effectiveness. Effectiveness of the system may be measured by charting the student's communication initiations, responses, ability to follow directions for a particular classroom task or activity, and ability to independently use the system without prompting. Most importantly, evaluation and data collection are tools you can use to determine the impact of communication successes and failures on a student's life.

Selected References

Beukelman, D.R., & Mirenda, P. (2005). *Augmentative and alternative communication: Management of severe communication disorders in children and adults (3rd ed.).* Baltimore: Paul H. Brookes Publishing Co.

Cafiero, J. (2005). *Meaningful exchanges for people with autism: An introduction to augmentative and alternative communication.* Bethesda, MD: Woodbine House.

Carter, M., & Maxwell, K. (1998). Promoting interaction with children using augmentative communication through a peer-directed intervention. *International Journal of Disability, Development and Education, 45,* 75–96.

Donnellan, A. (1984). The criterion of the least dangerous assumption. *Behavior Disorders, 9,* 141–150.

King, T.W. (1999). *Assistive technology: Essential human factors.* Needham Heights, MA: Allyn & Bacon.

Lloyd, L., & Blischak, D. (1992). AAC terminology policy and issues update. *Augmentative and Alternative Communication, 8,* 104–109.

Musslewhite, C., & King-DeBaun, P. (1997). *Emergent literacy success: Merging technology and whole language for students with special needs.* Birmingham, AL: Southeast Augmentative Communication Conference Publications.

Parette, H.P. (1997). Family-centered practice and computers for children with disabilities. *Early Childhood Education Journal, 25,* 53–55.

Peters-Walters, S. (1998). Accessible web site design. *Teaching Exceptional Children, 30(5),* 42–47.

Schlosser, R.W., & Braun, U. (1994). Efficacy of AAC interventions: Methodologic issues in evaluating behavior change, generalization, and effects. *Augmentative and Alternative Communication, 10,* 207–223.

Schlosser, R.W., & Lee, D.L (2000). Promoting generalization and maintenance in augmentative and alternative communication: A meta-analysis of 20 years of effectiveness research. *Augmentative and Alternative Communication, 16(4),* 208–226.

Trollinger, G., & Slavkin, R. (1999). Purposeful e-mail as stage 3 technology: IEP goals online. *Teaching Exceptional Children, 32(1),* 10–15.

Quick-Guide #8

Creating Positive
Behavior Supports

Deborah L. Hedeen and Barbara J. Ayres

Quick-Guides to Inclusion
Ideas for Educating Students with Disabilities, Second Edition

Michael F. Giangreco & Mary Beth Doyle

Editors

Quick-Guides to Inclusion: Ideas for Educating Students with Disabilities (2nd ed.) © Michael F. Giangreco, 2007
Available through Paul H. Brookes Publishing Co., Baltimore, 1-800-638-3775

Dear Teacher,

You have worked hard over the years to establish an effective classroom management style. You take pride in your ability to teach all your students. Now, for the first time, there is a student in your classroom who is not responding to your predictable and structured routines and lessons. In thinking about the situation, is this a student who doesn't seem to pay attention to the rules, destroys the property of others, ignores others' personal space, talks back, refuses to work, and/or doesn't respond to the consequences that have been effective with other students during your teaching career?

It is typical to feel frustrated and overwhelmed by a student's difficult behaviors. You may be thinking, "I've tried everything and nothing works." You may also believe the student's placement in your classroom in not appropriate. These are not unusual responses to a situation that presents a challenge to your classroom management plan. While the behaviors appear to be difficult to address in the classroom, the solutions are often quite low-tech and user-friendly. Some students will need additional support in order to learn and understand how to interact and participate during classroom activities. A variety of strategies can be created and implemented by concerned adults and students who are working together to create positive learning environments.

The purpose of this Quick-Guide on positive behavior supports in general education classrooms is to provide you with a number of guidelines that we feel you might find helpful as you work collaboratively with others to address behavioral issues presented by students. We hope the guidelines offered in this Quick-Guide will help you get started with creating positive behavior supports for students who have difficult behaviors.

You can do it!
Deb and Barb

GUIDELINES-AT-A-GLANCE

1. Create a Student-Centered Team

2. Establish Common Educational Goals

3. Understand the Impact of Your Interaction Style

4. Identify the Message Behind the Behavior

5. Help the Student Feel a Sense of Control

6. Share Information with the Student's Classmates

7. Focus on Prevention

8. Teach New Skills

9. Respond in Positive and Supportive Ways

10. Evaluate Your Teaching and Your Interactions

Create a Student-Centered Team

A student with difficult behaviors may need additional support in order to learn how to interact successfully and participate with classmates and adults. As the teacher, your attention needs to go to all of your students, not just one, and a team approach will be more effective than attempting to go it alone.

It will be critical to create a student-centered team for solving problems and developing a positive behavior support plan. Individuals who know the student will be instrumental, as will team members, in providing helpful information related to the student's interests, strengths, and areas of need. As a team, your willingness to share styles and beliefs about teaching, your ability to brainstorm new behavior support strategies, and your sincere interest in learning from each other will establish an effective working relationship.

Members of a student-centered team may include the classroom teacher, classroom assistant, student's parent(s), school counselor, principal, or related service providers. In addition, including the perspective of the student can assist the team in developing a plan that would make sense and be motivating for the student. Classmates can also have very good insight into age-specific activities and clever ideas for adaptations. It may be necessary to consider involving an educational consultant as a team member. Involving someone who has different experiences and is not a member of the school staff can be very advantageous. Regardless of the number of team members, the most critical element is the ability to meet on a regular basis in order to support each other and the student.

In order to develop a positive behavior support plan, the team will likely need to use a problem-solving format to brainstorm strategies for: 1) preventing problems, 2) teaching new skills, and 3) responding in supportive ways. Ongoing student assessment through videotapes, digital photos, observations in a variety of settings, and interviews with significant people as well as the student will provide valuable information for the positive behavior support plan. A team can make a significant contribution in making it possible for the student to remain in the school setting through their sincere effort to ensure a student-centered approach in problem-solving difficult behaviors.

Establish Common Educational Goals

Once the student-centered team is established, it will be important for the group to determine common educational outcomes and goals for the student. All team members must make a commitment to supporting the student through difficult times while teaching new skills.

If team members doubt the problem-solving process, challenge the appropriateness of the student's placement in the school, or question the effectiveness of the positive behavior support plan, it is very likely that the student will not acquire the necessary skills to be successful in the school. Team members' beliefs and attitudes regarding how to include students who have difficult behaviors are as important to talk about as establishing common educational goals for the student.

When discussing goals and objectives for the student's individualized education program (IEP), it will be necessary to identify positive behaviors to teach instead of focusing on the negative behaviors. Because the difficult behavior is so prominent in all interactions with the student, it is easy to dwell on the problem. The following IEP goal is a common one that focuses on decreasing the challenging behavior:

Negative Goal: *To extinguish hitting and kicking behaviors toward others.*

Such a goal does not describe what skills will be taught in order for the student to interact in positive ways with classmates and teachers. In order for the behavior to change, teachers will need to change how they make sense of the student's behavior. The question we must ask is, *"What skills can we teach so the student will not need to use the problem behavior?"* The following goal is an example of how to address teaching a new skill:

Positive Goal: *The student will tap a classmate's arm to get his attention.*

As the team works together to develop a common language for positive educational outcomes for the student, you will observe positive behavioral changes in the student. How we think about and describe student behavior will dramatically affect how we teach new skills and interact with the student.

Understand the Impact of Your Interaction Style

3

There will be times when the student with difficult behaviors will push us to our limits and bring out the worst in us! Although it may be difficult to remain calm and supportive when the student is "pushing our buttons," it is exactly at that time when we must be at our best, remain stable, and continue to provide positive direction to the student. Each time the student uses the difficult behavior, it provides an opportunity for us to model and teach new behaviors. Our style or attitude may influence how the student will respond during difficult times. People respond to difficult behaviors in different ways. In an effort to understand your style it will be helpful to review videotapes of your interactions and collaborate with others to brainstorm possible ways that you can become more positive with the student.

Some people find themselves using an *overprotective* style. This style of interaction occurs because the teacher is afraid to interact with the student because of the difficult behaviors, and therefore is unsure of the student's skills. A teacher with this attitude is communicating a message to the student that he can do whatever he would like and that there are no boundaries. Others may use a style that is cold and *mechanistic*. The teacher's attitude is one of sticking to the established rewards and consequences and not bending to accommodate a student's ideas or personal needs. The message to the student is, "You don't matter, but the task does." Little attention is paid to preventing problems from occurring.

When teachers are confronted with difficult behaviors, they might find themselves adopting an *authoritarian* style. The attitude of the teacher is, "I'm the boss. This is my classroom and you will follow my rules." A teacher with this attitude will often rely on negative consequences in an effort to shape a student's behavior. The message to the student is, "You will conform to the rules or be removed from the classroom."

As teachers, a goal of our interaction style should be one of *respect, relationship, and solidarity*. With this attitude, the teacher communicates a message to the student that, "We are in this together. You are a valued member of this classroom." This teacher is flexible, supportive, and resolves conflict with the student by providing positive support, even during the conflict. While we will find it difficult, if not impossible, to always remain calm and supportive, we should strive to develop this attitude as our classroom "umbrella."

Identify the Message Behind the Behavior

Have you ever felt like a student intentionally acts out in an attempt to ruin your day? Usually the behavior does serve a purpose and makes perfect sense to the student. Our job is to understand the purpose of the behavior in order to help the student use a different behavior that will result in positive interactions with classmates and adults. It is common for students who have limited verbal skills to use behaviors to "make things happen" in their school and home environments. We all communicate through our behavior, and behavior becomes a form of communication for many students. These difficult behaviors will continue being used until we assist the student in getting his needs met through the use of more positive behaviors.

There are five common purposes of behavior. The first purpose of behavior is *to get attention*. We are familiar with students using a variety of behaviors, such as hitting, yelling, throwing objects, or pounding on a desk to get the attention of others. Because the behavior is loud or intrudes upon our personal space, we pay immediate attention to the situation. The second purpose of behavior is *to escape or avoid*. A student may want to escape an activity because it is too easy or it is boring. Likewise, a student may avoid an activity because it is too difficult or the student is unsure of how to complete the activity successfully.

The third purpose of behavior is *to get something*. If a student does not have the ability to communicate her needs, she will do whatever it takes to fulfill the need. For example, if the student needs to use the bathroom or get a drink of water, she may run out of the classroom and through the hallway to accomplish the goal. The fourth purpose of behavior is *to play*. For example, the student likes to tap the teacher on the shoulder while laughing and then runs to sit in her desk. The teacher finds the behavior interferes with instruction, while the student views the behavior as her best attempt to be playful and interact with the teacher. The fifth purpose of behavior is *to self-regulate*. Continuous movement, such as rocking or swinging, foot or finger tapping, or jumping up and down, helps the child to focus, slow down, speed up, or feel less anxious.

When we problem solve as a team, videotapes and observation data will help determine possible purposes of behavior. The goal in identifying the communicative intent or purpose of the behavior is to select alternative positive skills that can be taught to replace the behavior as part of the positive behavior support plan.

Help the Student
Feel a Sense of Control

All children strive to feel a sense of control in their lives. Sometimes the student who has difficult behaviors just goes about getting this control in ways that we find difficult to understand and accept. This is the student who wants what he wants, when he wants it—NOW! As teachers, our first response might be to get firm, restrict privileges, and try to show him who is the "boss." However, teachers who are most successful in working with students who have difficult behaviors have found that, although they need to provide some overall structure and establish clear boundaries and expectations, they can also provide many opportunities for the student to feel a sense of control throughout his school day.

The student-centered team will want to carefully observe when the student feels the least amount of control during specific activities and events. This information will be helpful in developing opportunities for the student to feel a sense of control, therefore increasing the amount of time the student is engaged in academic activities.

There are a number of ways for the student to feel a sense of control in the classroom. First, post the daily schedule with picture symbols for the student who may not be able to read all words. When a student can anticipate and predict the upcoming events, anxiety lessens and a sense of control in knowing the plan is very comforting. Second, establish clear routines and transitions. For example, if the student arrives at school each day agitated, a specific routine will usually help the student transition more smoothly into the school day.

Third, teach turn-taking skills by structuring activities that clearly inform the student of the teacher's turn for student learning and the student's turn for free time. Students want to know when it will be their turn to engage in the activity they are so eager to do. Fourth, provide choice-making opportunities throughout instruction (e.g., where to sit, selection of partner, or order of activities). For example, during a reading lesson, the students may be asked to read a story, answer questions to the story, and write in their journals. By changing the order of activities, the student may have greater success with first writing in the journal and then reading the story. Fifth, combine materials of interest with activities of least interest. It will be easier to motivate a student to complete a math assignment if he enjoys using his colored markers instead of a pencil.

Share Information with the Student's Classmates

6

When a student who has difficult behaviors is educated in a general education classroom, it is typical for classmates to observe and question the behaviors of the student and the responses of the adults. It is important to recognize that classmates will model the attitudes and behaviors of the adults in the setting. From our experiences, when the teacher actively involves the student as a member of the classroom, then the classmates will include and interact with the student as well. Although we have always been concerned with confidentiality of students receiving special education services, the fact that we do not say anything about a student's behavior does not mean other students are not aware of the situation.

We feel it is important to talk honestly with classmates so they can begin to understand why the student is using certain behaviors. Sharing accurate information with classmates is better than students developing their own reasons to explain the behavior and questioning the responses of adults.

Before engaging classmates in discussion, it will be critical to have parental involvement when developing the information to share with classmates. Some parents may not want to directly participate, but will give permission for you to work closely with classmates to ensure a successful school experience for their child. We have known parents of elementary- and secondary-age students who have visited the classroom to share ideas for creating positive ways to interact with their son or daughter.

Many students will be excited to offer their ideas, suggestions, and specific strategies to assist a student with difficult behaviors. Students are much more supportive of their classmates when they are given accurate information and an invitation to problem-solve with adults. Sometimes it will be advantageous to include all classmates when problem-solving difficult behaviors, while at other times a more intimate circle of friends will be able to provide support in subtle ways. There will be situations when including the student with difficult behaviors in meetings and smaller group discussions will be necessary in order to role-play and model specific behaviors and new skills.

The most effective way to deal with difficult behaviors is to prevent them from ever occurring. The key to prevention is prediction. If you can predict when a challenging behavior is most and least likely to happen, and why, you will be able to create environmental changes that will minimize the possibility of occurrence. It is much easier to be proactive and change the physical environment, the instructional environment, or the social environment in order to establish positive routines for the student rather than waiting for the behavior to occur and then responding. The following example provides a variety of prevention techniques used to successfully support Sarah in her fourth grade classroom.

The *physical environment* includes the classroom, other areas within the school, or area outside the school. Each morning Sarah walked by the teacher's desk and knocked her pencil container and books off onto the floor. To address this behavior, the teacher created an alternate walking route, so Sarah no longer passed by her desk. Another situation that was difficult for Sarah was waiting after recess to enter the school with her classmates. Sarah would bang on the outside door, scream, and cry. Some of her classmates decided to bring little toys to recess so she would have something to do while waiting with them before returning to their classroom.

The *instructional environment* may be adapted by changing the difficulty, amount, or sequence of work. Sarah would become frustrated when she was not able to complete her work when the other students did. When students wrote a sentence for each of their 20 spelling words, Sarah used a picture schedule to guide her work as she wrote 10 of the spelling words, matched the word with a picture, and then typed the words on the computer. When students completed a math worksheet with two-digit multiplication problems, Sarah placed dinosaur counters on numbered cards for one-digit addition problems and then checked her work with a calculator.

The *social environment* involves changing how and when people interact with each other. During a science project, Sarah would hit her partner in order to get his attention. Placing the student across from her encouraged Sarah to use her voice to get his attention. Even though there was a classroom assistant to provide additional support for Sarah, the teacher made an effort to interact and provide feedback to Sarah related to her assignments and class participation.

Teach New Skills

8

Many successful teachers work to prevent problems while actively teaching new skills. For some students, the ability to effectively communicate their thoughts or feelings will cause them to use other forms of behavior in order to get their needs met. These behaviors may include hitting, swearing, throwing objects, or refusing to participate. Students use these behaviors as an effective means to accomplish their goals. So, our job is to teach new, more acceptable ways to communicate the same message.

In Guideline #4, we explained the importance of identifying the message or purpose of the behavior. This information will be very helpful in determining the new skill to teach. For example, one student often pinched the teacher during reading group. The student had learned that if he pinched, the teacher would remove him from the group and he would not have to work. Once the teacher realized that the student did not know another way to ask to leave the group, she decided to actively teach this new skill by presenting a card that said, "Take a break." She assisted him to point to the card, take a short break, and then return to the reading group.

The following examples describe how to identify the student's behavior, think about the purpose behind the behavior, and teach a new skill so the student no longer needs to use the difficult behavior.

Behavior: Student grabs classmate at recess

Purpose: To get classmate's attention

Teach: Student will tap classmate on shoulder

Behavior: Student runs out of classroom

Purpose: To get something—a drink of water

Teach: Student will give a picture symbol of water fountain to adult

The student may not respond immediately to your new teaching strategies. Continuous modeling and active teaching of new skills will show the student that there are more effective ways to communicate and interact with others. Your positive interactions with the student will encourage successful participation over time.

Respond in Positive and Supportive Ways

9

A positive behavior support plan emphasizes prevention and teaching versus focusing on how to *react* once the behavior has occurred. We have found when teachers primarily *react* to a student's behavior without considering prevention and teaching, the adult is unsure of what to do and the response may be emotionally charged. In those situations, teachers often regret how the situation was handled. When a teacher *responds* (rather than reacts) to a difficult situation, he or she is calm, confident, and consistently follows the positive strategies developed to assist the student when students' behaviors are challenging. We see a difference between *reacting* to a student's behavior and *responding* as part of a positive behavior support plan.

Even though the majority of your interactions with the student will focus on preventing behaviors and teaching new skills, there will be times when a student will display behaviors that you cannot prevent. It will be important that you support the student during the difficult times so that no one is harmed and the environment is restored while allowing all participants to maintain a reasonable degree of dignity. After everyone has had some time to reflect on what happened, a team meeting will be beneficial to discuss additional supports the student may need and to review the existing response strategies.

Additional supports for the student may include creatively engaging the student in the activity at hand so that you can continue teaching. If the student has chosen to go to a different place in the room, then take the materials to the student so that he can continue working. If the student is refusing to work, then provide some choices so that he can select one thing to do. If the student is starting to tire, then let the student know how much work is left before a break can be taken. If the student makes negative comments about working, continue providing positive feedback by smiling and using encouraging words.

It will take time for new skills and behaviors to be used consistently by the student. The adults will need to shadow the student initially in order to guide the student in using the positive behavior. There is an element of give and take—of negotiation—in helping to solve a challenging situation. It is not merely an attempt to control another person, but rather to understand and reach a mutually acceptable solution.

Evaluate Your
Teaching and Your Interactions

10

Creating positive behavior supports is an ongoing process that requires constant attention and reevaluation. Although the field historically took a more simplistic view of behavior change, we now recognize that it is a complex process that requires concentrated effort by a team of people over time.

By developing behavior support plans that address prevention, teaching, and responding, we are initially making our "best guess" as to what might be effective. These best guesses will need to be refined as we learn more about the student and the purpose of his behavior.

Careful observation and evaluation of your teaching will provide important information regarding how effective the positive behavior support plan is in replacing difficult behaviors with new skills. Assessing the teaching of new skills as well as the quality of the interactions will ensure positive experiences for the adult and student. Working with a student who has difficult behaviors can be very challenging and viewed by many as not very enjoyable; therefore, it will be critical to establish routines that will be fun and interesting to both the adult and student.

We have mentioned in other guidelines that videotaping the student is an extremely effective form of evaluation. By capturing segments of the student's day on videotape, you can assess the areas that have been described in this Quick-Guide, such as your interaction style and attitude toward the student, the message or purpose of the behavior, prevention strategies, new skills that need to be addressed, and positive, supportive ways to respond. Asking others to view and critique the videotaped footage with you is an excellent way to get feedback and direction. Segments of the videotape may also be used as a teaching tool for others who work with the student. In some situations, it will be appropriate for the student to review the videotape in order to show the specific behavior of concern or as a way for the student to observe improvement of behavior.

In addition, requesting that team members observe within the classroom during difficult times, and during successful times, will help you gather necessary information that will allow you to modify your plans. You and your team members are encouraged to reconsider intervention support plans and to make necessary changes that will allow the student, and the adults, to achieve success.

Selected References

Ayres, B.J., & Hedeen, D.L. (2003). Creating positive behavior support plans for students with significant behavioral challenges. In T.R. Berkeley, M.S.E. Fishbaugh, & G. Schroth (Eds.), *Ensuring safe school environments: Exploring issues—seeking solutions* (pp. 89–105). Mahwah, NJ: Lawrence Erlbaum Associates.

Chandler, L.K., & Dahlquist, C.M. (2002). *Functional assessment: Strategies to prevent and remediate challenging behavior in school settings.* Columbus, OH: Charles E. Merrill.

Crone, D.A., Hawken, L.S., & Horner, R.H. (2004). *Responding to problem behavior in schools: The behavior education program.* London: Guilford Press.

Crone, D.A., & Horner, R.H. (2003). *Building positive behavior support systems in schools: Functional behavioral assessment.* London: Guilford Press.

Daly, E.J., Noell, G.H., & Witt, J.C. (2000). *Functional assessments: A step-by-step guide to solving academic and behavior problems.* Longmont: Sopris West.

Fad, K.M., Patton, J.R., & Polloway, E.A. (2000). *Behavioral intervention planning: Completing a functional behavioral assessment and developing a behavioral intervention plan.* Austin, TX: PRO-ED.

Hedeen, D.L., Ayres, B.J., & Tate, A. (2001). Charlotte's story: Getting better, happy day, problems again! In M. Grenot-Scheyer, M. Fisher, & D. Staub (Eds.), *At the end of the day: Lessons learned in inclusive education* (pp. 47–72). Baltimore: Paul H. Brookes Publishing Co.

Horner, R.H., & Repp, A.C. (Eds.). (1999). *Functional analysis of problem behavior: From effective assessment to effective support.* Belmont: Wadsworth Publishing.

Jackson, L., & Panyan, M.V. (Eds.). (2002). *Positive behavioral support in the classroom: Principles and practices.* Baltimore: Paul H. Brookes Publishing Co.

Lucyshyn, J.M., Dunlap, G., & Albin, R.W. (Eds.). (2002). *Families and positive behavior support: Addressing problem behavior in family contexts.* Baltimore: Paul H. Brookes Publishing Co.

Steege, M.W., & Watson, T.S. (2003). *Conducting school-based functional behavioral assessments: A practitioner's guide.* London: Guilford Press.

Section IV

Curriculum & Instruction

RITA RETURNS TO DIG UP THE
ROOTS OF SPECIAL EDUCATION.

Quick-Guide #9

Universal Design for Learning

Bridget Dalton and David Gordon

Quick-Guides to Inclusion
Ideas for Educating Students with Disabilities, Second Edition
Michael F. Giangreco & Mary Beth Doyle

Editors

Dear Teacher,

So often in our discussions about how best to educate all students in inclusive classrooms, we search for ways to help learners adapt and adjust to established curriculum and instruction. When we pursue inclusive opportunities from that perspective, the onus is on the student to accommodate standard approaches. Less frequently do we seriously consider changing our curriculum or our instruction. Classroom goals, methods, materials, and assessments are seen as fixed walls that learners must somehow climb over. Students with disabilities (e.g., physical, intellectual, sensory, learning), along with those having English-language barriers, exceptional talents, emotional or behavioral problems, or simply their own unique learning styles and preferences, may face significant challenges when confronted with one-size-fits-all curriculum and instruction.

Universal Design for Learning (UDL) aims to remove those barriers. It starts from the premise that the curriculum and instruction should adapt to people, not the other way around. UDL offers a blueprint for creating flexible goals, methods, materials, and assessments that accommodate a wide array of learner differences. Drawing on recent advances in understanding how the brain learns and leveraging the power of new digital technologies, UDL provides practical strategies for expanding learning opportunities.

In the following pages, we'll provide an overview of basic UDL principles and share some practical solutions based on our classroom research and that of our colleagues at CAST (http://www.cast.org). You'll see how those new technologies make it possible to truly customize and individualize curriculum and instruction for students. We hope these ten guidelines will help you better serve the variety of learners you encounter in your own diverse classrooms.

Good Luck,
Bridget & David

GUIDELINES-AT-A-GLANCE

1. Recognize Each Learner's Strengths and Needs

2. Understand How the Learning Brain Works

3. Understand How UDL and Assistive Technology Fit Together

4. Differentiate the Means of Presentation

5. Offer Students Multiple Pathways to Learning

6. Engage Learners in Multiple Ways

7. Use Ongoing Assessment to Improve Instruction

8. Provide Flexible Supports for Literacy

9. Develop New Literacies Using Technology

10. Listen to Students and Learn from Them

Recognize Each Learner's Strengths and Needs

Today's teachers have a challenging assignment. They are expected to help an increasingly diverse mix of students learn to high academic standards. Yet experienced teachers know that any classroom may include students with very diverse learning needs as well as strengths.

To help all students maximize their learning potential, we need to begin by recognizing just how different each learner really is. Advances in neuroscience confirm what teachers know from experience: the way each student learns is highly individual. Students' patterns of processing information, approaching strategic tasks, and engaging with content are as unique as their fingerprints (Meyer & Rose, 2000; Rose & Meyer, 2002).

Universal Design for Learning provides a flexible framework for responding to such individual differences. The "universal" in UDL suggests helping all students succeed in the way that works best for each individual. It means recognizing and responding to individual needs and strengths by providing appropriate scaffolds, supports, options, and choices (Rose & Meyer, 2002).

Of course, educators don't work in a vacuum. The degree to which they can customize learning to meet individual needs depends on factors such as their experience and the resources and support at their disposal. UDL won't lead to the perfect classroom; there is no such place. But it does show how expanding the range of options and supports for learners from the outset can bring us closer to the goal of reaching and teaching all learners.

Fortunately, advances in technology and the availability of digital text make such differentiation more possible today than previously, when the time and effort it took to transform print-based materials into accessible versions was prohibitive. Certain barriers to learning materials can now be lowered with a few keystrokes. Some digital learning environments can also aid teachers in differentiating instruction itself with built-in comprehension scaffolds and assessment supports. When used as part of a universally designed curriculum, such new media help us shift the burden of adaptation from students to where it belongs, the curriculum itself.

Understand How the Learning Brain Works

New medical technologies enable us to peek inside the brain and see what happens as learning takes place. The result is an appreciation for the great variety in how individuals approach similar learning tasks.

Building on the work of the Russian psychologist, Lev Vygotsky (1896–1934), UDL correlates three essential elements of learning: 1) *recognition* of the information to be learned, 2) application of *strategies* to process that information, and 3) *engagement* with the learning task. These three elements neatly correspond with the neural networks uncovered by brain research: the 1) *recognition*, 2) *strategic,* and 3) *affective networks* (Meyer & Rose 2000; Rose & Meyer, 2002). See Table 1 for additional details.

Table 1. Comparison of brain network and Universal Design for Learning principles

Brain network	Universal Design for Learning principles
Recognition networks make it possible to receive and analyze information, recognize patterns, concepts, and relationships (e.g., understanding narrative structure; knowing what biodiversity means).	Provide varied and flexible methods of presentation. Give learners various ways to acquire information and knowledge—the "what" of learning.
Strategic networks make it possible to generate patterns and develop strategies for action and expression (e.g., contrasting narrative texts; producing biodiversity exemplars).	Provide multiple pathways for reaching goals. Offer students alternatives for developing skills and demonstrating what they know—the "how" of learning.
Affective networks fuel motivation and guide the ability to establish priorities, focus attention, and make choices (e.g., feeling challenged to continue reading a narrative text; choosing to study biodiversity).	Provide multiple options for engagement in order to help learners get interested, challenged, and motivated—the "why" of learning.

Understand How UDL and Assistive Technology Fit Together

3

UDL is often thought of as just another term for assistive technology (AT) or as an approach that would do away with assistive technology. Both perceptions are wrong. Assistive technology plays a critical role in helping students adjust to barriers inherent in traditional curriculum; UDL aims to eliminate barriers at the point of curriculum design. Assistive technology may support learners' independence, but its value is limited if barriers to learning persist in the curriculum in the same way that a wheelchair's value is limited if a building has only stairs.

Learning supports in a UDL curriculum are found on many levels. In some cases, supports are needed to improve access to information. Individuals with physical, sensory, learning, or intellectual disabilities may need AT in order to participate in the general education curriculum. For example, those with low vision may benefit from text-to-speech readers and computer-screen enlargers, while individuals with physical disabilities may be helped by adaptive keyboards or voice-recognition software.

Since the aim of UDL is to make *learning* more attainable, technology should be implemented in ways that support learning goals (Rose & Meyer, 2002). This is true for all learners, with and without disabilities. For example, a student might find it more engaging to read a passage about the *Red Badge of Courage* in digital text format with text-to-speech, linked vocabulary supports and synchronized highlighting than to read the traditional printed text version. If the assignment's goal is to build knowledge of the U.S. Civil War—rather than to decode text—then providing these supports to all students as an option can make that learning goal easier to achieve, by letting students focus on the content of the text rather than decoding the text itself.

However, if the goal of the assignment is specifically to build reading fluency, then providing decoding supports may actually interfere with a student's access to learning by eliminating the learning challenge. The goal of UDL is not to eliminate challenge—which is essential to learning—but to reduce extraneous barriers that are not core to the learning goals. Teachers in the UDL classroom know that simply reducing barriers to *access* is just a first step to reducing barriers to *learning*.

Differentiate the Means of Presentation

Our recognition networks in the brain enable us to decipher patterns of information and determine key features. But because no two individuals approach a learning task in exactly the same way, it is necessary to differentiate the presentation of information to reach and teach more learners (Rose & Meyer, 2002).

One way is to select and present multiple examples of whatever concept, point, or fact is trying to be conveyed. For example, in a lesson on photosynthesis, one might display different images of growing plants, including text, photos, scientific diagrams, and animations. A teacher might compare and contrast the life of plants in cold and warm climates to demonstrate how photosynthetic principles work in greatly diverse conditions. Students come to understand that photosynthesis is not something that happens just in warm climates or in wet ones, but can take place in dry, cold places, too. Multiple examples such as these can help students from diverse backgrounds better understand the key features of photosynthesis.

Such lessons may also require extra attention to background knowledge. What students already know about a subject affects how quickly and how well they acquire new knowledge on that subject. Differentiated presentations of information can provide more diverse students with more opportunities to "latch on" to an idea by making connections between what they already know and the topic at hand.

Fortunately, flexible new multimedia tools increase our options for presentation. Digital text, audio, video, and animation combine with traditional print materials to offer students a rich palette of learning materials. Text-to-speech is an example of a technological tool that supports individual differences in recognition. English language learners and students with learning disabilities are just two examples of the kinds of individuals who benefit from this alternative to one-size-fits-all printed text. Digital materials can be especially powerful when they provide links to background information and decoding supports. With such resources, teachers can more easily provide diverse pathways to learning (Leu, 2000).

Offer Students
Multiple Pathways to Learning

Our daily newspapers are filled with praise for independent thinkers, risk-takers, and innovators who find a way to "get the job done," whatever that job may be. Our daily speech is filled with praise for individual approaches: "To each his own," we say. "There's more than one way to skin a cat." "Different strokes for different folks." Indeed, brain research confirms what teachers already know: that the way individuals tackle challenges and how they express themselves can vary greatly from one person to the next.

UDL curriculum supports learners in taking different approaches to achieving common goals (Meyer & Rose, 2000; Rose & Meyer, 2002). One way this is accomplished is by presenting students with different models of skilled performance. This helps demonstrate the essential features of a successful performance while also highlighting the appropriateness of applying individual creativity to the task of finding out what works best.

Learners also benefit from lots of practice with supports. Like training wheels for the child learning to ride a bicycle, learning supports enable the practice of complex skills and activities in a safe way. As skills develop, these supports and scaffolds are gradually withdrawn, just as the parent's hand steadies the back of the bike once the training wheels are removed, until finally that too is taken away.

Providing relevant, ongoing feedback is also an important way to support students on diverse learning paths. As in the master-apprentice environment, such formative assessments help learners improve their work as they go along, making successful outcomes more likely.

Providing students with multiple avenues for expressing what they know and demonstrating what they can do is also essential. The same student who struggles to write an essay on the origins of the Civil War might be able to demonstrate a wealth of knowledge on the topic by creating an on-line, hyperlinked concept map, giving an oral narrative account, or writing and performing a folk ballad that shows Northern and Southern perspectives. By a "different strokes" approach in the classroom, we help students see that there are multiple pathways for lifelong success.

6   Engage Learners in Multiple Ways

Teachers know that getting students motivated and interested in learning is essential to school success. Emphasizing the "why" of learning is as important as the "what" and the "how" of learning. In the UDL model, providing appropriate levels of challenge and support is a key to engaging students (Rose & Meyer, 2002). Students who are not challenged get bored. Those who are overly challenged can get frustrated or afraid. Vygotsky (1978) wrote about helping students find their "zone of proximal development" (p. 85), where challenge and support are balanced according to each individual learner's needs.

Providing basic access supports is essential to engagement. For example, for students with low vision, adjusting font sizes, colors, or styles can be vital; without such simple access supports, the students might give up on a reading assignment that they otherwise would be motivated to accomplish. Providing supports in learning strategies may also be necessary for sustained work. For example, when both Mary and Jamal are assigned to write an essay, Mary may require writing strategy supports (e.g., sentence starters, model paragraphs, vocabulary help) to keep from getting frustrated by the assignment, while Jamal needs the challenge of writing without those supports to keep his interest.

Providing students with choices and flexibility in content, tools, and learning context can make the curriculum more engaging. In math class, learning division and percentages may seem pointless to young basketball fans—until, that is, it provides an opportunity to bring their background knowledge to bear on projecting the career statistics of Lebron James or Dwayne Wade and comparing them with an NBA legend such as Michael Jordan. With this assignment, the numbers suddenly have relevance and students are able to have the extended practice they need to develop critical skills. Once they've mastered the skills, the students demonstrate to classmates how they calculated the projections.

Having options and a relevant audience for their work (their peers) gives students more reason to invest their time and energy in becoming enthusiastic experts on a challenging topic. Having appropriate challenges and supports also engages learners as they become more attuned to what they need to develop learning skills for life.

Use Ongoing Assessment to Improve Instruction

Flexible, ongoing assessment is a core tool in any UDL classroom. Measuring and evaluating student progress toward learning goals enables teachers to adjust their instruction to meet individual student needs. Ongoing assessment is also a way of helping students learn to self-regulate and self-manage their own learning processes. It's a way of raising their awareness and understanding of their own strengths, weaknesses, preferences, and styles.

Of course, for assessments to be helpful, they must be accurate, and accuracy depends on defining precisely what knowledge and skills are meant to be measured. For example, when measuring students' ability to compose a coherent narrative text, it might make sense to provide scaffolds for mechanical skills, such as spelling, reading, and text entry (either through voice recognition or word processing) or to use additional media, like images and sounds, to scaffold motivation. These supports will help students with disabilities, for whom print is not easily accessible, to focus more effort on the skills and knowledge in question. This gives teachers a clearer picture of progress in that area and enables them to make appropriate adjustments in instruction. Of course, if the assessment is intended to measure the mastery of writing mechanics themselves, you wouldn't scaffold these skills, but you still might offer other supports, such as use of sound, images, or prompts that help students self-monitor their progress and develop editing skills.

Some universally designed, computer-based learning environments leverage the power of digital, interactive technologies to make ongoing assessment easier to provide at the point of instruction. Students can perform quick checks of their work to determine their progress and identify barriers to learning (Rose & Meyer, 2002). At key places in a lesson, the computer may prompt them to review and comment on their work. They may create a multimedia work log in which they record and play back audio notes, type comments, or load images related to their learning. Animated agents can assist the process by providing models and hints that support this self-evaluation. When reviewed with a teacher, these varied media can provide students with timely insights into their performance and the learning processes that underlie that performance.

8 Provide Flexible Supports for Literacy

Though technology in the classroom has not always lived up to its promise to improve classroom learning, a growing body of research documents the benefits of technology supports, especially for literacy (Dalton & Strangman, 2006; Kamil, Intrator, & Kim, 2000). Once text is in digital format, its representation can be transformed to provide all students access to the content. But access to the content alone isn't enough. Students often need supports and scaffolds for building critical thinking skills that characterize skilled readers and writers (Leu, Kinzer, Coiro, & Cammack, 2004).

The literacy program, *Thinking Reader*®, is an example of a universally designed learning environment. All students have access to the same content (i.e., full-text, age-appropriate novels) but with varying scaffolds and supports. *Text-to-speech* (TTS) and *read-aloud* functions are two examples of accessibility supports that can be helpful for students with weak decoding skills and fluency. The flexibility of digital environments allows students to choose, in consultation with their teacher, the level of support that their confidence or skills warrant. In addition to background knowledge and vocabulary support, students are prompted at certain points in the text to think strategically about their reading and respond to questions about the text. Animated characters act as skilled mentors, offering model responses and giving students feedback about their own responses. These interactions are captured in on-line work logs so that teachers and students together can discuss how students are performing.

In our work, we have seen that the multiple supports and avenues for success offered in a universally designed environment can re-energize and re-engage discouraged readers and writers. Our colleagues (Rose & Meyer, 2002) have described one student with significant learning disabilities who found it all but impossible to compose a paragraph of narrative text. When that same student was given the opportunity to use sound or images to develop first drafts of his compositions, the barrier to writing was broken. He began adding words to the picture-text, and before long he was writing text without fear. His enjoyment and competence in using pictures to compose fueled his motivation to learn a new medium—writing.

Develop New Literacies Using Technology

9

nformation and communication technologies are driving students' everyday interactions. They build social networks with instant text-messaging, on-line chat rooms, cell phones, and multimedia blogs. They go on-line to download music and video, swap pictures, or buy clothes and sporting goods. As technologist Marc Prensky has noted, those of us who did not grow up with these new, ubiquitous technologies often feel like cultural immigrants; we don't speak the language nearly as well as our younger, digital "natives" (Prensky, 2000).

Because these powerful resources are so familiar and engaging to students, they offer teachers new opportunities to reach all learners (Leu et al., 2004). However, they also require a broader understanding of literacy. Although instruction in traditional reading and writing is necessary, students also must develop the skills needed to: 1) gather facts and opinions from diverse information sources (e.g., reading, viewing, listening); 2) analyze and synthesize this information; 3) evaluate sources for credibility and sufficiency; 4) form points of view and plans of action; and 5) express themselves effectively and appropriately using different media (Leu, 2000).

One helpful example of integrating print and digital literacies was titled, "A Digital Journey to Altoona's Past." This award-winning project—a collaboration among high school students (from English, computer science, and art classes), their teachers, and historians in Altoona, Pennsylvania—featured a web site of historically accurate, multimedia interactive stories for elementary school students. The English class students interviewed local historians, conducted research, and wrote period stories about their town. Art students illustrated the stories with recent and old photographs, drawings, clip art, and animation. Computer science students created interactive web pages where young readers could type in their name and the names of a few friends and family members, and they would become characters in a story. You can read the stories online at http://aahs.aasdcat.com/9a/default.htm. The project helped students reach important benchmarks across the curriculum at Altoona High School. The resulting series of engaging and informative stories reached beyond classroom walls, to become a part of the community memory—not to mention part of the larger literature on multimedia literacy instruction by winning a prestigious award from the *International Reading Association*!

Listen to Students and Learn from Them

Understanding and meeting the needs of diverse learners begins with listening—*really* listening—to students themselves. Listening to students is not only a matter of being polite, it is a key teaching strategy for raising the achievement of all learners. Listening in this sense means more than just hearing. It means looking for clues between the lines, for hints and insights that will make us more responsive to student needs.

Listening is a critical assessment tool, less formal than tests and quizzes, but potentially more telling. Teachers who ask students questions during the course of a lesson, conduct interviews with individual students, or solicit student ideas through multiple venues are gathering invaluable data about their students' progress or lack of progress. When Ms. Clark listens to Janine describe the causes of the Civil War during a brief discussion, she is amazed to learn that her student knows a lot more than she demonstrated on the multiple choice test earlier that day. They discuss the quiz, and Janine reveals that tests create high levels of anxiety and that "just talking about" a subject is more comfortable. Suddenly, Ms. Clark has a new perspective on how she measures classroom learning.

So listening is a way of understanding what excites students as well as what barriers to learning they face. What sound like complaints (e.g., "This book stinks," "I hate to write," "What are we doing this for?") may be openings for genuine conversations about the media and materials we use in our classrooms—and what the point of that day's learning really is.

When it comes time for a major unit test on the Civil War, Ms. Clark offers her students choices in demonstrating their knowledge. Janine's multimedia composition features clips of Civil War folk songs—from both archival and contemporary recordings—and images from painters and photographers of the time. Ms. Clark is wowed by the performance. She's glad she heard what her student was saying about the "what, how, and why" of learning.

Selected References

Dalton, B., & Strangman, N. (2006). Improving struggling readers' comprehension through scaffolded hypertexts and other computer-based literacy programs. In D. Reinking, M.C. McKenna, L.D. Labbo, & R.D. Keiffer (Eds.), *Handbook of literacy and technology (2nd ed.)*, Mahwah, NJ: Lawrence Erlbaum Associates.

Kamil, M.L., Intrator, S.M., & Kim, H.S. (2000). The effects of other technologies on literacy and literacy learning. In M.L. Kamil, P.B. Mosenthal, P.D. Pearson, & R. Barr (Eds.), *Handbook of reading research, Vol. III.* (pp. 771–788), Mahwah, NJ: Lawrence Erlbaum Associates.

Leu, D.J., Jr., (2000). Literacy and Technology: Deictic consequences for literacy education in an information age. In M.L. Kamil, P.B. Mosenthal, P.D. Pearson, & R. Barr (Eds.), *Handbook of reading research, Vol. III.* (pp. 743–770). Mahwah, NJ: Lawrence Erlbaum Associates.

Leu, D.J., Jr., Kinzer, C.K., Coiro, J., Cammack, D. (2004). Toward a theory of new literacies emerging from the Internet and other information and communication technologies. In R.B. Ruddell & N. Unrau (Eds.), *Theoretical models and processes of reading (5th ed.)* (pp. 1568–1611). Newark, DE: International Reading Association.

Meyer, A., & Rose, D. (2000). Universal design for individual differences. *Educational Leadership, 58*(3), 39–43.

Prensky, M. (2000). *Digital game-based learning.* New York: McGraw-Hill.

Rose, D., & Dalton, B. (2002). Using technology to individualize reading instruction. In C.C. Block, L.B. Gambrell, & M. Pressley (Eds.), *Improving comprehension instruction: Rethinking research, theory, and classroom practice* (pp. 257–274). San Francisco: Jossey-Bass.

Rose, D., & Meyer, A. (2002). *Teaching every student in the digital age: Universal Design for Learning.* Alexandria, VA: ASCD.

Rose, D.H., Meyer, A., & Hitchcock, C. (2005). *The universally designed classroom: Accessible curriculum and digital technologies.* Cambridge, MA: Harvard Press.

Vygotsky, L.S. (1978). *Mind in society: The development of higher psychological processes.* Cambridge, MA: Harvard University Press.

Quick-Guide #10

Reaching and Teaching Diverse Learners Through Differentiated Instruction

Robi M. Kronberg

Quick-Guides to Inclusion
Ideas for Educating Students with Disabilities, Second Edition

Michael F. Giangreco & Mary Beth Doyle

Editors

Quick-Guides to Inclusion: Ideas for Educating Students with Disabilities (2nd ed.) © Michael F. Giangreco, 2007
Available through Paul H. Brookes Publishing Co., Baltimore, 1-800-638-3775

Dear Teacher,

Your classroom is probably more diverse than it ever has been. Your students have a myriad of learning characteristics and interests. You have some students who struggle with reading, while you have others who seem to be able to read everything. You might also have students who speak a primary language other than English. Some of your students love attending school, and others find little relevance in what school has to offer. Your task of teaching this diverse set of students is a daunting one—especially with the additional pressure many teachers feel about testing and standards.

Before you succumb to feeling totally overwhelmed ... stop and reflect on what you already know and do. You already recognize learning differences among your students. You know when to push some students and when to lighten the pressure on others. You have learned to alter your lesson plans to better meet the needs of your students. Better yet, you are learning how to proactively plan your lessons to address the range of student needs and interests.

Differentiation is about both the art and craft of our teaching ... at the core of differentiation is our responsiveness to each student. Your skills of designing and implementing differentiated instruction may not be at the level that you would like, but you do have a starting point from which to build. You have the capacity to reach and teach all of your diverse students. The following guidelines are designed to provide you with ideas about important aspects of differentiation. Take differentiation one step at a time. Start at a place that feels comfortable—try a few new ideas, reflect on how they work, and build upon your successes. Share your ideas, as well as your frustrations, with your colleagues. Strengthening the skillfulness of your teaching has never been so challenging or so important.

Sincerely,
Robi

GUIDELINES-AT-A-GLANCE

1. Know Your Students

2. Develop a Community Respectful of Diversity

3. Create a "Working-With" Learning Environment

4. Clarify Your Instructional Focus

5. Ensure that All Students Have Access to the Curriculum

6. Expand Your Instructional Repertoire

7. Design Ways for Students to Show What They Know

8. Assess Throughout Your Instruction

9. Teach Students How to Be Effective Learners

10. Develop a System of Organization and Management

Know Your Students

The most important aspect of your diverse classroom is, of course, your students. Your ability to effectively reach and teach your students depends upon knowing your students—their interests, learning styles, strengths, needs, and skills.

Knowing your students will provide important information to assist you in establishing meaningful instruction and curricular priorities. It will provide a lens through which to understand their passions, be guided by their needs, and be informed by their learning preferences.

There are many possibilities for getting to know your students. Students' interests can be discovered: 1) by designing interest inventories, 2) having students interview each other, 3) facilitating a class discussion, 4) observing students, and 5) having conversations with them. Differentiation will be enhanced as you: 1) guide students to particular reading selections, 2) design learning center activities that incorporate student interests, 3) encourage students to pursue in-depth investigations that capitalize on a passion, or 4) develop activities that invite students to learn in ways that are engaging and meaningful.

Your students reflect a mosaic of life experiences and learning characteristics. Students' background knowledge and prior experiences can be determined through teacher inquiry: "How many of you have ever been to a museum?" "Who can describe a mammal?" "Who can apply the concept of "supply and demand" in a way that is relevant to a teenager?" Knowing students' readiness for particular concepts and skill levels will assist in making instructional decisions. Selecting learning outcomes at the correct level of difficulty can be determined through pre-assessment or teacher knowledge of student performance. Understanding what your students bring to each learning experience will inform you as to how best to design instruction at each student's level of challenge.

Remember that your students will have different learning styles and learning preferences. Some students will learn best by listening, some by watching, and others by doing. Learning preferences are also influenced by gender, culture, ways of processing, and ways of interacting. Knowing the learning styles of your students will assist you in designing a balance of instructional opportunities.

Develop a Community Respectful of Diversity

2

Establishing a sense of community is an essential ingredient for creating a successful differentiated classroom. All students want to contribute, be respected, and be cared about.

Your classroom will provide fertile ground for helping students learn how to value differences, appreciate commonalities, and come to deeper understandings of such complex issues as fairness, cooperation, equity, and justice. Teachers concur that building a classroom community takes time and intentionality. Students need support in understanding why differentiated instruction is important and how a differentiated classroom creates a learning environment where all students can experience academic success.

Proactively establishing classroom expectations is important. For example, a fifth-grade teacher establishes expectations in context of teaching about the preamble of the U.S. Constitution. After learning about the purpose, the students create their own preamble—one that will guide their behavior throughout the year. In a first-grade class, the students identify four to five classroom expectations. The students then work in small groups, with each group painting a picture of classmates following the expectation successfully. For example, one group paints a picture titled "This is a picture of us taking turns." The pictures are displayed in the classroom and visually remind the students to follow their expectations. Many teachers find that class meetings are helpful vehicles for addressing issues, mediating conflict, planning instructional activities, and in general, working together as a community of learners.

Identifying student strengths and highlighting the array of strengths present among students is also important. A high school biology teacher provides his students with information about learning styles and multiple intelligences as a way of increasing self-awareness. He encourages his students to form lab teams composed of students with complementary strengths. All students learn to use their learning profile to guide choice making and to enhance reflection.

The time taken to create a classroom community is time well spent. Mutual respect and understanding form a strong foundation on which to build a differentiated classroom.

Create a "Working-With" Learning Environment

3

Differentiated classrooms are learning environments where teachers and students work together to create relevant and meaningful learning opportunities. Creating a "working-with" classroom environment means that teachers and students share decisions about instructional activities, routines for accomplishing classroom tasks, ways in which students might work together, and how students can demonstrate their learning. Teachers who create "working-with" learning environments encourage students to build responsibility for monitoring their work habits, making choices to enhance their learning, self-assessing their quality of work, and helping make decisions about how the overall classroom is functioning. Students take an active role in their own learning!

For example, a second-grade teacher asks students to reflect on their progress toward important benchmark skills and establish a goal to assist them in making progress toward mastery. During a fifth-grade class meeting, a teacher asks her students to discuss how different tasks might be assigned in order to complete a cooperative group project. An eighth-grade teacher frames the targeted learning outcomes for an upcoming unit and asks her students to work in small groups to brainstorm instructional activities that would assist the students in reaching their benchmarks. A high school government teacher asks each of her students to select two peers who will provide feedback on the student's semester project.

"Working-with" environments are sometimes messy and unpredictable. When you ask for student input, you don't always know what to expect! The benefits, however, are far-reaching. Students acquire lifelong skills of self-directedness, share responsibility for their learning, learn to appreciate the value of different opinions, and benefit from the ideas of their classmates. A "working-with" environment creates a classroom community where everyone is a teacher and a learner. As the old adage goes, "Whoever is doing the most work is doing the most learning." In differentiated classrooms, students' shared responsibility contributes greatly to the quality of their learning.

Clarify Your Instructional Focus

Thoughtful differentiation requires clarity of instruction. As you plan each unit of study, identify appropriate standards and benchmarks, specify desired learning outcomes, and establish clarity in three key areas. First, determine what you want your students to *know*. In each unit, there are probably certain facts that you want your students to master. For example, it may be important for students to know that oxygen is a gas, to identify characteristics of insects, to list key events during the Civil War, or to define parts of speech.

Second, be clear as to what you want your students to *understand*. Each unit should engage the students in understanding relevant concepts and principles. For example, it may be important that students understand the concept of measurement and an accompanying principle that there are many different methods and systems of measurement. Conceptual understanding provides students with the "big picture" and frequently provides continuity of learning between instructional units.

Third, be specific in what you want students to *be able to do* as a result of their engagement with the curriculum. The skills that you target for your students may involve: summarizing information, utilizing a graphic organizer, interpreting data, solving an equation, writing a persuasive essay, or giving an oral presentation.

Clarity of your instructional focus is at the heart of differentiation. It is in the combination of the factual, conceptual, and skill-based areas that coherent learning opportunities are created. Once you have established clarity, you will make many decisions as to how to support students in learning. You must decide how best to instill facts so that students are able to learn and remember. Some students may need to utilize a specific learning strategy to assist their memory, while other students will learn the desired set of facts independently.

You must also decide how each student can best understand the concepts and principles. Some students will need concrete experiences, while others will be ready for abstract connections. Some students may need to work with applications that affect their immediate life, while others are able to stretch themselves with less familiar applications. Achieving student mastery of the identified facts, concepts, and skills will require thoughtful differentiation.

Ensure that All Students Have Access to the Curriculum

Differentiated instruction is an inclusive way of teaching and learning. Ideally, planning for differentiation occurs within a collaborative framework. Hopefully, the collaborators include both general and special educators. When varied expertise areas are included, curricular planning becomes supportive of all students' learning needs. As voiced by one middle school team, "We try not to modify the general education curriculum. As a team, we create curricular activities that are accessible to as many students as possible regardless of their challenges."

As teachers proactively plan how to ensure accessibility to the curricular content, they consider a variety of options for differentiation—both in the depth and breadth of content, as well as how each student best acquires the content. For example, in a science unit on insects, a third-grade teacher encourages some of his students to explore how different insects adapt to environmental factors. His plans for other students involve identifying familiar insects and investigating their characteristics. A few students will spend several days in the library doing research.

In preparing for the unit, he has gathered a "tub" of resources that include grade-level reading material, resources rich with photographs and light on words, several audiotapes, a list of web sites, and several three-dimensional models of insects. In collaboration with a special education colleague, he has also included a teacher-made "unit dictionary," which captures essential vocabulary words and key concepts. By providing varied resources that capitalize on student interest and varying needs, this teacher supports all students in accessing the curriculum.

In creating access to a standards-based curriculum, a middle-school language arts teacher focuses on a monthly theme or an essential question in his literature units. For example, a guiding question might be: Does courage always involve sacrifice? Students choose to read a variety of novels or short stories that capture the theme of courage. This allows for accessibility to the curriculum, both in readability levels as well as student interests. While all students are expected to respond to a set of questions from the perspective of the main character as well as their own perspective, the teacher and his students negotiate several acceptable options for the format of response. Both visual and linguistic options are offered. This allows for accessibility to the curriculum based on students' learning preferences.

6 Expand Your Instructional Repertoire

Differentiation is all about creating multiple pathways for learning. Standards provide the targets for learning. Differentiated instruction provides the various routes through which students attain mastery of identified learning outcomes. It is both the artistry and the skill of teaching that enables a teacher to continually expand the instructional repertoire in order to better meet the diverse needs of students.

For example, a learning outcome in language arts involves knowing specific literary elements. The teacher strives for all students to reach mastery in understanding the element of setting. Based on teacher knowledge of students, instructional options are created. One student, who struggles with English, uses a sequential graphic organizer to identify aspects of setting. This student also has access to a picture dictionary to assist with the language demands of the task.

Another student uses a software program that provides a list of descriptive terms and then creates a web of categories. Two other students work together to create an alternative setting and then analyze how the new setting would alter the story. After all the students have had opportunities to understand setting, the teacher facilitates a large group activity in which students share their understanding of the role of setting in literature.

In a differentiated classroom, it is accepted that students learn differently. What works for one student doesn't necessarily work for another. Don't forget to use your students as resources; they can share responsibility in suggesting various routes to a common destination. As one high school student remarked, "Words on a page don't talk to me. I need to be able to work in groups and talk about the stuff we need to learn."

Many of the instructional strategies that embody differentiated instruction are not new to educators. Rather, teachers are using such strategies as learning centers, guided reading, project-based learning, and learning contracts, with a renewed sense of urgency and a refined focus of how to build greater differentiation into those tried and true strategies. Examine the instructional strategies currently in your instructional repertoire . . . start with a few of your favorite strategies and push yourself to incorporate greater differentiation within those strategies. Both you and your students will find enthusiasm for learning and greater success!

Design Ways for Students to Show What They Know

7

In addition to creating multiple pathways for learning, differentiation also involves designing a variety of ways in which students can integrate and demonstrate what they have learned. Often thought of as products or projects, these culminating activities encourage students to synthesize what they have learned.

Differences in students' interest, strengths, and needs will naturally lead to differences in how students demonstrate what they have learned. Incumbent on the teacher is careful selection of product options to guarantee that any selected option will provide the student with the opportunity to demonstrate mastery of the stated learning objectives.

An eighth-grade math teacher has developed three culminating activities for the unit on ratios, proportions, and percentages. Students select from: 1) making a three-dimensional replica of an item that is 225% larger than the original item; 2) designing an activity that would clarify the relationships between ratios, percentages, and proportions; or 3) finding examples in one's life (captured by drawings, words, or photos) which depict relevant applications of ratios, percentages, and proportions. The teacher provides clear expectations as to what each product must include. The teacher and the students have reviewed and agreed upon the task elements and quality indicators in the rubric that will be used to evaluate the finished projects.

As you plan for product differentiation, be mindful that students often require assistance with both the content focus of the project as well as the logistics of how best to successfully complete the project. Be prepared to offer support for the student who needs content clarification as well as the student who needs help with how to organize materials or develop a checklist to keep track of project tasks and timelines.

A sixth-grade teacher supports students who struggle with organization by coaching them to make a file folder organizer with pockets. On each pocket (envelopes cut in half and glued inside the file folder) students write their research paper topics. As the students take notes, they place the index card in the corresponding pocket.

8 Assess Throughout Your Instruction

Assessment and differentiation are integrally linked. In differentiated classrooms, assessment occurs throughout instruction. It serves to inform both the teacher and the student of the current level of understanding, progress, effectiveness of teaching and learning, and areas in need of improvement or enrichment.

Formative assessment, done at the beginning of instruction, informs a teacher as to the range of "starting points" for each student. At the beginning of a science unit, a middle school teacher asks her students to write a best-guess definition of the word "catalyst." Based on their responses, the teacher designs a differentiated activity at the beginning of the unit that allows each student to work from his or her starting point. A second-grade teacher encourages students to begin a unit by brainstorming ideas about a particular concept. She then creates a class web to help students begin to sort and label aspects of the concept. Not only are the students able to benefit from the background knowledge of their classmates, the teacher is able to informally assess what her students know about a particular topic.

Assessment can also be done throughout instruction. A first-grade teacher checks in with her students throughout instruction using the colors of a stop light. Students indicate green if they are "good to go," yellow means "I need more practice," and red indicates, "I just don't get it."

A sixth-grade teacher helps her students self-assess their progress on a four-week project by creating a "benchmark timeline" of weekly tasks. At the end of each week, students initial the timeline, indicating where they are in the task sequence. Each week, students initial with a different color pen. This visual aid provides a picture of progress, as well as indicating to the teacher which students might be having difficulty with task pacing.

Summative assessment, done at the end of instruction, provides feedback as to how well students have mastered learning outcomes. In the spirit of differentiation, summative assessment should also allow for individual differences and strengths. Be creative, think inclusively, and ask students how they can best demonstrate what they have learned. A written paper-and-pencil assessment doesn't work for everyone!

Teach Students
How to Be Effective Learners

Differentiated instruction changes the roles of students as well as teachers. In differentiated classrooms, students are active participants in the learning process. Student responsibilities include demonstrating such skills as: 1) making effective choices, 2) being self-directed, 3) organizing learning materials, 4) following directions, 5) completing tasks, and 6) working cooperatively with classmates. Teachers must provide many guided opportunities for students to build competence and confidence in the skills needed to be productive and responsible learners.

Providing choices to students is a powerful motivator. Students need to learn how to make choices that will support their learning. A first grader might complete the "must-do" activity at the learning center and then choose between two "can-do" learning center activities.

A fourth-grade student might select three activities from a menu of nine activities in order to increase his understanding of the Underground Railroad. A fifth grader might be asked for input about a classroom seating arrangement. A seventh grader might meet with his teacher to select a culminating project at an appropriate level of challenge. A high school student might select which projects to include in his art portfolio.

Facilitating a successful differentiated classroom will also be enhanced by student skills of self-directedness. Teaching students of all ages how to structure and manage their time is essential. Elementary students might be taught to follow a learning contract, in which tasks are specified but each student selects the order in which he or she completes the tasks. Middle school students might develop a list of resources necessary to complete a multi-faceted assignment. A high school student might take the initiative to meet with a teacher in order to self-advocate for a helpful instructional accommodation.

Cooperative skills also need to be taught and nurtured. A kindergarten student could work on sharing materials. A fourth-grade class might designate a student to complete a summary of the day's activities for an absent classmate. High school students might routinely edit each other's written work. Students need ongoing support to become effective learners. Seize those teachable moments, and offer lots of learning opportunities!

Develop a System of Organization and Management

Reaching and teaching all of your students can feel like an overwhelming task. In addition to sharpening your instructional skills, collaborating with colleagues, and supporting students in taking an active role in their own learning, you will also want to develop some routines for organizing and managing your differentiated classroom. Here are some tips:

1. Have students practice "organizational logistics." Provide opportunities to practice the simple things (e.g., moving between learning centers, obtaining materials, utilizing cooperative role cards, putting supplies away). This can help the instructional activity go more smoothly.

2. Develop set routines for giving directions. Multiple tasks, often requiring different directions, can be confusing. Establish routines that simplify directions. Color-coding works well. For example, teach students that if they are in the blue group, or are working on the blue set of tasks, then the materials are in the blue folder and the directions are written in blue on the overhead.

3. Give students responsibility for being accountable. You don't have to feel responsible for everything! If students in your class routinely turn in assignments, put them in charge of record-keeping. Simply attach a list of student names to the outside of the assignment folder. As students turn in assignments, it is their responsibility to check off their name. You can, at a glance, see who has yet to turn in the assignment.

4. Utilize your students as resources. Designate class experts who can offer assistance to classmates in a myriad of ways. Implement an "Ask three before me" rule to encourage students to seek out classmates for help. Put your classroom community of teachers and learners to work!

5. Set yourself "off limits" from interruptions. During targeted times throughout the day (e.g., when you are facilitating a small instructional group), let the students know that you are not to be interrupted. To visually remind the students, wear something colorful and easily noticed. Mardi Gras beads work well, as does a scrunchy on your wrist, or a colorful hat or headband.

Selected References

Benjamin, A. (2002). *Differentiated instruction: A guide for middle and high schools.* Larchmont, NY: Eye on Education.

Coil, C. (2004). *Standards-based activities and assessments for the differentiated classroom.* Marion, IL: Pieces of Learning.

Cushman, K. (2003). *Fires in the bathroom.* New York: The New Press.

Gregory, G. (2004). *Data driven differentiation in the standards-based classroom.* Thousand Oaks, CA: Corwin Press.

King-Shaver, B., & Hunter, A. (2003). *Differentiated instruction in the English classroom.* Portsmouth, NH: Heinemann Press.

Heacox, D. (2002). *Differentiating instruction in the regular classroom.* Minneapolis, MN: Free Spirit Press.

Northey, S. (2005). *Handbook on differentiated instruction for middle and high schools.* Larchment, NY: Eye on Education.

Silver, H., Strong, R., & Perini, M. (2000). *So each may learn: Integrating learning styles and multiple intelligences.* Alexandria, VA: Association for Supervision and Curriculum Development.

Tomlinson, C., & Allan, S. (2000*). Leadership for differentiating schools and classrooms.* Alexandria, VA: Association for Supervision and Curriculum Development.

Tomlinson, C. (2001). *How to differentiate instruction in mixed-ability classrooms (2nd ed.).* Alexandria, VA: Association for Supervision and Curriculum Development.

Tomlinson, C. (2003). *Fulfilling the promise of the differentiated classroom.* Alexandria, VA: Association for Supervision and Curriculum Development.

Tomlinson, C., & McTighe, J. (2006). *Integrating differentiated instruction and understanding by design.* Alexandria, VA: Association for Supervision and Curriculum Development.

VanderWeide, D. (2004). *Different tools for different learners.* Peterborough, NH: Crystal Springs.

Wormeli, R. (2006). *Fair isn't always equal.* Portland, ME: Stenhouse.

Quick-Guide #11

Co-Designing
Responsive Curriculum

Alice Udvari-Solner

Quick-Guides to Inclusion
Ideas for Educating Students with Disabilities, Second Edition

Michael F. Giangreco & Mary Beth Doyle

Editors

Dear Teacher,

As educators we are in a profession that allows, and often requires, us to be creative on a daily basis. Just as architects and engineers design structures for living, we design environments for learning. Our curricula, instruction, and assessments are the tools we use to construct these learning places. Through our curriculum decisions and planning, we have the power to create learning environments that are rich, exciting, interactive discovery zones for all students.

As we include students with disabilities in general education classes, we should reconsider what we have taught in the past and its relevance for our current students and their needs. Teachers who successfully include students with very diverse learning needs recommend taking a multifaceted view of curriculum design. Rather than thinking about curriculum as a predetermined set of facts and knowledge that the entire class must master, it should be considered a dynamic, ever-changing body of information that provides many learning options for every student. Quite simply, designing responsive curriculum is creating multiple paths to learning. Teachers do this by rethinking what they will teach or what they have taught in the past and by identifying what is appropriate for specific students to learn.

Thoughtfully designing curriculum is just one part of our creative endeavor as teachers that help keep our classrooms lively and responsive to the needs of students. The guidelines that follow outline key points that will help you and your team members talk about curriculum and develop multiple learning avenues together.

Good Luck!
Alice

GUIDELINES AT-A-GLANCE

1. Plan Curriculum Together as a Team

2. Decide What Your Team Means by "Curriculum"

3. Create a Student-Centered Curriculum

4. Get to Know Your Students' Abilities and Interests

5. Develop a Range of Learning Outcomes

6. Use the Learning Outcomes to Focus the Curriculum

7. Match Learning Outcomes and Experiences

8. Use Active and Interactive Instructional Approaches

9. Look for Ways to Differentiate Learning

10. Next Year? Revise, Refine, and Revive!

1   Plan Curriculum Together as a Team

In the past, teachers were expected and even encouraged to act as sole decision makers about the curriculum and instruction for their specific classes. The classroom teacher determined what was important to teach, designed learning activities, developed all the instructional materials, and carried out the instruction—alone.

As our classrooms have broadened to include students with more diverse learning needs, it is no longer realistic to expect classroom teachers to teach in isolation. To do our jobs well, communication, cooperation, and collaboration among team members are essential. This kind of teamwork forms an important building block in creating inclusive classrooms.

Discussions and decisions about what to teach and how to teach are critical components of collaboration between general and special educators. If we intend our classrooms to be truly accommodating to students with diverse needs, then our curricula and instruction must be flexible and open to input and change. Meeting weekly to discuss upcoming curricular activities with colleagues who are involved in the educational programs of your students with disabilities will facilitate common understanding, shared decision making, and joint responsibility for carrying out necessary instructional preparation.

Planning together regularly in advance of instruction provides time for all team members to offer input and use their expertise in the design of curriculum and instruction. When teams do not prioritize "up-front" planning, appropriate methods of differentiation are rarely employed and educators often feel they must adapt on the spot because instruction is out of sync with the needs of specific learners.

In weekly collaborative team meetings, the general educator can present ideas for upcoming curricular activities or topics to the team for discussion and development. The special educator can make suggestions for ways that the students with disabilities can participate in the instruction, as well as suggest potential adaptations, accommodations, or supports. If the unit has been taught in the past, it is important for the team to reflect on how it was structured, what worked, and what didn't work. The team can further define learning outcomes and activities, keeping particular students in mind who have unique learning needs. During these discussions it is critical that the team consider ideas as "under construction" so that all members can contribute to the development of the curriculum.

Decide What Your Team Means by "Curriculum"

As you begin the year and prepare to include a student with disabilities in your classroom, it will be important to have a brief conversation with team members about the meaning or definition of *curriculum*. As you plan together with special educators, parents, and related service providers, a common understanding of the term should help team members be more efficient in their communication with one another, facilitate joint planning of instructional activities, and help the team determine when variations in learning activities are necessary.

Generally, educators can think of the *explicit curriculum* as selected content and planned learning experiences that have educational outcomes. Most teachers see curriculum as much more than just subject matter. Often, teachers want to connect content with important values, concepts, opinions, interactions, and learning strategies that they want their students to acquire. This is sometimes referred to as the *implicit curriculum*. It is important to acknowledge both the explicit and implicit curriculum in your team discussion.

Some teachers are committed to a multicultural approach to curriculum planning. Fostering equity, understanding of cultural diversity, and respect for human differences are guiding elements across all subject areas in this educational approach. Integrated thematic curriculum (also referred to as thematic teaching, theme study, and learning across the curriculum) is another common approach. Here, different subject areas (e.g., math, reading, social studies) are meaningfully connected to each other in the classroom and the school community using a central theme, issue, or topic as a focus. Some classrooms use inquiry- or problem-based curriculum that allow teachers and students to investigate selected topics or issues through personal and collective research.

As you articulate the framework that supports the approach to curriculum design within your team, be certain to discuss the implications for your students with disabilities. For example, inquiry-based curriculum often begins by posing a broad instructional question and then soliciting questions from students to guide investigations. The team will need to consciously plan how students with disabilities will be active participants in this critical process. Whichever approach is used within a school or classroom, it should be defined and discussed. Then, everyone will be "on the same page" when they discuss the needs of specific students.

3   Create a Student-Centered Curriculum

If we looked into any American classroom during the first week in September, it would be evident that students' learning takes place in different ways and at different rates. Each student enters school with a different level of understanding and with unique personal strategies for learning. So it only makes sense that curriculum may differ based on the needs of students.

In the past, teachers thought of curriculum as a rigid set of predefined facts and skills that all students had to master to demonstrate achievement. The quantity of information acquired and then measured with standardized assessments took precedence. Educators used these narrow guidelines of facts and skills to determine what was important to teach, rather than using knowledge about their students to shape the curriculum. These inflexible approaches to content set up many students, particularly nontraditional learners, to fail in the general education classroom.

In contrast, a student-centered curriculum reflects the culture and experience that learners bring to the classroom as well as their current academic and social abilities. A student-centered approach acknowledges that learners will benefit from different aspects or facets of the curriculum. This basic sense of individualization is at the heart of inclusive practice. Adaptation to, or differentiation in, curriculum usually means making variations in the scope, depth, breadth, and complexity of what is taught based on knowledge of the learner. The purpose of differentiating curriculum is to make each learning experience more relevant and meaningful.

A common misconception is that when a student with disabilities is included in a general education class, the teacher must make exceptional variations in the curriculum. In reality, when a student-centered approach is employed, the teacher uses her knowledge of students' unique learning styles and abilities to influence content and complexity of curriculum for any given student. A student-centered approach promotes the philosophy that adaptation and differentiation are commonplace and necessary for every student in some aspect of learning. Understanding a student's past learning experiences, cultural identity, prior knowledge, educational priorities, and current interests is the first step in individualizing goals and learning outcomes.

Get to Know Your Students' Abilities and Interests

4

Uncovering and explicitly soliciting your students' abilities and interests are critical steps in developing a responsive and student-centered curriculum. Assessing your students in formal and informal ways will help you develop and shape relevant curricular themes and units of study. For example, asking yourself the following simple questions and reflecting on what you have observed can reveal pertinent details about your learners. In which activities do your students choose to participate? Which topics elicit excitement? Which issues prompt concern, questions, or inquiry?

Additionally, discovering students' areas of expertise can be as easy as asking, "What do you do well, in and out of school?" "What have you learned from your family, neighbors, and friends?" or "What have you taught others?" For older students, you might ask, "Within this topic (e.g., astronomy, French Revolution, Greek mythology), what would you really like to know, and how would you like to demonstrate your new knowledge?" Such questions are just as relevant for a student with disabilities as they are for other students in the classroom. However, you may need to rely on family members, peers, and past teachers to help identify, elaborate, and share the experiences of students with disabilities who do not communicate in traditional ways. It is impossible to know everything about your students at the start of the year. Instead, this understanding will be enhanced and strengthened with each shared teaching and learning experience.

A ninth-grade English teacher developed an expertise profile of his students based on questions similar to those posed above. He discovered interests, experiences, and abilities among his students that included botany, clothing design, speaking fluent Spanish, cooking, video gaming, storytelling, creative writing, hip-hop music, drumming, drama, and electronic "know-how." He found out that Julie, a student with Down syndrome in his class, had lived in South Africa while in elementary school.

During a unit on folklore, the teacher tapped the experiences of his students by allowing them to select stories from various regions and countries. Julie shared tribal artifacts and literature with the class, including stories from her own childhood experiences in South Africa. Based on the class profile, the teacher structured learning opportunities within the context of this curricular unit for students to act out selected folk tales in costume, rewrite endings or morals to traditional stories, prepare regional dishes to share during performances, and investigate the origins and evolution of storytelling and musical performance associated with specific folk tales.

5   Develop a Range of Learning Outcomes

Your first "window" into the learning abilities of a student with disabilities may be reading a student's individualized educational program (IEP). Using this document, you will be able to identify high-priority goals that should be infused into the daily rhythms of the school day. For example, if one of your students has a goal to initiate conversation using an augmentive communication system, you can emphasize this objective at the start of each class, during class discussions, in small-group or cooperative learning sessions, while at lunch, and during any social or free-time activity. It also is important to plan how an IEP goal, like the one above related to communication, can be applied in other curricular areas (e.g., science, social studies, math).

Individualized learning outcomes that are at different levels are also referred to as multilevel goals. Based on the student's unique needs, skills, interests, and abilities, these student-specific curricular goals can and should affect the scope of the curriculum. You may adjust learning outcomes for a particular student by: 1) teaching the same curricular topic but with a more or less complex focus, 2) addressing the same content but requiring the student to use different response modes to demonstrate her knowledge (e.g., to speak rather than write, to point rather than speak), 3) changing the expectations in the level of mastery, degree of quality, or quantity of the curricular requirements, or 4) focusing on similar content but having functional applications. For example, in a fifth-grade unit about state history and westward expansion, a learning outcome for students based on district curriculum standards was: Students will be able to compare and contrast changes in contemporary life with life in the past by looking at social, economic, political, and cultural elements. A multi-level goal for a student with disabilities in the class that addresses the same content but with less complexity was: By the end of the unit, Madeline will be able to use the words *past* and *present* to identify symbols, objects, and activities that belong to the 19th century from those of today.

Be aware that your student will be able to learn much more than what is identified in the IEP. Acquiring, extending, refining, and using knowledge meaningfully are all elements of what we want students to know and be able to do. Just as you want to build skills in your students without disabilities, you should also define sensible learning outcomes within each area of curriculum for students with disabilities. Some of these outcomes may be related to and guided by district or state curriculum standards.

6 Use the Learning Outcomes to Focus the Curriculum

earning to Conduct Research was a unit under consideration in Ms. Lopez's seventh-grade class. In the past, the goals of the unit focused primarily on grade-level literacy standards for writing a traditional research report. Ms. Lopez had selected the following general learning outcomes for all students: 1) to use note-taking strategies to gather information from written sources, 2) to read for facts and summarize main ideas from reference materials, 3) to paraphrase findings in one's own words, and 4) to use reference skills in the school or local library to select relevant resources.

The class included a student with multiple disabilities who used nonverbal strategies for communication. Other class members included students with advanced abilities in math and science, students with learning disabilities, and students who spoke English as a second language. Keeping the original literacy standards in mind, the educational team selected learning outcomes for the students with advanced math and science backgrounds that challenged their current knowledge base. The goals for these students were: 1) to investigate findings about a recent local or national research project; 2) to gather, analyze, and report quantitative data from the project; 3) to utilize the Internet and call on local experts and researchers for data collection; and 4) to predict, speculate, or theorize about the effects of this research.

For several students with learning disabilities, organizational strategies surfaced as important outcomes. Their goals emphasized sorting and prioritizing information, sequencing content, and validating findings with multiple sources. The student with multiple disabilities needed opportunities to practice and refine communication skills. Therefore, his learning outcomes focused on using his augmentative communication device to conduct interviews as a research-gathering technique and to convey information in a presentation to the class with visual aids and a voice-output device. These examples of learning outcomes represent multilevel variations of the curricular standards expected of all students. Although the goals differed in focus, depth, and breadth among these students, there were clear avenues for each learner to access and gain meaning from the curriculum related to conducting research.

Match Learning Outcomes and Experiences

7

An educator's job is not only to determine the goals within the curriculum but also to design the learning experiences that lead toward those objectives. Based on the goals selected for learners in Ms. Lopez's seventh-grade classroom, the educational team decided that students could produce an individual project or participate in a group investigation. The teachers asked students to select a topic related to an aspect of environmental protection. Students were allowed to choose their methods of research, presentation format, and whether to prepare an oral or written report. A group was formed that included the student with multiple disabilities as well as a student performing above grade level. This student group investigated pollution of a local watershed. They had opportunities to achieve student-specific learning outcomes through interviews with university researchers, communication with environmental protection agencies via the Internet, and the development of a final oral presentation. As the teaching team defined these multilevel outcomes for key students, the overall curriculum was expanded and enriched, allowing each learner to participate meaningfully. A planning web, illustrated in Figure 1, shows how the team differentiated the curriculum so that it reflected the educational goals of the class members.

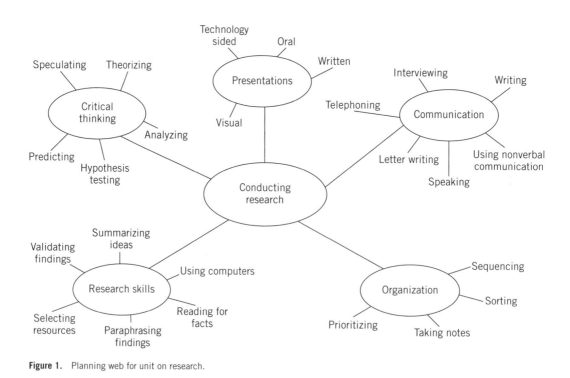

Figure 1. Planning web for unit on research.

8 Use Active and Interactive Instructional Approaches

Students with diverse learning needs often have difficulty retaining and applying knowledge when information is presented to them in isolation or in a passive manner. Additionally, instruction that relies heavily on the traditional methods of lecture, independent seatwork, whole-class question-and-answer, or discussion can leave many students struggling to understand and participate.

Alternatively, active and interactive instructional approaches offer many more avenues for involving and engaging students with disabilities. As a case in point, consider how Ms. Lopez redesigned her instructional approaches from traditional formats to more active methods. To introduce the unit about conducting research, Ms. Lopez typically provided a lecture outlining the use of resources and the elements of a good written report. Given the diverse class, lecture as the instructional approach was not a good match to the learning styles of many of her students. To increase engagement and understanding, Ms. Lopez collaborated with the special educator to adapt her unit introduction by first handing out newspapers, magazines, telephone books, encyclopedias, videotapes, computer software, names of resource people in the school building, and books.

After arranging students to work independently, in pairs, or in small groups, the teachers posed this challenge to the class: "Given these resources, find relevant information for a report on a current environmental issue." As the students explored the resources, Ms. Lopez and the special educator moved around the room to answer questions and observe the students' problem-solving methods. After 30 minutes of exploration, students were asked to share their research strategies, problems, and successes with the material. Both educators were able to follow up with key teaching points regarding the research process, which now made more sense to students after examining various resources. Using this active learning format, Ms. Lopez and her co-teacher engaged all learners, promoted understanding by discovery, and assessed the students' use of resources.

Games, simulations, role-play, interviews, activity-based and experiential instructional approaches utilize multisensory experiences with real objects, events, processes, and relationships. The use of these active methods provides the structure by which students can best access the curriculum.

Look for Ways to Differentiate Learning

9

So far we have noted that designing differentiated curriculum involves redefining relevant learning goals, expanding or shaping the content, and selecting responsive instructional approaches to reflect curricular decisions. These changes are often all that is necessary to support the inclusion of most students with disabilities in general education classrooms. However, some students may need additional considerations to maximize participation and learning.

You may need to change or vary the physical classroom environment, the instructional materials or media, the teaching strategy, ancillary support, management techniques, or method of assessment. For example, the teacher of the ninth-grade English class studying folklore used several of these other elements of differentiation to maximize Julie's participation. To help Julie (the young woman with Down syndrome) learn her lines as narrator for the folktale performance, she needed a written script with simplified language. Each page of the script had only four lines of large type; these were in bold print to reduce visual distractions. To help read her lines with proper timing and inflection, a classmate recorded the script on audiotape with appropriate pauses so that Julie could recite the lines after hearing a model.

During skit practices, the speech-language pathologist joined the class and worked with Julie's group to demonstrate ways that all students, but Julie in particular, could improve speech fluency, tone, and articulation. During the actual performance, Julie had a difficult time reciting her lines accurately while still keeping track of the sequence of the skit. A classmate provided support by gently tapping her arm as a physical cue to begin or to stop the narration at appropriate times. Julie's grade for the unit was based on meeting her language and communication goals, cooperating within the group, and producing a one-page summary of the origin of the folktale. This description illustrates changes in instructional materials, the use of student-specific teaching strategies, *effective* use of ancillary staff and peers for natural support, and alternative assessment systems. Each of these decisions represents an element of differentiation that may need to be employed to maximize a student's participation.

10 Next Year? Revise, Refine, and Revive!

Thinking about curriculum in a flexible, multilevel manner helps us to revive and rejuvenate our current teaching practices. This is not something we do once and stop. Instead, ongoing school renewal hinges on individual teachers engaging in self-reflection and making efforts toward personal change. If at the beginning of the year you catch yourself saying "This is the way I've always taught the unit on wolves," stop, and ask yourself a few important questions: "Is the scope and complexity of the curriculum appropriate for all the learners in my classroom this year?" "What do I know or need to know about my students' abilities and expertise that will help me make decisions about the curriculum?" "Do I need to devise specific goals to make the curriculum accessible and more meaningful for some students?" "Should I consider new or different active learning strategies that better match my students' strengths?"

The answers to these questions will depend on the unique makeup of your class membership (which will change every year) and put you in the mind-set to be responsive. This process of critical questioning provides an opening for new and creative thinking, and promotes the notion that the curriculum is dynamic and flexible.

Each year you will need to renew old relationships and forge new collaborative relationships with special educators, support staff, and parents. Therefore, educational teams will revisit and revise curricular decisions if necessary. Knowledge should be shared about successes or challenges with particular students so that information gained from prior teaching experiences can be expanded, reinforced, or improved upon.

Teachers who maintain their commitment to collaborative teamwork have found that, with each new school year, communication with colleagues becomes more efficient and ideas are developed more readily based on the successful endeavors of previous years. Use simple, agreed-upon strategies to differentiate your curriculum; this will help make your general education classroom an environment in which all students, including those with disabilities, can thrive.

Selected References

Jorgensen, C. (Fall, 2005). The least dangerous assumption: A challenge to create a new paradigm. *Disability Solutions, 6*(3), 1, 5–9, 15.

Jorgensen, C. (Ed.). (1998). *Restructuring high schools for all: Taking inclusion to the next level.* Baltimore: Paul H. Brookes Publishing Co.

Kluth, P. (2003). *"You're going to love this kid!": Teaching students with autism in the inclusive classroom.* Baltimore: Paul H. Brookes Publishing Co.

Kluth, P., Straut, D., & Biklen, D. (Eds.). (2003). *Access to academics for all students: Critical approaches to inclusive curriculum, instruction, and policy.* Mahwah, NJ: Lawrence Erlbaum Associates.

Tomlinson, C.A., & McTighe, J. (2006). *Integrating differentiated instruction and understanding by design: Connecting content and kids.* Alexandria, VA: Association for Supervision and Curriculum Development.

Udvari-Solner, A., Causton-Theoharis, J., & York-Barr, J. (2004). Developing adaptations to promote participation in inclusive settings. In F.P. Orelove, D. Sobsey, & R. Silberman (Eds.), *Educating children with multiple disabilities: A collaborative approach* (4th ed.) (pp. 151–192). Baltimore: Paul H. Brookes Publishing Co.

Udvari-Solner, A., & Kluth, P. (in press). *Joyful learning: Active and collaborative learning in the inclusive classroom.* Thousand Oaks, CA: Corwin Press.

Udvari-Solner, A., Villa, R., & Thousand, J. (2005). Access to the general education curriculum for all: The universal design process. In R. Villa & J.Thousand (Eds.), *Creating an inclusive school (2nd ed.)* (pp. 134–155) Alexandria, VA: Association for Supervision and Curriculum Development.

Wiggins, G., & McTighe, J. (2005). *Understanding by design (2nd ed.).* Alexandria, VA: Association for Supervision and Curriculum Development.

Quick Guide #12

Instructional Strategies

Michael F. Giangreco and Lia Cravedi

Quick-Guides to Inclusion
Ideas for Educating Students with Disabilities, Second Edition

Michael F. Giangreco & Mary Beth Doyle

Editors

Dear Team Member,

Everybody is concerned about the quality of instruction offered by our schools because, in one way or another, it affects everyone in our community. When the learning characteristics of a student with a disability present a challenge, the reflection, problem solving, and action required to address those needs helps us gain new insights and skills we can apply to help other students learn, and ultimately we can become better teachers.

It used to be assumed (wrongly) that general education teachers could not contribute successfully to teaching students with disabilities—that was one of the key rationales for placing those students in special education classes. In far too many special classes, students with disabilities encountered low expectations, limited access to peers without disabilities, too much instructional downtime, and questionable curriculum. In a small number of select situations, students did receive quality instruction, sometimes referred to as systematic instruction. While the instruction may have been technically stellar, too frequently it: 1) was applied to questionable curriculum content, 2) was applied out of context, 3) limited student access to typical places, activities, and relationships, 4) provided insufficient opportunities for generalization across settings and people, and 5) insufficiently addressed students' learning styles.

Placement in an inclusive class sets the stage to address these problems—but placement is not enough. The challenge is to apply these time-tested ideas about good teaching, including systematic instruction, in new and contextually viable ways. These are instructional strategies you already know, though possibly by different names. Remember, the principles of teaching and learning do not change just because a label has been put on a child—so individualize what you already know about good teaching.

Good Luck!
Michael & Lia

GUIDELINES-AT-A-GLANCE

1. Know Each Student's Characteristics and Learning Styles

2. Establish Shared Expectations

3. Plan How Learning Outcomes Will Be Addressed

4. Provide Sufficient Learning Opportunities

5. Involve Everyone in Whole-Group Instruction

6. Use Good Teaching Methods

7. Use More Good Teaching Methods

8. Use Even More Good Teaching Methods

9. Collect Data on Student Learning

10. Use Data to Make Instructional Decisions

Know Each Student's Characteristics and Learning Styles

It may seem almost too obvious to mention, but good instruction begins by knowing your students' characteristics and learning styles across a variety of dimensions. There is an unproductive tendency in special education to focus too much on a student's disabilities or perceived deficits. Although disability characteristics are important to consider, it is a student's attributes and abilities that will be equally, if not more, helpful in designing instruction and selecting environments conducive to learning. For example, knowing that a student is blind eliminates certain visual approaches to instruction, but doesn't provide constructive information to build upon.

Conversely, knowing that a student has good tactile discrimination and hearing abilities is much more useful from an instructional standpoint than simply being aware that a student is blind. Knowing that a student with physical disabilities cannot effectively point using his hand again eliminates certain options, but knowing he has excellent control of his head, eyes, and breathing opens options to point using eye gaze, a head pointer, or a pneumatic "sip and puff" switch attached to a computer.

There are many potential sources of information about student characteristics, such as parent interviews, reports from support service specialists, direct observations, and conversations with last year's teacher—but nothing can replace the knowledge you will gain through ongoing, personal teaching interactions with your students who have disabilities.

Ask yourself what you know about the student's abilities, attributes, and characteristics in these categories: 1) *Cognitive* (e.g., has good categorization and memory skills); 2) *Physical* (e.g., has consistent motor control over head movements side to side; has functional use of right hand); 3) *Sensory* (e.g., can orient toward the source of sounds; prefers using materials with smooth textures); 4) *Social/Emotional* (e.g., has an even temperament; very sociable; enjoys interactions with peers); 5) *Motivational* (e.g., is motivated by participation in games and activities); 6) *Interactional* (e.g., prefers working in small groups); 7) *Creative* (e.g., likes drawing and participating in performance art; likes folk music). Use these categories to design instruction that builds upon each student's strengths and abilities.

2 Establish Shared Expectations

A common source of anxiety for classroom teachers is not having an understanding of what others, such as parents, administrators, and special educators, expect of them: "Do you expect me to teach this student most or all of what the other students without disabilities are learning?" Whether the answer is "Yes" or "No," it is important to ensure everyone shares a common expectation of what the student should learn and who will be responsible for teaching. Although this conversation needs to occur among the adults involved in teaching a student, all too often the student is inappropriately left out of this loop.

Good instruction requires that students be aware of their teachers' expectations regarding preparation for class (e.g., homework), participation in class, targeted learning outcomes, and how learning will be assessed (e.g., products, outputs, other demonstrations of learning). Expectations should be at an appropriate level of difficulty so they offer a challenge but are reasonably attainable. Students should share ownership of their own learning. This may include options such as being involved in determining IEP goals, making choices about content or assessment within teacher-generated parameters, or self-monitoring progress. Self-advocacy and choice making are critical skills that should be intentionally taught and practiced.

A good place to start is for the team, including school personnel and the family, to identify a small, individualized, set of priority learning outcomes. Next, agree on a set of additional learning outcomes that reflect a broad-based educational program to ensure students' access to the general education curriculum. Many students with disabilities also need general supports that are provided to or for them (e.g., specialized equipment, positioning, personal care needs) to allow for their participation in class.

It can be helpful to summarize these three categories of the educational program: 1) priority learning outcomes, 2) additional learning outcomes, and 3) general supports, on a one- or two-page Program-at-a-Glance. Clarifying expectations using this type of concise listing can assist in planning and scheduling, serve as a helpful reminder of the student's individualized needs, and provide an effective way to communicate student needs to all teachers, including those in specialized areas such as art, music, and physical education.

Plan How Learning Outcomes Will Be Addressed

3

Planning an inclusive lesson requires the teacher to creatively integrate many pieces of knowledge about individual students, groups of students, the environment, potential learning materials and activities, as well as the subject matter and learning outcomes. This planning begins by knowing the individual learning outcomes targeted for each student during a lesson, regardless of whether it is a large or small group.

Although students with disabilities may have all or some of the same learning outcomes as the rest of the class during a lesson, at times their learning outcomes are different. The learning outcomes may be slightly or significantly different in scope or content within the same curriculum area (e.g., social studies). At other times, a student's learning outcomes may be from a different curriculum area than the rest of the class. For example, a student may be participating in a science experiment, but focusing on communication and literacy outcomes (e.g., describing an observation verbally and in writing). When it's not obvious which individualized learning outcomes are best suited to particular class activities, team planning can be facilitated by using variations of the *Osborn-Parnes Creative Problem-Solving Process* or other problem-solving approaches (see the reference list at the end of this Quick-Guide more information).

Once the class activity and learning outcomes have been identified, a series of basic questions should be asked and decisions made to plan the lesson. First, "What will I do as a teacher?" This includes factors like environmental arrangement, student groupings, materials, directions given, and extra cues provided. Second, "What will it look like when the student responds correctly?" This should be observable behaviors, and need not be limited to a single type of correct response. Third, "What will you do if the student responds correctly, does not respond, or responds incorrectly?" You must be prepared for all the various possibilities (e.g., correct responding, incorrect responding, nonresponding, partial responding, or mixed correct and incorrect responding). This may include components like feedback, reinforcement, correction procedures, prompts, additional time for responding, or additional opportunities for responding. Fourth, "How will you describe, measure, and document student progress so that it can be used to facilitate learning?" Remember, instruction is a cyclical process, so use what you learn to adjust your plans.

Provide Sufficient Learning Opportunities

Most students require frequent opportunities to interact with content or to practice a skill in order to learn it. This is true for students with disabilities as well, and sometimes they need even more opportunities.

As you consider how learning outcomes will be addressed in classroom activities, think about the various opportunities you can provide for students to experience those outcomes. For example, if a student has the learning outcome "initiates interactions with peers," consider appropriate times when that skill could be practiced within various activities.

One implication of providing a sufficient number of learning opportunities distributed throughout the day and week is that the team must intentionally focus on a set of important learning outcomes that they can reasonably address and also plan activities that purposely provide opportunities to work on multiple learning outcomes. For example, many academic, communication, and social skills (e.g., writing, instruction following, describing, turn taking) can be embedded across numerous activities throughout the day.

If students are working in pairs or small groups, opportunities to interact are naturally occurring and appropriate. Using a matrix with class activities across the top and a student's goals down the side can help identify intersections of learning opportunities. Remember, it is okay to ask for help. There are people in your school, or available to your school, to help you identify opportunities for your students.

With the need for multiple opportunities to interact with content, as well as to practice skills at different times and in different situations, comes a need for the student to experience consistency. If you have decided to cue or reinforce a skill in certain ways, you and other classroom staff (and maybe even students) need to feel comfortable enough with those procedures to be able to be consistent in their use.

To be truthful, this is sometimes difficult, and mistakes may be made—that's unavoidable. What is important is that you are thinking consciously about what you are doing and how you are doing it. As you consider consistency, think beyond the immediate classroom staff to special area teachers, office staff, cafeteria workers, and schoolmates. Only pursue this extent of consistency in situations where it is critical. Some naturally occurring variations can facilitate generalization across settings, people, and cues that are desirable for optimal functioning and participation.

Involve Everyone in Whole-Group Instruction

5

Teachers group students for instruction in a variety of ways, depending on the nature of their goals. Whole-group instruction is among the most frequently used arrangements. Although it can be a challenging format to individualize, it is possible and necessary to do so. Establish early on that everyone is expected to participate. Have students clear their desks of any materials unrelated to the lesson at hand, and make sure that the physical environment is arranged to facilitate participation. Move among your students, rather than standing in one spot. Make it a practice to call on students randomly, rather than only those same students who always seem to raise their hands.

Help students get ready for learning by creating an agenda and using other advance organizers that activate prior knowledge and introduce key vocabulary and concepts. Use graphic organizers, such as concept maps or webs and timelines, to identify main points, illustrate steps in a process, and show relationships between ideas. Individualize, by varying the amount and complexity of the questions you ask, to match what you know about individual students.

Remember the importance of wait time, cueing, and using both positive and negative exemplars. You may need to provide some students with disabilities questions ahead of time, so they can be ready to participate; this might involve extra learning time, having written notes or graphics, or preprogramming a communication device. In addition to calling on individual students, intermix whole-group questions that require all students to respond simultaneously, chorally (when age appropriate), using thumbs-up or -down, or by writing on individual white boards to get a quick sense of students' understanding, knowledge, reactions, or feedback. Use "think–pair–share" and other quick grouping strategies to facilitate peer-to-peer interaction and provide variety within whole-class instruction.

Help your students to develop and use mnemonic devices to remember content or processes. For example, ROY G BIV cues students to the colors in the spectrum, and COPS—Capitalization, Overall appearance, Punctuation, and Spelling (Lewis & Doorlang, 1999) is a great way for students to remember how to proofread written work. These are just a few things you can do to enhance whole-group instruction and ensure that students with disabilities are appropriately included.

Use Good Teaching Methods

6

Many students with disabilities respond favorably to the same teaching methods that are effective with students who do not have disabilities. Some of these common methods include: modeling and demonstration, class discussion, repeated exposure and practice, guided discovery, experiments, field-study, participatory activities, use of multi-media technology, use of question-asking strategies, use of manipulative materials, educational games and play, use of positive and negatives examples, corrective feedback, and individual or small group projects.

Challenges arise when students do not progress adequately using typical instructional methods. In such cases, instruction must be augmented using more precisely applied methods. What follows here, as well as in Guidelines #7 and #8, are some instructional methods that can be applied within the context of typical class activities. Don't be intimidated by the technical names that come from the field of applied behavior analysis, because you will recognize that you have used many or all of these strategies before.

Selection of these instructional methods should be based on: 1) which method, or combination, is most likely to be effective based on your knowledge of the student's characteristics, 2) the nature of target learning outcome, and 3) which method can be applied in the most socially appropriate or status-enhancing way in typical settings.

For example, if you are a teacher of primary grade students and typically use stickers or smiley faces to acknowledge students' progress or accomplishments, it may be appropriate to do so for a student with a disability in your class. Conversely, if you are a high school teacher who never uses stickers or smiley faces with your teenage students, it would be inadvisable to use them with students who have disabilities.

If you've ever taught a child to tie his or her shoelaces or do long division, you may have used *task analysis.* Task analysis involves taking a skill and breaking it down into its component parts of student behavior to facilitate learning. Task analyses can include fairly large chunks of behavior, or those that are quite small—this depends on the complexity of the task and the skill level of the student. Each step in a task analysis has a built-in cue that serves as a naturally occurring prompt for the next step. You may find that a student is having a problem with a particular part of a skill and that may be the only part that needs to be task analyzed.

Use More Good Teaching Methods

If you've ever taught someone dressing skills, at school or at home, you've probably used some form of *chaining.* Forms of chaining include: 1) *continuous chaining* (teaching all the steps of the task analysis); 2) *forward chaining* (teaching the steps of the task analysis from the beginning until the student makes an error; instruction proceeds only after the step is mastered); and 3) *backward chaining* (prearranging a task so that all the steps are complete except the last one; the last step is taught until it is mastered, and then you sequentially move backward through the sequence until you reach the beginning).

When using *backward chaining* to teach a student to zip a coat, the teacher would do all the steps except pulling the zipper up the last few inches. The student would then be expected to pull the zipper up from half way, then from near the bottom. The last step taught would be joining the two parts of the zipper together. This approach can be motivating, because it ends in successfully completing the task. It can be especially effective when a skill is taught in context and followed by a natural and desired consequence (e.g., "After you zip up your coat, it will be time to go outside for recess.").

If you've ever taught a child how to ride a bike, cross the street, or dial a phone, you may have used *errorless learning.* Errorless learning refers to guiding a student through a task using sufficient prompts so that the student can be successful as quickly as possible while making as few errors as possible (hopefully none). Errors are interrupted as they occur, and guidance is provided. In some cases, it can be important to back up and have the student repeat the last step they completed correctly, then guide him through the step where he had difficulty. As the student becomes more proficient, the guidance is faded. Errorless learning provides more opportunities for practicing a skill correctly, and is useful for tasks where errors just won't do (e.g., crossing the street).

If you've ever taught a child how to read a face clock, you may have used *cue redundancy.* Cue redundancy is when you exaggerate the relevant dimension of a cue to discriminate between it and other cues. For example, when teaching the difference between the hour and minute hands on a face clock, length is the relevant dimension (not color or shape). Using cue redundancy, you would exaggerate the difference in length by making the hour hand very short and the minute hand very long, and then fade toward more typical lengths.

Use Even More
Good Teaching Methods

I f you've ever taught a child how to compose a story, you've probably used *shaping.* Shaping is simply reinforcing increasingly proficient approximations of skill. For example, in composition, teachers expect increasing detail, description, spelling accuracy, and proper use of grammar. Shaping is, by its very nature, a developmental process of starting where the child is and moving forward at an individualized pace. Shaping acknowledges and reinforces what a student can already do, and then pushes him another step or two further toward proficiency or advanced skillfulness.

If you've ever taught a child early handwriting skills, you've probably used *prompts*, *cues*, and *fading.* Prompts and cues include approaches such as full physical guidance, partial physical guidance, modeling, verbal directions, questions, reminders, or encouragement, and visual clues. Prompts and cues can be provided prior to or following student responding. Prompts and cues should be faded as quickly as possible. Using dotted letters in handwriting instruction is a cue that eventually will be faded.

If you've ever taught a child to say "Thank you" in response to receiving something, you've probably used *time delay.* Time delay refers to the pairing of two cues simultaneously (zero delay). The established cue is one you know the student will respond to correctly, and the desired cue is the one you would like the student to respond to, particularly a natural cue. For example, when teaching a young child to say "Thank you,", you want the child to respond to the natural cue of receiving something. You can start by simultaneously pairing the natural cue, such as receiving something tangible like a toy, drink, or cookie, with the established cue, "Say, Thank you," knowing the child is capable of saying or approximating, "Thank you." You would release the item to the child once he says, "Thank you." Once this is consistently established, a time delay (e.g., a couple of seconds) is inserted between the natural cue and the extra cue, and is gradually increased. When the time delay is long enough, the student responds "Thank you" before receiving the extra cue. Extra cues are often faded simultaneously as the time delay increases (e.g., "Say Thank you;" "What do you say?"). Time delay can be especially valuable for teaching students who are not imitative.

9

Collect Data on Student Learning

Teachers often have an intuitive sense of how their students are progressing. In order to validate those impressions, or sometimes to challenge them, it is important to gather additional information through various forms of systematic data collection. Encourage your team to establish a disposition that values data collection, to maintain professional accountability and as a vital step in the teaching/learning cycle.

When measuring progress, you must first focus on the learning outcomes that have been identified for the student and translate them into behaviors that you can observe and document. A relatively small number of student learning outcomes (e.g., IEP goals) may require individualized data collection that you can establish with the special educator or related services personnel.

Learning outcomes that come from the existing general education curriculum can often be assessed using the same methods as the rest of the class. Start by selecting methods for evaluating behaviors that make sense and tell you what you want to know. There are many ways to do this, and you probably already use a number of them. Quizzes, tests, projects, observations, demonstrations, and work samples can all be used to measure progress. These various methods can tell you information like: 1) the percentage of accuracy the student has achieved, 2) the frequency with which the student uses a skill, 3) the rate at which the student accomplishes a task, 4) the quality of work the student generates, 5) the duration of time a student's attention can be sustained, 6) the number of steps in a series (e.g., from a task analysis) that the student can successfully complete, or 7) the extent to which a student's valued life outcomes have improved as a result of working on certain learning outcomes.

The data collection methods you choose and the information you seek should be directly related to the student's learning outcomes. For example, think back to the learning outcome mentioned in Guideline #8: "initiates interactions with peers." Given that stated outcome, you might want to use observation as a method to measure the frequency of interactions during small groups with classmates. Whatever the learning outcomes, the data collection method should be agreed upon by the student's team, and the data should be collected by a variety of team members, including the student when appropriate.

Use Data to Make Instructional Decisions

10

Now you have some ideas about how to collect data about students' progress toward their learning outcomes. What's next? The data that you collect can be used in an active way to help you to understand students' current and future instructional needs.

In order to do this, you first need to think about: 1) the level at which each student is currently performing, 2) the level at which the student needs to perform in order to be considered accomplished, 3) how much time it might take for the student to meet this goal, 4) how frequently you will collect information about the student's progress, and 5) when you should review the data to see if goals have been reached. If data is simply collected—not reviewed and used—it may as well not be collected at all.

Once you have some data to look at, you need to ask yourself what the data is telling you. It may show that the student: 1) is ready to move forward and pursue a new learning outcome or a higher level of performance related to the existing outcome, 2) needs more time to accomplish the outcome, or 3) requires more or different teaching strategies. It would not be unusual for the data to suggest more than a message for future action.

After the team has decided what they think the data means, it is time to consider possible actions based on your knowledge of the student and situation, to select a course of action, and to take that action. Your action doesn't have to be earth shattering; it can be small and simple yet still be potent, because it establishes a pattern of action based on data review. As Alex Osborn once stated, "A fair idea put to use is better than a great idea left on the polishing wheel" (Parnes, 1988, p. 37).

Though it is common and appropriate to consider instructional and curricular changes, in some cases you may also want to change your data collection method. Your existing methods may not be providing you with the information you are seeking, or may not be sensitive enough to detect modest levels of progress—this is particularly important for students with severe disabilities, who have slower rates and inconsistent patterns of learning. Whatever you decide needs to happen instructionally, it has been informed by the data you have collected.

Selected References

Alberto, P.A., & Troutman, A.C. (2005). *Applied behavior analysis for teachers (7th ed.).* Upper Saddle River, NJ: Prentice Hall.

Giangreco, M.F., Cloninger, C.J., Dennis, R.E., & Edelman, S.W. (2002). Problem-solving methods to facilitate inclusive education. In J.S. Thousand, R.A. Villa, & A.I. Nevin, (Eds.), *Creativity and collaborative learning: A practical guide to empowering students, teachers, and families (2nd ed.).* Baltimore: Paul H. Brookes Publishing Co.

Giangreco, M.F., Cloninger, C.J., & Iverson, V.S. (1998). *Choosing outcomes and accommodations for children: A guide to educational planning for students with disabilities (2nd ed.).* Baltimore: Paul H. Brookes Publishing Co.

Kameenui, E.J., & Carnine, D. (1998). *Effective strategies that accommodate diverse learners.* Englewood Cliffs, NJ: Prentice-Hall.

Lewis, R.B., & Doorlang, D.H. (1999). *Teaching special students in general education classrooms (5th ed.).* Upper Saddle, NJ: Prentice-Hall.

Parnes, S.J. (1988). *Visionizing: State-of-the-art processes for encouraging innovative excellence.* East Aurora, NY: D.O.K. Publishers.

Rainforth, B., & Kugelmass, J.W. (2003). *Curriculum and instruction for all learners: Blending systematic and constructivist approaches in inclusive elementary schools.* Baltimore: Paul H. Brookes Publishing Co.

Snell, M.E., & Brown, F. (Eds.) (2006). *Instruction of students with severe disabilities (5th Ed.).* Columbus, OH: Merrill/Pearson Education.

Turnbull, A.P., Turnbull, H.R., & Wehmeyer, M.L. (2007). *Exceptional lives: Special education in today's schools (5th ed.).* Upper Saddle River, NJ: Prentice Hall.

Vaughn, S., Boss, C.S., & Schumm, J.S. (2003). *Teaching exceptional, diverse, and at-risk students in the general education classroom (3rd ed.).* Needham Heights, MA: Allyn & Bacon.

Villa, R.A., Thousand, J.S., & Nevin, A.I. (2004). *A guide to co-teaching: Practical tips for facilitating student learning.* Thousand Oaks, CA: Corwin Press.

Section V

Literacy & Numeracy

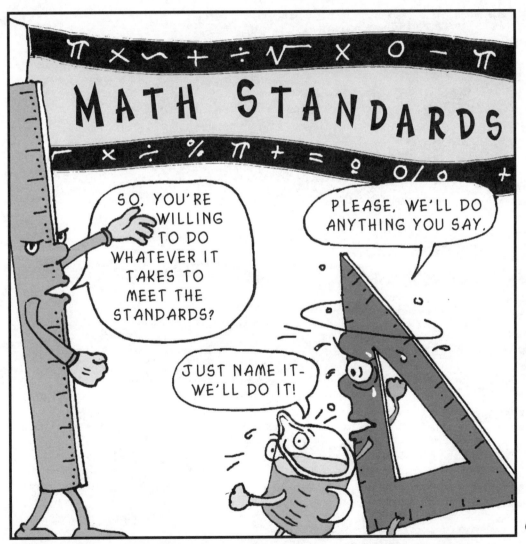

Quick-Guide #13

Supporting Literacy
Learning in All Children

David A. Koppenhaver and Karen A. Erickson

Quick-Guides to Inclusion
Ideas for Educating Students with Disabilities, Second Edition
Michael F. Giangreco & Mary Beth Doyle
Editors

Quick-Guides to Inclusion: Ideas for Educating Students with Disabilities (2nd ed.) © Michael F. Giangreco, 2007
Available through Paul H. Brookes Publishing Co., Baltimore, 1-800-638-3775

Dear Teacher,

Finding ways to teach all of the students in your class to read and write presents unique challenges. The students come to your class with diverse abilities, experiences, and interests. The climate surrounding your classroom is politically charged, and the demand for positive literacy outcomes, usually with a strong emphasis on end-of-grade reading test scores, is great. In many schools, you have restricted choice in the kinds of materials and strategies you are to employ. Increasingly, you are being asked to teach students with significant learning needs with whom you may have little experience or familiarity, and little or no specific training.

The 10 guidelines in this Quick-Guide are intended to provide you with decision-making support as you face these many challenges. Each guideline is followed by a brief explanation that will help you identify the successful and effective strategies you already have in your arsenal, as well as those areas in which you might seek new or additional strategies. At the end of this Quick-Guide, you'll find selected references that will help you learn more about literacy instruction, assessment, and the use of assistive technologies to support all students in learning to read, write, and communicate.

This Quick-Guide is not intended to be read as the "right way" to teach. It is, instead, organized around some principles and practices of successful classroom literacy instruction. We hope that it helps you find a balance in your classroom that will benefit all of your students.

Read (and Write) On!
David and Karen

GUIDELINES-AT-A-GLANCE

1. Focus Literacy Activities on Communication

2. Use Words to Teach Letters and Sounds

3. Provide a Balance of Instruction

4. Make Materials Accessible for Every Student

5. Make Activities Accessible for Every Student

6. Provide Diverse Materials and Models

7. Support Students Before, During, and After Reading

8. Use a Word Wall

9. Teach the Writing Process

10. Perfect Practice Makes Perfect

Focus Literacy Activities on Communication

Meaningful, purposeful communication is at the heart of learning to read and write. Students who learn that they can use reading and writing to investigate areas of interest, share their ideas, thoughts, and feelings, or interact with new people understand that the primary purpose of literacy is communication. Without a focus on the communicative functions of literacy, instruction can teach skills such as letter and word identification, phonics, and spelling, but that instruction won't lead to lifelong use of those skills.

In the early stages of learning to read and write, this focus on communication means that instruction should target the functions of print rather than the forms. Students who are just learning about letters, sounds, and words should be learning why those aspects of print are important. For example, an emphasis on communication in early literacy instruction would result in students learning how and why their name is used in print. They would have multiple opportunities to write their names, letter by letter, for real purposes each day (e.g., attendance charts, special activity sign-ups, assignments), and they would see models of their name being written and used for real purposes each day. They would not copy or trace their name, use a name stamp, or otherwise select or write in a manner that emphasized the quality of the product over an understanding of the process. For children with significant physical disabilities in particular, this requires careful selection of alternative means of selecting individual letters and writing letter by letter.

For more sophisticated readers and writers, a focus on communication means that instruction supports students in selecting their own topics for writing and their own purposes for reading. Writers who select their own topics and audiences learn to pay attention to mechanics and other writing conventions in order to communicate in a way that their chosen audience can understand. Readers who select their own purposes learn that a single text can be read for multiple purposes and understood in a number of different ways. Instruction focused on literacy as communication supports these more sophisticated readers and writers as they refine their skills through meaningful application.

Regardless of a student's level of competence in reading or writing, focusing literacy instruction on communication increases the potential impact of the instruction and the likelihood that the skills will be used across contexts for a lifetime.

Use Words to Teach Letters and Sounds

2

An important component of beginning reading instruction is effectively teaching letters and sounds. Related to letter and sound knowledge are *phonological awareness*, the ability to hear and manipulate sounds in oral language, and *phonemic awareness*, the ability to hear and manipulate phonemes, the smallest units of sound in oral language. It is tempting to teach these skills in isolation since they can be easily parsed, but they are very difficult to apply and generalize when they are taught in isolation.

Using words to teach letters and sounds integrates the skills and teaches their application from the beginning. Use words that are meaningful to the student, beginning with first names and other words that they are likely to see often. For example, schools are full of exit signs that glow red and attract the attention of many students. Those signs provide a highly visible means to introduce and refer repeatedly to E, "like EXIT." Another common example is a student's first name. For a short period of time, most young children think that every word they see that begins with the same letter as their name *is* their name. Use that to support your students in learning both the name and sound of the letters that start their names.

Words also serve as important *mnemonics*, or memory aids, as students learn letter names and sounds. Letter names and sounds can be paired with the names of food items and actions. Students can learn the name of the letter J by seeing it on the JELL-O® box, and the sound it makes by saying the whole word and isolating the beginning sound from the whole word. They can also learn the letter J by associating it with jumping.

As you work to teach letter and sound knowledge, use a variety of approaches that encourage generalized understanding from the beginning rather than rote learning of a routine, song, individual book, or other words-based letter and sound instructional strategy. The power of being able to identify letters and the sounds associated with them lies in being able to use that knowledge to read and write words. Using words to teach letters and sounds is one way to increase the likelihood that students will understand their importance and apply them meaningfully in their efforts to read and write.

3   Provide a Balance of Instruction

Whether you call it balanced instruction, comprehensive instruction, or instruction that addresses the individual needs of every learner in the class, effective literacy instruction requires more than a single approach or a focus on a single set of skills. Effective literacy instruction requires the conscious combination of instructional approaches and activities that address all of the literacy learning needs students present, both individually and collectively. Balance in literacy instruction ensures that students receive the systematic, teacher-directed instruction they need in order to learn many reading and writing skills while also having regular opportunities to apply and refine those skills through self-directed reading and writing activities.

In classrooms with a diverse group of students, you must continually make adjustments to address the needs of all students. By creating a balance in your instruction, you avoid the pitfalls of eclectic approaches that take a little of this, maybe a lot of that, and some more of something else, without conscious attention to the whole that is created by the parts. Balance means that teachers make a conscious effort to provide specific amounts of different instructional approaches that reflect all of the components of research-based reading and writing instruction.

One type of balance many teachers have found successful is to devote 30 or more minutes each day to four different approaches: 1) comprehension, 2) composition, 3) word-level instruction, and 4) self-directed reading. In developing comprehension, you teach strategies for understanding different kinds of texts through reading and listening. In composition, you teach writing with an emphasis on self-selected topics, short and focused teacher-directed lessons, lots of interaction among student authors and with the teacher, and opportunities to write initial drafts focused on communication, with later drafts edited for convention. In word-level instruction, you teach phonics, word recognition skills, and strategies for reading and spelling unfamiliar words. In self-directed reading, you create an environment where students share their interests in different kinds of reading and writing experiences, to increase their motivation to read and write beyond the classroom while providing an important opportunity to develop independent and automatic application of skills taught during other parts of the day. The end product of this, or any comprehensive approach to literacy instruction, is that every student's needs are met every day.

Make Materials Accessible for Every Student

A book isn't a book, nor a pencil a pencil, if a student isn't able to use it. We need to adapt or create tools for literacy learning that students with physical impairments can hold, students with sensory impairments can see or hear, students with intellectual impairments can understand, and all students are motivated to use.

As you consider the ways in which to create or adapt tools, begin by identifying the purpose of the materials in their original form. It is important that the adapted version provides equal opportunity to achieve the same purpose as the original. For example, a book on audiotape without an accessible print or Braille version provides important access to the story itself for a child who has visual impairments, but doesn't provide the same opportunity to develop print awareness or reading fluency as the original book. In the same way, a bank of pictures provides important writing supports to a child with significant physical impairments, but it does not provide the same opportunity to develop spelling and sentence writing skills as the original pencil.

In addition to determining the purpose of the materials to be made accessible, you should consider six types of learning differences: 1) communicative, 2) cognitive, 3) physical, 4) sensory, 5) affective, and 6) attentional. These differences are significant because they affect the relative success or difficulty that students experience when using standard materials. Students may have significant differences in one or more of the six areas and may, therefore, require multiple adaptations to existing materials in order to use them successfully.

Some of the most common means of adapting standard materials can be accomplished with simple, everyday materials. For example, build up a pencil with some molding clay, make the pages in a book easier to turn by slipping a large paperclip onto the bottom corner of each, or make a piece of paper easier to write on by taping it to the top of a 3-inch, three-ring binder with the fat side facing away from the student. Numerous high-tech solutions are also available to make reading and writing more accessible for every student. Whatever solutions you find, don't allow the time it takes you to make the material accessible exceed the time the student will spend using it!

Make Activities Accessible for Every Student

There is an important difference between the accessibility of the materials that students use during literacy instruction and the accessibility of the instructional activities themselves. As teachers, we need to design our instruction so that it targets the varied needs of students and engages them actively as learners. Students need to understand the directions of each activity. They need time to think before other students blurt out answers. They require a means to ask questions.

A first step toward making activities accessible for every student is to begin using "every-pupil-response" strategies for group activities. Every-pupil-response strategies allow you to monitor each child's understanding and attention at the same time. A common example is a thumb up for "Yes," or a thumb down for "No." The teacher poses a Yes/No question, "Do you think the boy is going to win?" and asks everyone to show their answer on the count of three. At a glance the teacher can see all of the responses, and few demands have been placed on the students. A related strategy to make activities more accessible is to incorporate more choice-making. Offer choices that include multiple responses that are plausible rather than a single correct response. Then point to and read each option aloud while students use an appropriate every-pupil-response technique to indicate their choices. The combination of these two strategies will make group activities far more accessible to students who otherwise would be uninvolved or struggling to keep up.

Modeling is another important strategy that will help make activities accessible to all students. Students with disabilities rarely see others reading and writing with the adapted tools and materials they must use. Teachers regularly model writing for nondisabled students throughout the day. They write information on the board, in notes, or in lists, and think aloud as they use chalk, pens, markers, and the computer. It is important for teachers also to model use of the adapted pencils, modified books, or unique response modes of students with disabilities in their class. This benefits not only the students with disabilities, who learn better how to use their particular tools and materials, but it also legitimizes for other students the use of those tools and materials.

6 Provide Diverse Materials and Models

As teachers, we want to help our students not only learn how to read but also to choose to do so. We can help students make personal connections to literacy through both the materials and the instructional activities we bring into the classroom.

Find reading and writing materials that the student can (and wants to) use. Entice students with cover art by standing some books upright on your shelves. Place books in strategic locations where students congregate, such as bathrooms, halls, the lunchroom, or the drinking fountain. Try to include at least 20 different kinds of reading materials per student in your class, including newspapers, magazines, books, close-captioning, music CDs and lyrics, web sites, catalogs, brochures, atlases, student-authored books and multimedia projects, posters, charts, and anything else that might be interesting to one or more students. Be sure to include examples of fiction, nonfiction, directions, poetry, and drama, ranging from easy reading (including wordless picture books and comics at all grade levels) to extended text.

Remember that reading materials are just decorations until students choose to explore them. Find interesting ways to share and read books. Some teachers have bedtime reading day, when students wear pajamas, bring flashlights and pillows, and read with the lights out. Others have beach reading day, when students bring beach blankets, umbrellas, sunglasses, and sprinklers and read outside. One teacher has a Greek lyceum day each Friday, when her third graders wear togas, drink grape juice, eat cheese and crackers, and discuss their readings with one another. Few of us choose to sit in hard chairs at desks to do pleasure reading, and for students, who don't yet know the pleasures of reading, the more real the experience the better.

Remember also that all books are not equally accessible to students with disabilities. Teachers can get service clubs, fraternities, and parent volunteers (or teach their own students) to scan their reading collection. Then they import the images into *My Own Bookshelf* (http://www.softtouch.com), *KidPix Studio Deluxe* (http://www.riverdeep.net), or other multimedia software, record a child reading the text aloud, and keep this adapted version in a pocket in the back of each book for those students needing alternatives, and for others who just want a change of pace.

Support Students Before, During, and After Reading

In guiding students' reading to improve comprehension, part of your role as a teacher is to carefully design supports to account for what happens before, during, and after the reading of a text. Rather than assign reading and ask questions after students finish, you teach students before they begin reading. You help them identify what they already know that applies to the day's reading, or you help them build new background knowledge as needed. You preteach key vocabulary, discuss illustrations, or remind students of the elements of a typical story (or other text structure). Many teachers find that video clips (e.g., fee services such as http://www.unitedstreaming.com or free services such as video searches at http://www.altavista.com) and photos (e.g., image searches at http://www.google.com) are helpful learning supports before reading.

Next, you may ask students to predict what might happen or what they might learn from the text. In various ways, you help students establish a purpose for their reading, such as sequencing key events, comparing and contrasting two characters, describing the setting and why it matters, determining the main idea, and so on.

As students then read, provide the level of support each student needs to address the purpose for reading successfully. You might have the class chorally read, ask students to partner with a classmate, or read silently. You might read aloud to the class, or stop every page or two to review the purpose or take notes on a wall chart. You might work with a small mixed-ability group to provide models and more intensive support to some students as the rest of the class reads independently or with partners.

Following the reading, have students remind you, and each other, of the purpose for reading, and guide students to reflect on the reading purpose. Guide students in discussing the text. Ask open-ended questions, and encourage student conversations with one another. Prompt students to consider their own thinking and reading strategies with questions like, "What made you think of that?" or "Where does it say that in the book?" or "How do you know?" Engage students in related art, cooking, drama, music, and writing activities, not as busywork but rather to facilitate deeper processing of important ideas they have just read.

Use a Word Wall

8

Word walls help students learn to read and spell words accurately and automatically. They are literally entire classroom walls where five words are added each week, arranged alphabetically by first letter. Students learning at a different pace than their classmates may use a file folder as their individual word wall. Students who cannot speak often use their communication device with the words programmed accordingly. Regardless of the particular physical format required by the student, the word wall provides a support for students in learning to read and spell words encountered throughout the day. Over the course of a year, a word wall helps students learn approximately 150 sight words and acquire dozens of strategies to read and spell familiar and unfamiliar words.

Like any teaching strategy, the word wall is most effective when used thoughtfully. The wall includes words that occur frequently in text (e.g., *the, of, or*), have common spelling patterns (e.g., *tire, map, sing*), or are meaningful in the classroom culture (e.g., *survivor, idol*). The words are written with thick, dark magic markers on sentence strips, then block cut to emphasize the word shape, and glued onto a dark background to visually emphasize that shape and the spelling. Homophones (e.g., their, there, they're) and words that have similar sounds (e.g., am, an) are placed on different colored backgrounds, and color is used for visual contrast in all of the words. Words remain on the wall all year, and students learn to use the wall in reading and spelling throughout the day.

Word wall instruction encourages students to look carefully at spelling patterns and provides ongoing, varied repetition of all the words while emphasizing new words each week. Daily 15-minute activities with the word *wall* are selected from an infinite number of possibilities, including concentration, hangman, silly sentences, guess the covered word, word bingo, word graphs, card games like "War," chants, raps, and more. Successful teachers make sure that no instructional activities eliminate students from participation because of error; they know that students need practice in order to learn. Teachers can find clear photographs of word walls and many more teaching ideas at web sites such as *The School Bell* (http://www.theschoolbell.com), *abcteach* (http://www .abcteach.com), and *Teachers.Net* (http://www.teachers.net).

Teach the Writing Process

9

Writing is a complex act—essentially thinking on paper. To write effectively, students must think simultaneously on multiple levels about the ideas they want to convey. Writers consider what knowledge their audience already has about their message; word choice, grammar, and spelling rules; and other considerations. Students must learn both individual skills and the ability to juggle these skills in fluent writing.

It is important for students to pick their own topics, if they are to become independent writers, and there are many helpful strategies for those who find this difficult. Many teachers help students brainstorm topics of interest early in the year (e.g., favorite places; movie stars; athletes; pets; friends; things that make you happy, sad, frightened, angry). These lists are stored in the students' writing folders for reference as needed. Other teachers use journals as topic sources. Others use "Can't Stop Writing" for a few minutes at a time occasionally: students begin writing non-stop, and write "I can't think of anything to write" any time they get stuck, until they think of something else to write. Still other teachers engage students in play, science, cooking, art, and other activities to provide direct experiences that can be written about.

Several technologies assist students in generating topics or brainstorming ideas. Inexpensive digital cameras (less than $20 in many discount stores) provide a visual record for supporting memory and language. Photos can be imported into *Inspiration* or *Kidspiration* (http://www.inspiration.com) to prompt student ideas and language.

After students generate an idea, they must create a text. This can be done by dictating to a scribe, handwriting, typing, using alternative keyboards (e.g., *Intellikeys* from http://www.intellitools.com), and using a variety of software. Two of the more useful tools are spelling prediction programs and talking word processors (e.g., *Co:Writer* and *Write:OutLoud* from http://www.donjohnston.com). Be sure to respond to students' initial drafts as meaningful, even when the meaning may not be obvious. For example, students may scribble, combine letters in apparently random ways, or spell words unconventionally. Demonstrating an interest in the students' message is one of the most powerful motivators of conventional spelling and grammar in later drafts. An "author's chair," where students read aloud what they have written, is another way to encourage developing writers' motivation and attention to convention.

Perfect Practice Makes Perfect

Practice makes perfect. You've heard that mantra echoed by your parents, teachers, coaches, band or chorus director, and friends as encouragement in your struggles to learn new skills. You probably have repeated it yourself to friends, colleagues, and your own students. For a few, often gifted, individuals, practice does make perfect. Larry Bird was said to have shot 1,000 jump shots every day, and now he's in the Basketball Hall of Fame. Madeleine L'Engle writes and studies daily and has won the Newbery Medal and numerous other literary prizes.

Most of us, however, never achieve perfection, despite hours, days, and even years of practice. That experience with failure leads some of us to lose interest and quit. You can observe this phenomenon in your next teachers' meeting. Ask all those who took instrumental lessons as children to raise their hands. Next, ask how many of those individuals still play an instrument today. Typically, few hands remain in the air.

One of the keys to maximizing practice time is to attempt to provide students with perfect practice. That is, we want students to practice skills accurately and well day after day, in order to develop the fluency and ease needed to become successful and lifelong readers.

There are a variety of ways to attempt to implement this ideal in your literacy instruction. In reading comprehension lessons, provide students with texts at or close to their reading level, read the same text on successive days for new purposes, and design comprehension tasks in which students regularly achieve 80% or greater success.

As students attempt to learn abstract letter names and the associated sounds, connect the letter names and sounds to known words, actions, foods, student-made and illustrated alphabet books. *Making Words*, a familiar activity to many teachers, provides lots of successful practice in spelling as students are guided in systematically manipulating a limited set of letters (e.g., *e, i, l, n, s, t*) as they spell one-letter words, two, and so on (e.g., *l, it, is, in, tin, sin, sit, site, list, listen*).

Choose seatwork or homework tasks that provide students with opportunities to practice skills already learned in class rather than new tasks. The goals are to increase student success, reduce frustration, and increase the odds that what students learn through practice is accurate and, ultimately, applied successfully in real literacy.

Selected References

Allington, R.L. (2005). *What really matters for struggling readers: Designing research-based programs (2nd ed.).* Needham Heights, NJ: Allyn & Bacon.

Center for Literacy and Disability Studies web site. Retrieved May 17, 2006, from http://www.med.unc.edu/ahs/clds/.

Cunningham, P.M., Hall, D.P., & Sigmon, C.M. (2000). *The teacher's guide to the four blocks.* Greensboro, NC: Carson-Dellosa.

Erickson, K.A., & Koppenhaver, D.A. (1998). Using the "write talk-nology" with Patrik. *Teaching Exceptional Children, 31 (1)*, 58–64.

Erickson, K.A., & Koppenhaver, D.A. (2007). *Children with special needs: Reading and writing the four blocks way.* Greensboro, NC: Carson-Dellosa.

Erickson, K.A., Koppenhaver, D.A., & Cunningham, J.W. (2006). Balanced reading intervention and assessment in augmentative communication. In R.J. McCauley and M.E. Fey (Eds.), *Treatment of language disorders in children* (pp. 309–345). Baltimore: Paul H. Brookes Publishing Co.

Erickson, K.A., Koppenhaver, D.A., & Yoder, D.E. (Eds.). (2002). *Waves of words: Augmented communicators read and write.* Toronto, Canada: International Society for Augmentative and Alternative Communication Press.

Koppenhaver, D.A. (2006). Home page. Retrieved May 17, 2006, from http://faculty.rcoe.appstate.edu/koppenhaverd/.

Koppenhaver, D.A., Spadorcia, S., and Erickson, K.A. (1998). Inclusive early literacy instruction for children with disabilities. In S.B. Neuman and K. Roskos (Eds.), *Children achieving: Instructional practices in early literacy* (pp. 77–97). Newark, DE: International Reading Association.

Musselwhite, C., & King-DeBaun, P. (1997). *Emergent literacy success: Merging technology and whole language for students with disabilities.* Litchfield Park, AZ: Special Communications.

Rasinski, T., & Padak, N. (2003). *Effective reading strategies: Teaching children who find reading difficult (3rd ed.).* Upper Saddle River, NJ: Prentice Hall.

Quick-Guide #14

Writing Matters

Patricia McGonegal and Nancy Talbott

Quick-Guides to Inclusion
Ideas for Educating Students with Disabilities, Second Edition

Michael F. Giangreco & Mary Beth Doyle

Editors

Quick-Guides to Inclusion: Ideas for Educating Students with Disabilities (2nd ed.) © Michael F. Giangreco, 2007
Available through Paul H. Brookes Publishing Co., Baltimore, 1-800-638-3775

Dear Teacher,

What could be more vital to the education of our students than good writing skills? At least as vital is the attitude students have toward writing. Part of our job as teachers is to encourage our students to recognize the value and importance written language has as a vehicle for helping them pursue opportunities in their lives, both within school and beyond. Come explore with us the simple, logical uses for language we can introduce to students, along with some specific methods for helping students with disabilities come to understand that writing is a valuable tool for thinking, communication, persuasion, and their own development as a self-determined people in the world.

An early step for any teacher is to put writing in perspective and recognize that we are all writers who are continually extending our writing skills and uses. Some of the same questions you might ask yourself about your own writing can be helpful as you think about supporting your students.

What kinds of processes, skills, and habits of mind do you find indispensable in your own writing life?

Do you ever write anything without a reason?

How much of the writing you do is meant for an audience?

When you need to write in a new form, do you find it helpful to refer to examples of what other writers have done in that form?

How important is feedback to you?

Where do you go for help with "correctness?"

Based on the work of teachers and researchers we know, we have assembled some tips that we hope will help you and your students become part of what Frank Smith calls, "The Literacy Club" (1987). We invite you and your students to join the club!

Good luck,
Tish & Nancy

GUIDELINES-AT-A-GLANCE

1. Provide Strategies for Beginning

2. Build Choice into Each Assignment

3. Introduce Writing in Many Forms into the Day

4. Write for Real Purposes and Audiences

5. Provide Models for Writing Forms You Are Assigning

6. Teach Skills and Conventions in Context

7. Ask for Reflection and Meta-Thinking Before, During, and After Writing

8. Give Honest, but Supportive, Feedback

9. Teach to the (Gasp!) Test

10. Be Part of a Community of Teacher Researchers

Provide Strategies for Beginning

When students have difficulty writing, what strategies do they use? Graham and Harris (2005) tell us that, compared to more skilled writers, the students who struggle seldom know or understand what strategies will help get the job done. Teachers can improve the performance of challenged writers by teaching them specific strategies; here are some to consider:

Graphic organizers: Visual sketches, drawings, and graphic organizers come more easily both for early writers and for students with special needs. A student's comfort level can be maintained when a new piece of writing begins with an uncomplicated, or even playful, chart, figure, or table.

Think aloud: For years, Graves (1994) has advocated teacher modeling by talking through a piece of writing on a poster or blackboard as students observe.

Literature circles: Daniels' (2001) roles for group members (e.g., facilitator, note taker, encourager) create a relaxed, yet organized, climate for writing students, who can pick up strategies from their peers.

Stop and Think Of Purposes (STOP): *STOP* can help a struggling writer to focus on the purpose for a paper. Once the purpose is established, the remainder of the paper often flows more easily (Graham & Harris, 2005, p. 55).

List Ideas and Sequence Them (LIST): LIST will help with another major challenge, namely organization (Graham & Harris, 2005, p. 57).

Begin a few times: If writers can be working in low-stakes situations, many will find it easier to begin. As long as a draft doesn't have to get a grade or be the "official" one, a student will relax and let things flow. Teachers can have students try two or more first drafts with assignments like, "Write this essay as a letter to your grandmother," then "Write another one as a letter to the editor." Teachers of students with disabilities know that their students become better writers with frequent opportunities to practice and review teacher-modeled tips.

Stress is often at the heart of difficulties in writing. Who doesn't avoid stressful situations? Defusing the tension can help our students get started, and once we begin, we're halfway home.

2   Build Choice into Each Assignment

Parents and teachers share the challenge: How much authority and responsibility is a child or teenager ready for? With too much choice, some writers will be overwhelmed; with too little choice, they may lose their sense of ownership and authority.

Atwell (1989) and Graves (1994) have given us models for how to strike the balance in writing workshops. Graves (1994) suggests that the teacher: 1) demonstrate choice of topic, form, and audience; 2) teach the skills as needed for these writings; 3) set up the classroom for access to resources and models—both human and text; and 4) allow for movement within the classroom when accessing resources is needed. Teacher support will require differentiation and individualization. Students' growth will depend on their maturity, writing experience, and the task's level of challenge— necessitating that the writing forms they're asked to take on be similarly differentiated and individualized.

Many teachers in early grades offer a wide range of choice to their writers. Stories, poems, reports, and interviews can be going on simultaneously. Even when students are all writing in the same form, for instructional or content-related reasons, we should seek to invest a sense of authority and responsibility in our young writers. Moffett's (1992) *Active Voice* assignments offer this choice, suggesting the task, but allowing the writer to select the content and focus; consider his survey assignment:

> Ask a number of people the same question or questions about something you want to know their view of, then summarize what they said or what you learned. First, think out your questions carefully according to what you want to find out and who you think it would be best to ask. When writing up, think of who you want to read these results. Post up, send to someone, or include in a class or local newspaper. (p. 89)

Using this activity offers writers a wide range of choices and interaction with their peers. Meanwhile, the teacher enjoys many teachable moments. This is an authentic way to gather information, sort and generalize, establish claims, and support conclusions.

When teachers can hand over a measure of authority and responsibility to their students, big dividends can be realized. Atwell (1998) tells us,

> When they can choose . . . students will write for all the reasons literate people everywhere engage as writers . . . they convey and request information, apply for jobs, parody, petition, play, explore, argue, apologize, advise, sympathize, express love, show gratitude, make money. (p. 75)

Introduce Writing in Many Forms into the Day

3

Think about the range of activities that happen in a classroom. Writing their way through diverse content and experiences, students can go beyond rote learning and reproducing facts to higher order thinking as they write to reflect, question, and evaluate what happens to them in the classroom (National Writing Project & Nagin, 2003).

Students can take turns being in charge of writing a daily log by recording content, activities, class happenings, and commenting on them in the style that suits each writer (e.g., straight reporting, in verse, as a drama, dialogue). Begin each day or each class by having a student read the previous day's log. This can help review the previous session, bring a student who was absent up to speed, and build a sense of community in the group. Class journals have been around for a long time. Let's reaffirm their use as a non-threatening vehicle for thinking in so many ways.

Start a class or unit with the prompt, "Write down as many things as you know about . . . (e.g., the moon, Saskatchewan, Mark Twain, the Periodic Table)." Students can look back at the end of a unit and feel proud of all they learned since that first writing.

Stop in the middle of activities to write opinions, questions, or predictions.

At the end of a lesson or unit, ask students about what they learned (e.g., a list, best and worst aspects, a question you still have, a prediction on what's next.)

Students love passing notes to each other. Capitalize on this with reciprocal notes about class learning. This invites audience-based composing. Writing beyond an audience of *me* encourages revision and shared ideas.

Daily lesson planning that allows the frequent opportunities to re-think ideas out loud for an audience (either the teacher, themselves, or classmates) elicits deeper thinking and deeper understanding of key concepts.

Connecting reading and writing to academic content areas such as math, science, and social studies gives teachers opportunities to instruct students with special needs in how to link their ideas across graphics, numbers, and symbols, to reach higher thinking skills through these connections.

4 Write for Real Purposes and Audiences

Think for a moment about the range of writings you do across a day. A typical list for a teacher might include the following examples.

- E-mail a friend or relative; send a note to a parent
- Draft an assignment for a course you're taking
- Create a meeting agenda or presentation
- Write an advertisement for a class, church, or club event
- Contribute an article or opinion piece to a professional journal
- Send a memo to colleagues or an administrator
- Take notes during a meeting, lecture, or reading
- Send invitations to a family celebration
- Note a reminder to a family member—or to yourself!

What a range we see here! Different audiences, different purposes, and different levels of formality are addressed across this list. Researchers, and common sense, tell us that the more ways we practice a skill, the more we will improve. Let's help students to cross-train in the same way, as they produce *real* writing for *real* audiences. A list of possibilities in any classroom might include

- An invitation to a classroom event
- Group or individual brainstorm list of "all you know about" a topic before a unit of study
- A timeline or schedule for assignments, chores, a vacation, or a single day
- Daily logs of classroom activities
- Survey of peer ideas about a unit of study
- Memos to teachers asking for help
- List of all you found out after a lesson, unit, reading, video, or field trip
- Memo to principal or cafeteria staff suggesting a school improvement
- Sequence of steps when planning a project, or report of how it went
- Notes from an interview with a staff or community member about content or a school issue

Nobody welcomes busywork, and there is neither support nor necessity for it in students' lives. Real writing is engaging. Students want to get the job done when there is a payoff worth writing for, and an audience who needs to hear about it.

Provide Models for Writing Forms You Are Assigning

5

Picture a typical television cooking show. The chef shows us the ingredients and the processes we need to make something wonderful before launching into the process with gusto. The chef then shows us the delicious finished product, pulling together the elements rolled into one great cake or a platter of Chicken Marengo. We're left thinking, "I can do that!" In the writing classroom, we can build in many occasions for demonstrating models for our students.

Teacher models: Graves (1994) urges us to write with our students. If we simply supervise, he suggests a student might think, "When I grow up, I won't have to write." Let's demonstrate the ways writing works in our lives, sometimes with a "think-aloud," where a teacher demonstrates the drafting of a piece, asking for and accepting student suggestions whenever possible.

Student models: Demonstrate how previous students handled this form or assignment. Save copies of good, mediocre, and poor persuasion, narratives, or reports from this year's class. Next year, with students' names removed, work those samples into your instruction: "Here's a story by a student from last year. What do you see happening here?" Help students to be explicit about the strengths and limitations of these examples.

Models from published authors: Moffett, in his *Active Voice* (1992) sequence of writing assignments, recommends collateral reading for each writing task. Are students writing persuasive essays? Why not read Marc Antony's funeral oration to see what classic persuasion looks like. Are students writing dialogue? Read the "substitute teacher" scene from *Stuart Little* (White, 1945, p. 90). Provide opportunities for students to discuss the readings, and help them make the links to their own writing.

Teachers of students with special needs often use display models of student writing on classroom walls, and in published copies of student work on display in bookshelves. This can encourage students to review and use these models as guidelines. A classroom can become a true community of literate people when we look beyond the assignment to the elements, the processes, and the challenges all writers share. Looking together at models can do this for us.

6 Teach Skills and Conventions in Context

Many of us remember a heavy emphasis on the grammar and mechanics of writing in our own schooling; some of us feel that we had little of the authentic writing instruction we value today. Most current researchers and many teachers know that it's less effective to teach grammar as a formal system than to teach it as students need it, watching carefully what they write and interpreting their errors as signposts for mini-lessons and teachable moments.

Real purposes and audiences, real models, real choice, and ownership are likely to engage writers to seek out correctness, as if they are finding the ingredients for a recipe they are preparing or the steps for a model they want to build. If our writing is going out into the world, or even among our peers, we will work to make it presentable. Some teachers use performance to drive home sentence structure and punctuation standards. If students are encouraged to read exactly what's written on each other's papers, their performance will highlight the editing needs because a wrongly placed word or comma sounds odd, and sometimes even funny!

Weaver (1996) suggests that teachers should teach and use grammatical skills and mechanical processes when they come up in discussion of literature or of students' writing. Thus we'll embed the concepts into what students need. We'll find a way to look at adjectives in memoir or poetry writing, citations in reports, or dialogue in narratives.

Students working in collaborative editing groups can scaffold and peer-teach while socializing. Likewise, teachers should be collaborating on determining grade, class, and project priorities so they are reinforcing rather than inadvertently re-teaching similar concepts. Our job here is to strike a balance, namely to refrain from making the medium the message, yet to teach the conventions of our language for clarity and communicative intent.

Students can use scoring grids as guides that show specific criteria to assess their own writing. They can apply these as well to models for judgment and comparison. Teachers can collect models, for example, for teaching and critiquing organization, composition, grammar, usage, punctuation, and other mechanics (Reeves, 2002).

Ask for Reflection and Meta-Thinking Before, During, and After Writing

7

We want students to be independent learners, ultimately to take on the task of thinking through their experiences and texts. Students, perhaps especially those with disabilities, benefit from a cultivated habit of reading their own writing, saying at times, "That doesn't make sense. Let me retry this, by writing it again another way." Engaged students have the motivation to look at what they are learning, and can stop and say, "What's going on here? I'd better read that again." Many students need some scaffolding to approach and complete the task. Writing some informal reflective notes to oneself can help support, enhance, and organize the writer and the writing task at hand.

Before: Writers in the real world rarely write without a notion of purpose. A few cues might help the early or unsure writer. A suggested list of these could be pasted into a writer's notebook or journal: *What is my reason for writing here? What is the main thing I want to say? What would be the best way to get started?*

During: Sometimes a writer can hand a paper to a reader for feedback. More skilled writers develop the ability to look at pieces in progress with new eyes, imagining a reader's reaction: If I were reading this for the first time, what part makes the most sense to me? What reasons will help convince a reader? As a reader, I'm most—or least—interested in this part. How logical is this next step? What might be another reason to add here? Can I predict the way this will end?

After: Reading again with "outsider" eyes, a writer might jot down reactions to a piece: What are three most memorable words, phrases, sentences, or ideas in this paper? Here's what I expected, or here's what I didn't expect. Here's what I don't understand. Here's what this paper reminds me of. As I read, here's a thought—or question—that came to me.

Writers who take on the responsibility for their thinking will write more and grow more. The option to use these cues and select which ones to use can help invest a writer with this power.

8 Give Honest, but Supportive, Feedback

Few elements of the writing process are as useful, or as threatening, as feedback from a reader. Here is the spot where the writer can soar with effective feedback or be stymied by feedback that is inappropriate, too general, or trite. In the case of many struggling writers, a teacher who sets out to fix everything at once may inadvertently subject the writer to feedback overload.

Graves (1994) recommends feedback that will "keep the writer writing." What might this look like? Many teachers find it useful to respond first as a reader, sending "I" messages that convey what's happening within the reader, rather than a "to do" list for the writer. It also seems helpful to speak of the paper's merits or flaws, rather than the writer's qualities. "I was excited by the part where . . . " or "I got confused when the paper goes into . . . " rather than, "You seem disorganized here" or "Why did you lead off with . . . ?" Constructive feedback is particularly effective early in the composing process, while ideas are being formed, and a writer might be more open to revising.

Once the writer feels supported and collegial toward the reader, some editing suggestions can help polish the paper. With fledgling writers, the best approach is to look at only one or two issues with each project. It's advisable for the writer to be aware of what we're currently looking at (e.g., introductions, conclusions, run-on sentences, paragraphing, punctuation). Sure, all of these elements, and others, are important to address, but it's counter-productive to take them on all at once!

Additional tips for giving feedback include: 1) be genuine; 2) be specific, not ambiguous; 3) praise consistently and sparingly (don't overdo it); 4) take time to review feedback with a student with special needs to ensure understanding and applications; 5) allow re-dos, retries, and do-overs; and (6) encourage students to take risks by down-playing errors.

If our classrooms are places where writers feel secure and free to take risks, we'll expand their capacity for accepting constructively critical feedback. If our class is a safe zone, when we see big needs in a paper, we can take more risks ourselves, delivering the news that there's lots of work to do, but we're working together to make it happen.

Teach to the (Gasp!) Test

Let's face facts, we can't teach without some measure of accountability, either for ourselves or for our students and their work. We know tests are here to stay, and while we must hold the line and not make test preparation our curriculum, we're shortchanging our students if we don't equip them to handle this genre ("the Prompt") while we're exploring all the others. Gere, Christenbury and Sassi (2005) suggest two simple guidelines: 1) let students "unpack" various writing test questions (prompts), and 2) help them recognize the elements of their writing process that will support them during testing.

Teachers, alone or with colleagues, can gather past writing prompts used in their school's or state's test. They then can help students analyze these questions, asking themselves, "What is the major point asked for here? (e.g., support or criticize the war). "Is there a suggested role I expected to take?" (e.g., you are a citizen writing a letter to your town council). "Which strategies could I try" (e.g., a point with examples; compare and contrast).

To help students see that these elements are authentic, use models from nontesting situations for students to analyze or argue. Look at magazine articles geared toward student interest and ability level; have them help you find them. Likewise, examine samples of student essays.

A common complaint about test writing is its on-demand nature, especially when contrasted with the more typical processed classroom writing at one's own pace. Granted, we can't bend the rules to allow collaboration or even conferring for feedback during testing. But a writer can still brainstorm, and if we help students to internalize revision strategies, a second look, even a second draft, will help our students toward test success.

By providing additional writing opportunities in daily lesson planning, teachers of students with disabilities allow students time to practice the writing skills learned before test taking, then give them authentic opportunities to practice before required tests. More opportunities to review, reapply, and generalize skills necessary for new learning all help students gain skills and become better test takers. Because test situations increase anxiety for many students, and especially for students with special needs, it will help to offer specific occasions for writing practice in nontesting situations.

Be Part of a Community of Teacher Researchers

Teaching writing and teaching in general are both such important callings. But what lonely occupations they can be as well. Does it seem logical to get a little help from your friends? Teachers who see themselves as part of a community of learners know that such collaboration enhances and enriches their practice.

Though they are very busy, teachers who are part of such learning communities keep abreast of advances in the field by reading professional journals. The research and related professional literature in these journals are at least as vital to our teaching professions as analogous research and literature are to our colleagues in other professional fields (e.g., law, medicine, sciences). Would you want to go to a doctor who didn't keep up on current medical advances? Many journals and other resources are now on-line, making it easy to access information and specify exactly what you are seeking. Books on teaching literacy abound as well.

Teachers typically like to talk with each other. They naturally confer with colleagues when they can. Enlightened school administrators (often informed by confident, assertive teachers) are making space in the in-service calendar to honor these conversations by sometimes using structured or semi-structured processes for dialogue. Together, these teachers might discuss recent research they have read in advance, critique student work, or share teaching ideas. Study groups are effective and practical ways to examine student behaviors and products, lessons, or curricular units.

Teachers in learning communities often participate in professional initiatives and organizations. National networks and their local affiliates, such as the National Council of Teacher and the International Reading Association, offer teachers useful readings, conferences, and on-line communities where their ideas are generated, questioned, and enriched. The Bread Loaf School of English focuses directly on helping teachers become *"smaller"* researchers, by modeling, encouraging, and supporting inquiry in our own backyards. Particularly useful to teachers is the National Writing Project web site (http://www.writingproject.org), where a dozen-year archive of articles is available specifically targeting research-based writing instruction.

Graves (1994) urges us to "Live the professional life." Teachers who have picked up this Quick-Guide already know the key to continually rejuvenating ourselves in our profession—we must continue to learn what we teach, namely communication, curiosity, and collaboration.

Selected References

Atwell, N. (1989). *In the middle: Writing, reading, and learning with adolescents.* Portsmouth, NH: Heinemann.

Daniels, H. (2001). *Literature circles: Voice and choice in book clubs and reading groups.* Portsmouth, NH: Stenhouse.

Gere, A.R., Christenbury, L., & Sassi, K. (2005). *Writing on demand: Best practices and strategies for success.* Portsmouth, NH: Heinemann.

Graham, S., & Harris, K. (2005). Improving the writing performance of young struggling writers: Theoretical and programmatic research from the Center on Accelerating Student Learning. *Journal of Special Education, 39,* 19–33.

Graham, S., & Harris, K. (2006). *Writing better: Effective strategies for teaching students with learning difficulties.* Baltimore: Paul H. Brookes Publishing Co.

Graham, S., Harris, K., Fink-Chorzempa, B., & MacArthur, C.A. (2003). Primary grade teachers' instructional adaptations for struggling writers: A national survey. *Journal of Educational Psychology, 95,* 279–292.

Graham, S., Harris, K.R., & MacArthur, C.A. (2006). Explicitly teaching struggling writers: Strategies for mastering the writing process. *Intervention in School and Clinic, 41*(5), 290–294.

Graves, D. (1994). *A fresh look at writing.* Portsmouth, NH: Heinemann.

Moffett, J. (1992). *Active voice: A writing program across the curriculum.* Portsmouth, NH: Heinemann.

National Writing Project, & Nagin, C. (2003). *Because writing matters: Improving student writing in our schools.* San Francisco: Jossey-Bass.

Reeves, D. (2002). *Reasons to write.* New York: Simon and Schuster.

Smith, F. (1987). *Joining the literacy club.* Portsmouth, NH: Heinemann.

Troia, G.A., & Graham, S. (2003). Effective writing instruction across the grades: What every educational consultant should know. *Journal of Educational and Psychological Consultation, 14,* 75–89.

Weaver, C. (1996). *Teaching grammar in context.* Portsmouth, NH: Boynton/Cook.

White, E. (1945). *Stuart Little.* New York: Harper & Brothers.

Quick-Guide #15

Making Math Meaningful for Students with Special Needs

Timothy J. Whiteford

Quick-Guides to Inclusion
Ideas for Educating Students with Disabilities, Second Edition
Michael F. Giangreco & Mary Beth Doyle
Editors

Dear Teacher,

When we think about teaching math to students with special needs, or any student for that matter, there is a tendency to focus primarily on teaching simple procedural knowledge, such as 3 + 4 = 7, or 5 x 8 = 40. Our assumption is that the successful completion of such procedural activities demonstrates mathematical achievement by students. Unfortunately, this type of procedural focus is too often accompanied by a bombardment of worksheets and other paper and pencil tasks, and seldom helps students to function in the real world where they will need to think about mathematical relationships and the types of numerical and quantitative problems that are part of everyday life.

Students with special needs can learn to think conceptually about the mathematical relationships around them and the type of math they will encounter on a daily basis through problem solving. By focusing on the language of mathematics and the use of manipulative materials to make mathematical situations real and meaningful, we can help students construct mathematical meaning that will serve them in the real world much more effectively than rote learning of simple mathematical procedures.

This Quick-Guide is designed to share some of the most foundational issues with you about making math meaningful for your students with special needs. In doing so, you will undoubtedly see that these very same approaches can be valuable learning strategies for a much wider range of students you encounter in your classroom. I've also included a list of some selected references if you decide to dig deeper into the teaching of math to your students with special needs. Students with special needs, like all students, should be given the opportunity to experience the joy and beauty of mathematics as well as the empowerment that comes with such understanding.

Good luck,
Tim

GUIDELINES-AT-A-GLANCE

1. Approach Math as Patterns and Relationships

2. Develop Your Own Understanding of Math

3. Explore Math as Language

4. Differentiate Between Knowledge and Understanding

5. Select Appropriate Manipulative Materials

6. Encourage Personally Meaningful Connections

7. Differentiate Your Math Instruction

8. Ensure Opportunities for Meaningful Practice

9. Use Instructional Technology

10. Assess Each Student's Math Learning

Approach Math as Patterns and Relationships

The human brain likes to use patterns and relationships when trying to remember or understand. When we can make meaningful, personal connections between what we experience and learn, we are more likely to be able to apply what we have learned to solve problems in our daily lives and appreciate the world around us. Patterns exist in all areas of math, not just in geometry. Multiplication, for example, can be seen as repeated addition. The equation 5 x 4 = 20 can be shown as 4 + 4 + 4 + 4 + 4 = 20. If you add one to both the numerator and denominator of fractions, they get larger in proportion to the whole, approaching, but never reaching one. For example, if you start with ½ and repeatedly add one to the numerator and denominator you get ⅔, ⅘, ⅚, ⁶⁄₇, and so on.

Many numbers make geometric patterns, such as *square numbers* (e.g., 1, 4, 9, 16). A less common and slightly more complex example is *triangular numbers* (e.g., 1, 3, 6, 10, 15, 21). Starting with the number one, *triangular numbers* are formed by adding the next number, as in 1 + 2 = 3, where 3 is the *triangular number*. To determine the next *triangular number*, take the sum (i.e., 3) and make it the first number in the next equation. The second number is one more than the second number in the previous equation. By adding these two numbers, you get the second *triangular number*. You have a pattern that looks like this: 1 + 2 = 3, 3 + 3 = 6, 6 + 4 = 10, 10 + 5 = 15, 15 + 6 = 21, and so on. Interestingly, if you add two consecutive *triangular numbers* together (e.g., 3 + 6 = 9; 10 + 15 = 25) you get a *square number*. While it is fun to see a pattern, the most important part of the experience, educationally, is to understand the relationship. This can be demonstrated effectively using a variety of manipulative materials (e.g., *Linker* cubes—see http://www.wrightgroup.com).

Another way of thinking about patterns when teaching students math is to explore errors students make in computations, or the misconceptions they might share when talking about a specific mathematical idea. Part of the excitement of teaching math is the search for an error pattern and subsequent underlying cause. This can be achieved by entering into a dialogue with the student, through which such misconceptions or lack of recall of factual information can be illuminated and addressed through appropriate activities. The identification of mathematical patterns is an effective way of helping students overcome misconceptions and develop more accurate recall of factual information.

Develop Your Own
Understanding of Math

The more we understand the math we teach, the better we are able to guide and facilitate student learning. A deeper understanding of basic or fundamental math ideas also helps us interpret students' unique mathematical constructs and ideas. One way of thinking about math is that all mathematical knowledge can be categorized as either *procedural knowledge* or *conceptual knowledge.*

Procedural knowledge comprises all the symbols and procedures we use in math (e.g., 248, 56.5, >, x, =, $, +, %, ½), singularly or in combinations. All *procedural knowledge* comprises a set of arbitrary conventions that are socially constructed and culturally defined. For example, it is an arbitrary, though longstanding, convention that we use two short, horizontal, parallel lines to represent an "equal sign"; it could have just as arbitrarily been two longer vertical lines.

Conceptual knowledge refers to ideas, concepts, and relationships that are a function of what Piaget called the *natural world*. Rational counting (i.e., the way we attach number names to groups of objects) is a piece of *conceptual knowledge*. Three is two and one more, but the word "three" refers to the group of three and not the last object counted. An angle, measured in degrees, is based on the concept of the rotation of a line, or ray, about a point, and is not a measure of distance. This concept is crucial to understanding why a 45-degree angle is always the same number of degrees, regardless of how long the rays of the angle are.

Understanding the difference between conceptual and procedural knowledge helps guide our teaching by making sure that we know exactly what we are teaching and expecting students to learn. It is important to know whether we are teaching a procedure, a concept, or the relationship between them. A subtraction algorithm (e.g., 79–35), could be used to solve several different types of word problem. The same algorithm could be used to solve: 1) a *separation* problem (e.g., if I have 79 cents and give you 35 cents, how many cents do I have left?); 2) a *comparison* problem (e.g., if I have 79 cents and you have 35 cents, how much more money do I have than you?); or 3) a *part-part-whole* problem (e.g., if you and I have 79 cents between us, and I have 35 cents, how much money do you have?). Each of these three conceptual knowledge problems can be solved using the same procedural algorithm.

Explore Math as Language

Math is more than a collection of symbols and procedures. By far the most important aspects of math are the structures and meanings we use when expressing and communicating mathematical relationships and ideas.

Like a traditional language, math has a syntax or structure that must be followed so that precise meaning can be communicated. The simple equation $3 + 4 = 7$ contains five symbols in a particular order that clearly identifies the relationship between the quantities. More complex equations require a particular sequence of operations to be solved correctly.

Math also has a complex semantic structure where the same symbol, or procedure, can represent a variety of meanings in just the same way that a single word such as "book" can have multiple meanings. The numbers on an analog clock face, for example, have two meanings, one for hours and one for minutes. Students learning to tell the time will need to know that the 3 can refer to 3 hours or to 15 minutes. There is, in fact, a third meaning attached to the 3, the metaphorical language of *quarter past* that refers to the fraction of the circle represented by the position of the 3. The use of such metaphorical language in math is critical to the construction of meaning, but it can lead to misconceptions and difficulty. For example, the use of the term *reduce* in the context of fractions can lead younger students to think that ½ is less than ¼ because the word *reduce* means to make smaller. Even the numbers are smaller when the fraction is renamed.

We must be careful to avoid the use of inappropriate metaphor such as "goes into," "borrow," and "take away," which can lead to confusion. The language we use when teaching math must be related to the concepts and ideas we want students to learn in a meaningful way. For example, when teaching children to count, it really helps develop their sense of cardinal numbers (numbers that express an amount) if we use the language "and one more" as in: "3, and one more is 4." When the last object is counted, the language "altogether" can be used to show that this number (i.e., 4) refers to the whole group and not just the last one counted. For example, "How many altogether?" or "Altogether there are 5."

Differentiate Between Knowledge and Understanding

4

Knowing a piece of conceptual or procedural knowledge does not imply that it is understood. We can know that the sun rises in the east, yet not understand why or how it happens. Turning an ignition key and shifting into drive will move a car forward without the driver having any understanding of how the internal combustion engine works. A student can know that 3 x 7 = 21, but have no understanding of the relationship between the quantities. Simply knowing one's multiplication facts is a form of rote memorization that doesn't help in solving problems.

There are, for example, several different concepts related to multiplication: 1) *repeated addition* (e.g., 7 + 7 + 7), 2) the *area concept* (e.g., 7 x 3 rectangle), and 3) the *multiplicative comparison* (e.g., What is 7 times as many as 3?). Each one is a completely different concept, yet all can be solved through the application of the 3 x 7 multiplication algorithm.

Understanding is developed and enhanced through the construction of relationships between different pieces of conceptual and/or procedural knowledge as well as through the identification of patterns. A student may know the procedural knowledge for solving a multiplication algorithm yet not know when to use the multiplication operation. Understanding which operation to use is the essence of problem solving. Once the operation has been selected, the problem-solving exercise is reduced to one of arithmetic as the solution is computed.

A student's procedural knowledge that ¾ is a symbol for a fraction, and conceptual knowledge that ¾ is three parts of a whole divided into four equal parts, can be significantly enhanced through understanding that the numerator is an adjective, a number describing a quantity, and the denominator is a noun, a number representing a particular part of a whole. To help children with special needs develop this idea, we can use a fraction manipulative such as fraction pies or squares with which students can count the fraction parts as if they were counting regular objects. Using fourth-sized pieces, they can count, and verbalize, one fourth, two fourths, three fourths, and four fourths, noting that the four fourths can be renamed as one whole. The counting pattern can then be extended with five-fourths, six fourths, and so on to develop the idea of mixed numbers; we can count fractional parts in the same way we can count anything.

Select Appropriate Manipulative Materials

Manipulative materials can help students construct concrete, meaningful concepts of abstract mathematical ideas when appropriate materials are selected. Because the characteristics of an individual manipulative material can have a significant effect upon what students learn, it is important to choose the type of material paying careful attention to the instructional intent. There are four types of manipulative materials. Unless otherwise noted, the materials listed below can be searched for online at http://www.etacuisenaire.com.

Concrete manipulatives are the most basic form and include those materials where the size of the referent is maintained throughout the manipulative (the piece representing 10 will be exactly 10 times larger than the piece representing 1). Examples of *concrete materials* are:

Digi-Blocks® (ages 5–12)
    http://www.digi-block.com/dbls/packit/packit.cfm

Cuisinaire® Rods (ages 6–16)

Counting bears (ages 5–12)

Base ten blocks (ages 6–16)

Representational manipulatives are those where one piece can represent a certain number of other pieces but is not proportional to the referent in size; sometimes colors are used to represent multiples. Examples of *representational manipulatives* are:

Unifix® cubes (ages 5–16)

MathLink® cubes (ages 5–16)

Please note that these materials can also be used as *concrete materials* as described above.

Symbolic materials are those materials where the number is symbolically represented. Examples of *symbolic materials* are:

Playing cards (ages 5–16)

Rook® cards (ages 5–16)
    htttp://thehouseofcards.com/retail/rook.html

Dominoes (ages 5–16)

Tools are manipulatives that can be used to help us measure and construct. Examples of *tools* are compasses, protractors, rulers, calipers, measuring cups, beakers, and shape templates.

The selection of the right manipulative for the concept or skill being learned is as important as the selection of the appropriate instructional strategy. For example, a rotating protractor will better develop the concept of angle as a measure of rotation than a semi-circular protractor, which tends to develop the misconception of angle as a measure of distance.

Encourage Personally Meaningful Connections

Real-world problems and real-world math activities help students make meaningful connections between what they learn in math class and how they can use their math knowledge beyond the classroom walls. When we make math instruction relevant to students' lives and interests, they are more likely to remember and understand the math concepts and skills they are learning. We also know from the results of research in *brain-based learning* that when students are emotionally invested in their learning they are more likely to remember and understand the concepts and skills they are using. To capitalize on these aspects of brain functioning, it is important to connect the math we are teaching with the interests, experiences, and dispositions of the students with whom we are working.

Numerous problem-solving strategies can be developed using a student's interests and experiences. For example, baseball, football, basketball, soccer, and other sports can yield many opportunities for developing mathematical thinking and skill development. Numeral recognition can be enhanced through the use of players' shirts with their numbers on the back as well as the small models of players available in toy stores. Box scores, rankings, records, team statistics, and individual player statistics provide a wealth of mathematical data at a more advanced level.

Meal planning and cooking also can be used to develop a variety of applied math skills, such as counting, measuring, estimating, computing whole numbers, and using fractions, time, and temperature. Daily events and routines provide many opportunities for developing and practicing mathematical ideas and skills. Lining up for recess can involve the use of ordinal numbers (e.g., first, second, third in line). Frequent references to the classroom clock or the student's watch (analog of course) throughout the day can help students learn to read the time and develop a sense of time. A trip to the grocery store can be used to develop math skills involving counting, weighing, computing, time, money, and interpreting numbers (e.g., calories and saturated fat on nutrition labels). There is also a wealth of mathematical opportunities on every car journey.

As teachers, it is important that we are aware and deliberate with the possibilities in the learning/teaching environment and beyond, so that we can take advantage of those unplanned moments when a particular concept or skill can become real and meaningful because of its link to an immediate experience.

Differentiate Your Math Instruction

The *differentiated classroom* is an ideal setting in which students with special needs can develop their math skills and concepts. The teacher in a *differentiated classroom* individualizes the selection of instructional strategies and academic content based on student needs. Students are strategically grouped in a variety of ways throughout the day to take advantage of the strengths and opportunities available through mixed-ability groupings, similar-ability groupings, and interest-based groupings.

Providing a variety of grouping opportunities allows teachers to observe students under varying conditions to ascertain which grouping options work best for them for specific instructional purposes. Varying grouping options also serves as a classroom management tool by keeping this aspect of instruction dynamic and interesting. It also can contribute to building a classroom community by ensuring that all students have the opportunity to work in groups with all of their classmates throughout the week. In many differentiated classrooms, student grouping typically occurs after the teacher has introduced the lesson topic. For some students with special needs, it may be advisable to pre-teach a skill or concept, so they are better prepared to participate in whole-class and small-group activities. Regardless of the grouping approach, students are encouraged to learn with and from each other.

Teaching strategies can also be differentiated. For example, during a lesson on multiplication, some students might be working on *multiplicative comparisons*, other students could be exploring the *area concept*, and another group could be investigating the idea of *repeated addition*; each piece of content representing a different level in the development of the concept of multiplication.

In terms of differentiation of materials, one group could be using a textbook, another group an on-line resource, while a third group could be using manipulative materials. Further differentiation could occur through the use of problem solving, in which the content of the problems could relate specifically to the interests of the students. This would help develop the student's emotional investment in the math class; an important characteristic of the *differentiated classroom* (Tomlinson & McTighe, 2006). Again, as noted in Guideline 6, the role of positive attitudes and dispositions in the development of mathematical concepts and skills should not be underestimated.

Ensure Opportunities for Meaningful Practice

Meaningful practice of both procedural and conceptual knowledge of mathematics is essential to the retention of math facts and procedures as well as the development of mathematical understanding. Meaningful practice increases the likelihood that newly learned concepts and skills are retained over time and sets the stage for students to generalize what they have learned and pursue more advanced learning outcomes.

One of the components of the *direct instruction model* of teaching is *guided practice*, in which the teacher provides differing levels of support as the student moves toward mastery. Varying levels of support can be provided through the careful use of manipulative materials, verbal questions or prompts, physical cues or prompts, as well as visual cues, graphic organizers (e.g., writedesignonline.com/organizers), and picture board stories.

Practice activities can require students to give an immediate response or involve *think time*, during which the students are given time to process and think through what they have been asked to do. This can help students develop recall strategies and improve accuracy. Immediate response, or speed drill, activities are typically those involving the recall of specific facts such as addition and multiplication facts. Such activities are not recommended for new learning, but may be appropriate in the context of a game, to reinforce previously mastered knowledge and skills, to help with retention, and to encourage automaticity (e.g., knowing multiplication facts). All students, especially those with special learning needs, need planned opportunities for repeated practice if they are to pursue skill mastery and retention.

There are many on-line, as well as textbook-based, resources that can be used in the practice phase of concept and skill development. But care must be taken to avoid making practice experiences dull, tedious, and meaningless for the student.

Practice activities that are motivating can include visual or auditory characteristics that can be very effective as long as they do not detract from the math involved in the activity. A web site that contains many excellent practice activities designed by students is called Ambleweb: (see http://www.amblesideprimary.com/ambleweb/numeracy.htm). Games such as those found at Aplusmath.com (see http://www.Aplusmath.com/Games/index.html) can also be used to motivate student learning.

Use Instructional Technology

The careful use of calculators, computers, Smartboards®, and other forms of technology can significantly increase the mathematical performance of students with special needs. Technology, including assistive technology, can be used to individualize instruction and aide in the process of differentiating instruction (See Quick-Guide Extra #3: Simple Technology to Encourage Participation).

Calculators come in may forms and sizes, from simple to incredibly complex. Adaptive calculators are available, for example, with Braille keys and audio output at many levels of cognitive complexity. Calculators can be used during problem solving for students who have difficulty remembering facts or the procedural knowledge of arithmetic. Simple problem solving involves the selection of an appropriate operation (e.g., addition, subtraction, multiplication, division), something no calculator can do. The calculator can take the arithmetical drudgery out of problem solving, so that the student's time and energy are focused on the act of problem solving. A selection of calculators designed for students with special needs can be seen at the NASCO® web site (http://www.nasco.com/specialeducation/Static.do?page=se_newsletter).

Computers provide all students with the ability to do things more efficiently and with a greater degree of complexity than traditional tools (e.g., paper and pencil). Word-processing programs such as Microsoft Word® and data analysis programs such as Microsoft Excel® can be used by students with special needs to communicate mathematically and manipulate data (e.g., graphing) more efficiently than by paper and pencil. They also allow students to have instant access to the world beyond the classroom through connection to the World Wide Web, where there is a growing resource of free or inexpensive on-line, interactive software.

Web sites such as the *National Center for Virtual Manipulatives* (http://www.nlvm .usu.edu/en/nav/vlibrary.html) and teacher-originated sites such as Ambleweb (http://www.amblesideprimary.com/ambleweb/numeracy.htm) provide teachers with free access to a variety of outstanding activities that can be used by any student with Internet access. These free, high-quality activities offer engaging opportunities for students to practice conceptually sound math. There are also web sites such as Portaportal (http://www.guest.portaportal.com/cgrimsmartboard) that are producing interactive activities designed specifically for use with the Smartboard® and other types of classroom presentation media.

10 Assess Each Student's Math Learning

An effective way of gaining insight into a student's mathematical thinking is through *interactive interviewing* that includes: 1) purposely selected learning activities, 2) observation, 3) asking targeted questions, and 4) a conversation between the teacher and student about his or her engagement in the activity. This allows teachers to better understand a student's conceptual and procedural knowledge, relational understanding, mathematical thinking, and use of math language.

The content of an *interactive interview* can be based on local standards or those of the *National Council of Teachers of Mathematics*. The results of an *interactive interview* can be used to plan instructional activities to pursue a student's IEP goals and to keep team members informed as to the nature of the students' mathematical thinking.

1. Select a specific piece of conceptual or procedural knowledge about which you want to explore the nature of the student's knowledge and understanding.

2. Construct a series of questions or activities relating to this topic that will allow you to engage in a dialog with the student.

3. Use appropriate manipulative materials so that the student can share and demonstrate knowledge and understanding.

4. Use follow-up questions to explore your hunches about the student's thinking.

5. Keep careful notes of the student's language and actions, and any help or clues you might give the student. Write down what the student does and says.

An *interactive interview* was used with a kindergarten student who was having difficulty counting from 1 through 100. When asked to count a group of 20 cubes, the student counted the cubes accurately but mumbled the words "thirteen," "fourteen," and "fifteen"; when he spoke them, all three words sounded similar. The student was then asked to continue counting cubes to 100. When he reached thirty cubes the same mumbling pattern began. Within the space of counting the next ten cubes, he mumbled words that included parts of numbers from the 30s, 40s, and 50s, and then said "sixty" (instead of "forty"). To remedy the situation, a toy telephone receiver was made from 2-inch diameter plastic elbow pipes glued together, which the student could then place between his mouth and ear so that he could practice verbally differentiating between number words. Sometimes, a mathematical difficulty is the result of something other than mathematics, such as mispronunciation in this example.

Selected Resources

Browder, D.M., Ahlgrim-Delzell, L., Pugalee, D.K., & Jimenez, B.A. (2006). Enhancing numeracy. In D.M. Browder & F. Spooner (Eds.), *Teaching language arts, math, and science to students with significant cognitive disabilities* (pp. 171–196). Baltimore: Paul H. Brookes Publishing Co.

Carpenter, T.P., Fennema, E., Franke, M.L., Levi, L., & Empson, S.B. (1999). *Children's mathematics: Cognitively guided instruction.* Portsmouth, NH: Heinemann.

Collins, B.C., Kleinert, H.L., & Land, L.E. (2006). Addressing math standards and functional math. In D.M. Browder & F. Spooner (Eds.), *Teaching language arts, math, and science to students with significant cognitive disabilities* (pp. 197–228). Baltimore: Paul H. Brookes Publishing Co.

Fosnot, C.T., & Dolk, M. (2001). *Young mathematicians at work: Constructing number sense, addition and subtraction.* Portsmouth, NH: Heinemann

Jitendra, A.K., Hoff, K., & Beck, M. (1999). Teaching middle school students with learning disabilities to solve multi-step word problems using a schema-based approach. *Remedial and Special Education, 20*, 50–64.

Jitendra, A.K., & Xin, Y.P. (1997). Mathematical word problem solving instruction for students with disabilities and at risk: A research synthesis. *Journal of Special Education, 30*, 412–439.

Maccini, P., & Gagnon, J.C. (2006). Mathematics instructional practices and assessment accommodations by secondary special and general educators. *Exceptional Children, 72*, 217–234.

Montague, M., & Jitendra, A.K. (Eds.) (2006). *Teaching mathematics to middle school students with learning difficulties.* New York: Guilford Press.

Sliva, J., (2004). *Teaching inclusive mathematics to special learners, K–6.* Thousand Oaks, CA: Corwin Press.

Tomlinson, C.A., & McTighe, J., (2006). *Integrating differentiated instruction and understanding by design.* Alexandria, VA: ASCD.

Tucker, B.F., Singleton, A.H., & Weaver, T.L., (2006). *Teaching mathematics to all children: Designing and adapting instruction to meet the needs of diverse learners (2nd ed.).* Upper Saddle River, NJ: Pearson Education Ltd.

Section VI

High School & Transition

SIMPLE ACCOMMODATIONS IN THE AGE OF LITIGATION

Quick-Guide #16

Taking Inclusion to the Next Level

Creating Inclusive High School Classrooms

Cheryl M. Jorgensen, Douglas Fisher, and Carol Tashie

Quick-Guides to Inclusion
Ideas for Educating Students with Disabilities, Second Edition

Michael F. Giangreco & Mary Beth Doyle

Editors

Dear Teacher,

As a high school teacher, you have the power to shape a young person's future. It's an awesome responsibility, but one that you have embraced. When a student with disabilities is enrolled in your class, you may wonder if you are prepared to meet this challenge. For many of us, neither our college education nor our past teaching experiences provide a compass, particularly if the student has significant disabilities. This Quick-Guide is meant to remind you that the values and skills that make an effective teacher for students without disabilities are the very same ones that will work for students with disabilities.

Before reading the ten guidelines, take a little trip into the past. Think about your own high school experience. What were the most important things you learned in high school? Was it the Pythagorean Theorem or the Periodic Table of the Elements? Do you still recall how to solve quadratic equations? More likely, you recall a love of literature, good writing skills, how to drive or repair a car, or how to get along with people. You learned that how you act with your friends is different from how you act at work. You learned how important it is to stand up for what you believe regardless of what the crowd does.

Which teachers do you remember with fondness and respect? It was probably the teachers who really knew their subject and loved teaching! They had high expectations and pushed you to do your best. They helped you see the relationship between what you were studying and your own life. They respected how you learned best and accommodated their teaching and testing styles so that you could really show what you knew. These memorable and effective teachers understood that learning could be fun, and they strove to make the material come alive for students. They created a community atmosphere in their class—a place where you always felt welcome with no fear of rejection or judgment. And so it is for students with disabilities. Good inclusive teaching doesn't come with a recipe, but perhaps this Quick-Guide will provide a roadmap for your journey.

Sincerely,
Cheryl, Doug, and Carol

GUIDELINES-AT-A-GLANCE

1. Teach Students Life's Most Important Lessons

2. Teach Students to Care About Learning by Caring About Them

3. Figure Out How Every Student Is "Smart"

4. Make Learning Relevant

5. Make Learning Cooperative

6. Use Universal Design Principles

7. Provide Supports as Naturally as Possible

8. Embed Social Justice Values in Your Classroom

9. Become a Reflective Practitioner

10. Advocate for Untracking and Inclusion

Teach Students Life's Most Important Lessons

The "one-year rule" in education says that we should teach students what we want them to remember a year after the class is finished. To make sense of this rule, think about your own students for a minute. Chances are, a year after the class has ended, most students would not remember all of the dates of the Civil War battles, nor the exact formula for converting moles to grams (or is it grams to moles?). However, you might reasonably expect them to remember the economic significance of the Great Depression, the themes from Romeo and Juliet that carry over into modern times, and the negative impact of pollution on the environment.

It is an even safer bet to assume that they will remember how their fear of reading Shakespeare dwindled with practice and success, the sense of satisfaction they felt when solving a difficult mathematical problem for the first time, and whether the concept of justice that they heard about in social studies class was practiced in their own school and community.

What does this "one-year rule" have to do with teaching students with disabilities? It reminds us that memorization of facts and figures is by far the most fleeting—and least important—aspect of schooling. It tells us that all students—not just those who can easily recite back those memorized facts—can learn together when the curriculum consists of the most essential knowledge about ourselves and our world, and when we focus on teaching skills for lifelong learning and working.

Today's educational landscape is filled with standardized testing requirements for teachers, and you may feel enormous pressure to "teach to the test." No student deserves a poor education to prepare them to do well on a poorly designed test. If the real purpose of education is to create citizens who can live in and contribute to a democratic society, then we must include all of our students in our classrooms and teach them "what matters most."

What matters most is not only just standards from the district or state curriculum framework, but also values such as tolerance, kindness, and fairness. An inclusive classroom that embodies these dispositions forms a strong foundation for teaching students the lessons of history and the tools of modern scientists, historians, writers, healers, and artists. With these tools, all students, including those with a label of "disability," can be successful learners and citizens in their communities.

Teach Students to Care About Learning by Caring About Them

2

What was it about school that made you want to become a teacher? Were your parents teachers? Did you love math or science or literature so much that you just had to share your passion with others? Was it a specific teacher in your educational career that really ignited your passion for learning because she cared about you as an individual? Perhaps it was a combination of many factors.

Students in high school—like all students—need teachers who care about them and about their learning. Believing that all students can and do learn is a core value that teachers in an inclusive high school share. These teachers believe strongly in giving every student the benefit of the doubt regarding their competence, even students who may have great difficulty paying attention, managing their emotions, expressing their thoughts in writing, or communicating in traditional ways. After all, we know that our own caring, passion for learning, and an expectation for success influence student performance!

The old adage, "They don't care how much you know until they know how much you care" characterizes high school learners. The teachers that adolescents respond to best are those who know their names, treat them with respect in the classroom, create a classroom climate that is free of humiliation, grade fairly, follow through with promises, and respect their privacy. Creating such a classroom climate doesn't come from a cookbook or a one-day workshop on behavior management.

Teachers show students they care the old-fashioned way. They get to know each student's interests, passions, talents, and challenges. They become involved in students' lives in and outside of school. They serve as coaches, mentors, chaperones, and they balance nonjudgmental acceptance with "tough love." Most veteran teachers have had former students return for a visit and thank them for not giving up on them, for keeping after them to work hard.

Isn't it interesting that many of these returning students had learning difficulties when they were in school? Excellent teachers often get their greatest reward not from teaching students who score 1600 on their SATs, but from students who struggle to learn and won't be successful without teachers who care and excel at their craft. Once students know that their teachers care, they are ready to learn the course content from teachers who are as passionate about their subject area as they are about their students' learning.

Figure Out How
Every Student Is "Smart"

Imagine that you are attending a teachers' conference, and when you walk into the lecture hall there are no tables and no chairs. Although the speaker's presentation is enlightening and humorous, after 15 minutes you notice that everyone in the room is starting to get a little "antsy." People begin to shift from foot to foot, and their attention wanders. One by one, they start to talk among themselves—some even leave the hall. Then you see a colleague who appears calm and comfortable, sitting in her wheelchair, taking notes. Who has the disability in this situation? In another scenario, imagine that you are teaching a biology class and a discussion of genetic engineering arises. You ask the students to debate the merits of selective abortion of fetuses with birth defects. A student in your class who has Down syndrome speaks haltingly but passionately about his right to life as a person with a disability. Having a student with a disability in your class elevates the discussion to a new level. In a manner of speaking, the student with Down syndrome has a unique kind of intelligence because of his disability.

It is often said that including students with disabilities requires that we look "beyond" their labels. We contend that we need to do something even more radical—we need to change our whole notion of what "disability" is and look at human differences as a natural form of diversity (Snow, 2005). Just as the notion of disability takes on a new meaning in the conference example above, so does the concept of "intelligence." Just because one of the standing teachers couldn't pay attention to the speaker while managing her sore feet doesn't mean that she isn't smart! We all know students who are great writers but are unable to carry a tune. Other students can fix a car, but can't write a coherent paragraph.

How "smart" people seem depends on how they are asked to demonstrate their smartness and what society values. Although adult society has a place for people of varied talents, schools focus almost exclusively on linguistic and logical-mathematical intelligence. Our challenge as teachers is to find out how every one of our students is smart, to teach using methods that tap into different intelligences, and to stretch all of our students to develop their talents in all areas. Within a unit on ecology, for example, a student who excels linguistically can write a paper describing the life cycle of a tree. A student who has spatial intelligence can create a landscaping plan that utilizes complementary trees and plants. A student who has naturalist intelligence can work in the field to build sustainable organic gardens shared by all community members (Armstrong, 2000). If we approach teaching this way, differences become ordinary and no students seem out of place in our classroom.

Make Learning Relevant

4

When high school classrooms are comprised of students of varying interests, talents, experiences, learning styles, and motivations, following a traditional, lecture-based approach to teaching just won't work. And if a high school uses block schedules, where students are in each class for 80 minutes, lecturing is guaranteed to lose even the most conventional learners! This is particularly true if what we want all students to know and be able to do goes beyond rote memorization and recall of a set of disconnected names, places, dates, and events. Designing units of study around an underlying "essential question" or in response to a real-life problem allows students to answer the question or solve the problem in unique ways that tap into their talents and bypass their academic challenges.

"What is worth fighting for?" is an essential question that might organize a semester's work in American History, from the Revolutionary War through Reconstruction. "If we can, should we?" might be the central question for a biology unit on genetics and heredity. "Who owns the land?" could frame a unit of study about the westward expansion of America during the early 1800s.

Posing these questions on the very first day of class would undoubtedly engage each and every student in a lively discussion that is based mostly on personal opinion and experience. The teacher then introduces and elaborates the content of the unit to help students make connections between the lessons of history and science and their own lives. The knowledge and skills that are important for students to learn, then, are the ones necessary for them to answer the essential question.

Teaching this way results in students learning depth over breadth, and requires teachers to make careful choices about what's most important to teach. Other content areas lend themselves to the use of "problem-based learning," where teachers engage students in studying and solving real-life problems such as, "Develop a school policy about fair and reasonable accommodations for the participation of students with disabilities in interscholastic sports," "Fill out an IRS 1040 form," or, "Design a business plan for a student-run school store." The skills that are taught are those that students will need in order to solve the problem, providing a focus for instruction that goes beyond basic acquisition of knowledge to practical application and synthesis.

Make Learning Cooperative

5

When a problem arises in your family, neighborhood, or community, are the best solutions discovered by people working in isolation, or are the most creative and practical ideas developed when people work cooperatively? We bet that you learned the most when you were in school from teachers who encouraged their students to work together on homework, labs, or projects. Instead of penalizing students for talking during class, they encouraged students to provide feedback to one another's efforts and to work on solving problems together. Their classrooms were a hotbed of activity and conversation, and you could just feel the excitement when students were encouraged to bounce ideas off one another.

Group activities are one of the ways that teachers ensure that learning is active and interactive and that instruction responds to the diverse learning styles of students. Effective grouping meets individual student needs, because activities are planned that value and build on differences in what students know and how they approach problems, and precisely because every student brings something unique to the group. Good teachers use cooperative group activities as an adjunct to whole-class instruction, one-on-one coaching, hands-on labs, problem-based lessons, and solitary learning activities like library research or reflective writing.

Instead of tracking and ability grouping, teachers in inclusive high schools use cooperative groups and peer supports to capitalize on student differences. In well designed cooperative group activities, each student has a specific role and several tasks to accomplish for the group. Cooperative group assignments are designed so that every member of the group must do his or her part to accomplish the activity. For example, in a social studies class, groups of students may adopt a country and develop a strategy for improving its citizens' literacy or health. Each group would need researchers, speech writers, chart makers, speakers, and liaisons to other countries. In a science class, students might work together to design a solar collecting panel that would power a boom box—blending intrinsic motivation to have music during seatwork time and cooperative learning!

Peer supports, another form of cooperative learning, can also be used in high school classes to ensure that students with disabilities participate in meaningful ways in the curriculum. For example, a classmate may provide a voice for a student who does not speak, take notes for a student who has difficulty writing, or redirect a student with attention difficulties. When all students learn together, each student learns more.

6   Use Universal Design Principles

The principles of Universal Design for Learning (UDL) offer a model for designing curriculum and instruction and for evaluating learning within a diverse high school classroom (Rose & Meyer, 2002). The key elements of these principles—many ways of presenting information, many ways of interacting with and making sense of information, and many ways of assessing learning—are incorporated into lesson planning by effective teachers.

The first principle of UDL is to support recognition learning by providing multiple, flexible methods of presentation. When teachers use flexible instructional media such as digital text, sound, images, and the World Wide Web, information can be made accessible for students with different learning styles and challenges. Imagine the power of teaching students about the Civil Rights era by having them listen to and watch Martin Luther King's "I Have a Dream" speech. Imagine supporting a student with poor reading skills by enhancing difficult text with definitions and examples of unfamiliar terms that are just one "click" away.

A second UDL principle supports strategic learning by providing multiple, flexible methods of students showing what they know. For example, a science teacher might give students choices for how they demonstrate their evolving understanding of molecular bonding, such as: 1) explaining the concept in writing, 2) using chemical symbols to show electron exchange, 3) drawing diagrams or building models of compounds, or 4) orchestrating a dance that shows how elements regroup to form new compounds.

A third UDL principle supports affective learning, providing multiple, flexible options for engagement that empowers students by giving them choices about the books they read, the biographies they write, the experiments they conduct, or the art that they create. When you think about the most rewarding learning experiences in your life—not just those that took place in formal schooling contexts—we bet that a common thread is that you chose what you wanted to learn about. Integrating all three UDL principles into unit and lesson design represents the art of teaching.

Provide Supports as Naturally as Possible

The provision of supports in a thoughtful way can make the difference between a student merely being "in" an inclusive environment—just physically present—and truly being "with" the other students—communicating, learning, and establishing social relationships. The first question we should ask is, "Can this student participate in this activity just like all the other students?" Many times the answer is "yes," and no extra supports are needed.

When students do need supports in order to fully participate, they tend to cluster in five interrelated categories. The first category of *physical, emotional, and sensory supports* might include: 1) assisting a student to move from his wheelchair to a stationary bicycle in physical education class, 2) providing and fading physical supports and prompts to assist a student typing out a message on an augmentative communication device, or 3) building in regular movement breaks for all students in the classroom.

The second category of support is related to *modifying materials and/or providing technology.* Teachers might convert test items that require written responses into multiple-choice questions that can be programmed into a student's augmentative communication device. They might support students' writing by using software like *Clicker 5* (Crick Software, 2005) that enables emergent readers and writers to compose sentences.

Personalized instruction, the third category of support, can be as simple as reinforcing directions or asking each student in the class a slightly different question during group discussions. Personalized instruction can be provided by the general education teacher or by special education personnel who provide one-on-one support to students with and without disabilities in the general education classroom.

In addition, allowing a student to build a model of a cell instead of writing a lab report can assess the same knowledge, but *personalizes the demonstration of learning*, an example of the fourth category of supports. For students with reading and writing challenges, teachers must assure that these difficulties are not allowed to be barriers to students' access to information or their demonstration of learning. Certainly, learning to read and write are essential life skills for all students, but these skills are not prerequisites to learning content from other subject areas.

And finally, some students may need *individualized grading plans* that represent a unique combination of their achievement of grade-level standards and their achievement of goals from their individualized education programs.

Embed Social Justice Values in Your Classroom

8

Preparation for college and the world of work are important goals of a high school education. However, it is also essential that we prepare our students to be contributing citizens in a democracy. One of the responsibilities of our citizenship is the ability to live peacefully with others who are different from ourselves and to fight injustice whenever we see it—in other words, to work for social justice.

To facilitate students' commitment to this cause, teachers can address social justice issues through the curriculum and through their personal actions. Rather than stopping the flow of a course to have "disability awareness week," teachers can identify natural opportunities to discuss these issues. While reading *Of Mice and Men* (Steinbeck, 1937) an English teacher might highlight the need for everyone to have friends and advocates. Social studies students might study the World War II T4 killing program, in which children with disabilities were the focus of Nazi experiments. In a child development course, the teacher might explore why people offer sympathy rather than congratulations when they hear that a friend has given birth to a child with a disability. In science, the teacher may discuss seizures during a lab on the central nervous system. In a building trades class, students might debate the merits of requiring universal accessibility in the design and building of public facilities. And in physical education, students might discuss issues related to "fairness" concerning the participation of students with disabilities in competitive sports.

Establishing norms for how students and teachers treat one another extends the commitment to social justice beyond the curriculum to everyday interactions. Banning the use of hate speech and teaching students to mediate disagreements are part of the "hidden" yet essential curriculum in inclusive schools. Some of the most successful inclusive schools are those in which students themselves become advocates for issues such as hunger relief, peace, and eliminating racism.

In one of the author's experience, a young man with a significant disability joined his school's "Peace" club. Discussions about violence against students with disabilities resulted in the students working with the school administration to revise the school's policy about bullying and respect for diversity. Teachers in inclusive high schools show students that striving for social justice is in their best interest, because there comes a time in everyone's life when we need others to stand up alongside us and for us.

Become a Reflective Practitioner

Taking on a new challenge like including students with disabilities tests many of the assumptions we all hold about teaching and learning. Like any other innovation, sustaining new practices and ways of thinking is probably harder than taking the first few steps. How do we avoid a return to the "status quo" or teacher burnout when we've got more questions than answers?

From our experience with inclusive high schools all around the country, teachers who engage in ongoing "reflective practice" seem to be able to keep up their enthusiasm, to work through tough problems, and to keep learning more about what works well. Taking reflection beyond the end-of-the-day thinking that we do on the drive home from school, however, means moving beyond our personal musings to making changes in our teaching that improve student learning. Because many minds are better than one, this is best accomplished by being a member of a small group of teachers who meet together regularly in "reflective practice groups."

Finding time together can be difficult to say the least, but many high schools are restructuring their schedules to give teachers a common planning period during the school day to do this important work. With the helpful guidance of a facilitator—who is sometimes a "critical friend" from outside the school— teachers can ask their colleagues to help them brainstorm ideas for inclusive teaching while they are planning a unit. They can work in pairs to observe in one another's classrooms, asking, "Is each and every student an active participant in both the academic and social life of this learning community?" They can reflect on "critical incidents" in their day-to-day teaching. They can learn how to ask themselves and one another probing questions ("What are the assumptions behind your thinking about John's refusal to do the work?") that help to uncover their assumptions about motivation, independence, learning difficulties, and beliefs about teaching. And perhaps most importantly, reflective practitioners examine student work as an indicator of how effectively instruction and supports were designed and implemented.

Although each of us undoubtedly has strong feelings about the merits of national educational policies such as No Child Left Behind, the requirement that schools be responsible for the learning of all students has promoted interesting conversations at the local school level. Schools that focus their reflective conversations on questions such as, "How can we narrow the gap between the achievement of students with and without disabilities?" demonstrate their commitment to all of their students.

10 Advocate for Untracking and Inclusion

As a teacher, you have a tremendous amount of control over what goes on in your classroom, and you may not think that you need to become involved in larger school debates about inclusive education in order to be successful with your students. You may wonder, however, if your job might be made easier if more teachers were willing to have students with disabilities in their classrooms, or if administrators provided more professional development about students with disabilities. You see the benefits of having students with disabilities in your own classroom, but you wonder why there are still separate special education classes, "low" and "high" level tracks, and alternative high schools. You sense that inclusion is the right thing to do, but don't have the resources to do it well.

In our experience, unless all teachers take on the role of "teacher as leader" in their schools, they will find that their own classroom practice is negatively affected by outdated philosophies, too little classroom support for students with learning challenges, limited time for regular collaboration with other teachers and support professionals, and a lack of quality professional development. All around the country, teachers are becoming involved in efforts to "untrack" schools and include all students.

In one of the author's experience, teachers from a nearby high school were all members of professional learning teams that worked together for a year to investigate and understand a variety of current educational issues and dilemmas. One such team focused on the inclusion of students with significant disabilities in their school. They read seminal and current research, used reflective practice protocols to solve problems related to instruction, and eventually made recommendations for changes in the school's course registration policies that improved access to rigorous academic courses by students with disabilities.

In another school, all teachers were members of action research groups who study one problem intensively over the course of the school year. One of these groups was dismayed by the poor performance of students with learning disabilities. After a year of study, the group proposed a number of changes to their English language arts curriculum that resulted in a more intensive focus on reading comprehension and writing.

Teachers like you—who may have started by making a difference in the life of just one student—are recognizing Margaret Mead's wisdom that "a small group of committed citizens can change the world. Indeed it is the only thing that ever has" (Warner, 1992).

Selected References

Armstrong, T. (2000). *Multiple intelligences in the classroom (2nd ed.).* Alexandria, VA: Association for Supervision and Curriculum Development.

Crick Software (2005). *Clicker 5* [Computer software]. Seattle, Washington: Crick Software.

Delisle, R. (1997). *How to use problem-based learning in the classroom.* Alexandria, VA: Association for Supervision and Curriculum Development.

Fried, R. (1995). *The passionate teacher.* Boston: Beacon Press.

Gardner, H. (1983). *Frames of mind: The theory of multiple intelligences.* New York: Basic Books.

Jorgensen, C. (2006). *Restructuring high schools for all students: Taking inclusion to the next level (2nd ed.).* Durham, NH: Institute on Disability.

Rose, D., & Meyer, A. (2002). *Teaching every student in the digital age: Universal design for learning.* Alexandria, VA: Association for Supervision and Curriculum Development.

Sizer, T. (1984). *Horace's compromise.* Boston: Houghton Mifflin.

Snow, K. (2005). *Disability is natural. Revolutionary common sense for raising successful children with disabilities.* Woodland Park, CO: BraveHeart Press.

Steinbeck, J. (1937). *Of Mice and men.* New York: Penguin Books.

Tomlinson, C.A. (1999). *The differentiated classroom: Responding to the needs of all learners.* Alexandria, VA: Association for Supervision and Curriculum Development.

Warner, C. (1992). *The last word: A treasury of women's quotes.* Upper Saddle River, NJ: Prentice Hall.

Quick-Guide #17

Transition from School to Adult Life

Katharine Shepherd and George B. Salembier

Quick-Guides to Inclusion
Ideas for Educating Students with Disabilities, Second Edition

Michael F. Giangreco & Mary Beth Doyle

Editors

Dear Teacher,

Have you ever wondered what happens to your students with disabilities after they leave high school? Unfortunately, state and national studies show that, without adequate supports, these former students may find themselves unemployed or underemployed, without access to postsecondary education and vocational education, and lacking connections to the community. In order to support students in achieving more positive adult life outcomes, the federal government requires that the individualized education programs (IEPs) developed for students with disabilities contain measurable postsecondary goals that build on students' strengths, preferences, and needs in areas such as employment, postsecondary education, community participation, and independent living (Individuals with Disabilities Education Improvement Act [IDEA], 2004). Although the transition component of the IEP is not required until the year in which a student will reach the age of 16, it is important for IEP teams to consider students' transition needs as early as the elementary and middle school years.

This Quick-Guide suggests guidelines that you may use to ensure that students with disabilities have the opportunities, options, services, and supports they need to advocate for themselves and to make a successful transition from school to adult life. Each guideline includes a brief description and examples of ways to make transition planning more student- and family-centered, collaborative, and effective. We encourage you to use these guidelines as you support your students in achieving their dreams and goals for life beyond high school.

Good luck,
Katie and George

GUIDELINES-AT-A-GLANCE

1. Plan Early

2. Build a Collaborative Team Around the Student

3. Make Transition Planning Student and Family Centered

4. Encourage Students to Advocate for Themselves

5. Develop Plans Based on Students' Strengths, Dreams, and Interests

6. Build Connections Between Students' Transition Goals and Curriculum

7. Identify a Range of Post–High School and Community Resources

8. Build a Network of Support in Your Community

9. Review the Plan at Least Once a Year

10. Remember, Transition Planning Benefits All Students

Plan Early

The Individuals with Disabilities Improvement Education Act (IDEA) of 2004 (PL 108-446) requires that IEPs for students with disabilities include goals and services that guide the transition from school to adult life. The transition component of the IEP must be developed, "beginning not later than the first IEP to be in effect when the child is 16, and updated annually thereafter" (IDEA 2004, Sec 614 [d] [1] [A] [I]). Early transition planning is important for several reasons.

First, early planning allows you and other team members to assess and identify a student's postsecondary education goals related to "training, education, employment, and, where appropriate, independent living skills" (IDEA 2004, Sec. 614 [d] [1] [A] [I]). The IEP team should use these goals as the basis for identifying the courses and experiences a student should have while in high school. Students who do not have a clear idea about what they would like to do after high school will thus have time to explore possibilities in their schools and communities, and their experiences may help them establish personal goals for the future.

Second, early planning allows students and their families to learn about community resources and supports that are available both during and after high school. Many of these resources have eligibility requirements and waiting lists that students and their families need to know about. Some students may need time to gather various documents needed to engage in work and postsecondary education, such as a Social Security card and birth certificate. They may also need to apply for various kinds of financial support available through Supplemental Security Income, Medicare, and other state and federal financial supplemental programs, including scholarships and financial aid to postsecondary institutions.

Third, early planning allows team members to identify representatives from adult services and/or postsecondary institutions who should be invited to attend future team meetings and/or to become team members. Finally, students and their families need plenty of time to make informed choices about the future and to learn how to advocate for themselves in their schools and communities.

Build a Collaborative Team Around the Student

Prior to the IEP meeting in which transition planning will be discussed, you will need to identify additional people who will need to be present to discuss transition issues. According to IDEA (2004) the transition team must consist of the student, his or her IEP team, and any adult services representatives whose agencies may be responsible for paying for future services to the student.

It may also be helpful to invite individuals who are not IEP team members, but who may be interested in assisting the student in transition planning. These individuals might include siblings, friends, grandparents, or other community members, who can provide unique perspectives on the student and links to employment, living situations, recreation, and other community opportunities. The team must meet annually to review the student's transition plan, but may meet more frequently to discuss progress on specific goals and activities.

As you consider team membership, it is important to weigh the pros and cons of large and small teams. Larger teams may provide more ideas and perspectives, but they may also be difficult to manage. You may wish to differentiate between team members who need to attend all transition-related meetings and those who should be invited to selected meetings for specific purposes. For example, a student's current employer does not need to attend all transition planning meetings, but you might want to invite the employer to attend an annual review at which employment goals will be discussed.

Transition teams should keep in mind the principles of collaborative teaming, such as being clear about the group's purpose, promoting a sense of trust and shared responsibility among all team members, encouraging equal participation during meetings, and identifying how the team will make decisions. Many collaborative teams find it helpful to use agendas and timelines, keep minutes, and identify action steps for future plans. Critical communication skills for collaboration include: active listening, perspective taking, conflict resolution, and problem solving.

It is helpful for teams to remember that, while collaborative teaming structures may be familiar to school professionals, they may be less familiar to parents and students. As such, you may want to identify group norms that address how the team will function and how all team members' voices will be heard.

Make Transition Planning Student and Family Centered

3

In order for students to become participating members of their schools and communities, the transition planning process needs to be student- and family-centered. By this, we mean that the transition planning process should be directed by students and family members and built around their ideas about what is most important in the student's life.

As a teacher, you can help to ensure that transition planning is student- and family-centered by encouraging teams to use one of a number of specific planning processes designed to support students and families in expressing and clarifying their vision for the student's future. Examples of these processes include: 1) *Choosing Outcomes and Accommodations for Children (COACH)* (Giangreco, Cloninger, & Iverson, 1998), 2) *Making Action Plans (MAPs)* (Pearpoint, Forest, & O'Brien, 1996), and 3) *Planning Alternative Tomorrows with Hope (PATH)* (Pearpoint, O'Brien, & Forest, 1993). These processes stress the importance of building strong relationships and good communication with students and families before, during, and after all transition planning meetings.

Before the annual transition planning meetings occur, it is important for the rest of the transition team to make sure that the student and family members understand the purpose of the meetings and that they understand their legal rights and responsibilities. The student and family members should be involved in choosing the composition of their IEP and transition teams, the times and places of meetings, and meeting agendas. During meetings, encourage student and family participation by using active listening skills, directing questions to the student and parents, and conveying a sense that you care about, and are open to acting on, what they want for the future.

It is critical to understand a family's context and to consider the ways in which cultural background and values may influence how family members define their hopes and dreams for the student. After meetings, you should continue to include the student and parents by touching base with them regularly, sharing information, reporting on students' accomplishments, and continuing to build a strong and ongoing relationship.

Encourage Students to Advocate for Themselves

An important aspect of making transition planning a student- and family-centered process is encouraging students to advocate for themselves (e.g., during planning meetings, in daily life) and to develop a sense of self-determination as they look to the future. Self-advocacy has been defined as an individual's right to identify and express personal needs, while self-determination relates to a student's ability to experience a sense of control over the future by making informed choices, setting goals, and taking responsibility for achieving those goals (Pierangelo & Giuliani, 2004; Wehman, 2006; Wehmeyer & Field, 2007). You can use transition planning as an opportunity to encourage self-advocacy and self-determination by involving students in a range of activities before, during, and after meetings. It is important to consider that students with varying needs may have a range of ways in which self-advocacy can be expressed.

Prior to meetings, you can help students prepare their responses to questions that are likely to be asked. Some students may become involved in identifying and sending out invitations to potential team members. During meetings, you should ask your student to be the first person to respond to questions that are posed, encourage the student to share previously prepared notes, and invite him or her to assume responsibility for carrying out specific responsibilities on the IEP and transition plan. You can also foster self-advocacy by creating a comfortable and relaxed atmosphere and encouraging the student to invite friends to meetings. Over time, students can be asked to take on increasing levels of responsibility during meetings, including cofacilitation.

Outside of planning meetings, you can promote self-advocacy and self-determination by providing the student with various opportunities to make choices about possible course of studies, extracurricular activities, and recreational activities, and by encouraging your students to express their needs in appropriate ways. Many students benefit from instruction in specific self-advocacy skills, such as self-assessment, goal setting, problem solving, communicating, and resolving conflicts. It is important to remember that self-advocacy means different things to different people and should be considered within the context of a student's age, culture, and degree of support needs. Additionally, consideration needs to be given to the fact that self-advocacy skills take time to develop and should be promoted beginning in the elementary and middle school grades.

Develop Plans Based on Students' Strengths, Dreams, and Interests

5

The student's strengths, dreams for the future, and needs provide the building blocks for his IEP and transition plan. In the context of transition planning, strengths refer to a student's personal qualities, skills, interests and preferences. The person-centered processes mentioned in Guideline #3 (i.e., *COACH, MAPS, PATH*) use strength-based approaches to planning. These strength-based approaches are an alternative to traditional models of planning and assessment, which tend to focus on identifying the student's areas of weakness in an effort to remediate them.

Strength-based planning focuses on what students can do rather than on what they cannot do. Dreams refer to what a student wants to achieve both during and after high school. Dreams may be related to particular chosen course of study, employment, postsecondary education or vocational training, independent living, health, relationships, community participation, or personal interests. Needs refer to the skills and opportunities that a student requires in order to live in the community and to pursue personal dreams.

Often students have not had many opportunities to talk about their strengths, dreams, and needs, so it is important to prepare them to do so before their transition planning meetings. During each meeting, invite the student, parents, and other team members to brainstorm and answer specific questions about the student's strengths, dreams, and needs in relation to the transition areas identified above. As you address a particular area, try using prompting questions such as "When you think about jobs you'd like to have, what do you see yourself doing one year from now? In five years? In ten years?" This information will be used later to identify goals, activities, and resources to be included in the student's IEP and transition plan, and to distinguish between short- and long-range goals.

Once again, it is important to think about a student's needs in terms of strengths rather than weaknesses, and to be sensitive to the cultural context within which students and families are identifying dreams and needs. For example, goals related to independent living, employment, and postsecondary living may be defined differently across cultures.

Build Connections Between Students' Transition Goals and Curriculum

6

Once IEP teams have identified strengths, dreams, and needs, they need to translate them into goals, objectives, services, and activities that will make up yearly IEPs and transition plans. One way to accomplish this is to develop a list of transition goals that articulate the student's dreams and goals in the areas of employment, postsecondary education or technical education, independent living, health, relationships, community participation, self-advocacy, and personal interests.

Next, you and the rest of the IEP and transition team should decide what needs to occur in the coming year in order to move the student closer to his long-term transition goals. The IEP team can then use these decisions to inform and identify annual IEP goals and related transition activities that are important for the student.

In addition, the team needs to consider the student's transition goals when designing his general course of studies. For example, imagine that a student with learning disabilities named George has told you that he wants to help build houses and plans to attend a technical school after high school to acquire additional skills. His IEP goals and objectives might be related to content such as: 1) improving organizational skills; 2) extending reading skills; 3) learning geometry, calculation, and measurement; and 4) preparing job applications. His course of study during high school should include courses of study required for admission to technical college and technical education classes of interest. In addition, George might benefit from volunteer experiences building homes (e.g., Habitat for Humanity), or work-based opportunities, such as job shadowing on a construction site or an apprenticeship with contractors and carpenters in the community.

It is important to remember that all educational goals, activities, and services should support a student's progress toward his transition goals and dreams. In other words, his dreams and long-term transition goals should provide the focus through which to develop the IEP, transition plan, and general high school curriculum. Some students with disabilities are assessed through alternative means, such as life-skills portfolios. These students' transition goals can be used as the basis of determining which life skills are most important to focus on, and what activities might be planned to help students achieve their goals.

Identify a Range of Post-High School and Community Resources

7

A number of available resources and supports help students to achieve their transition goals and become increasingly independent and connected to the community. As indicated in Guideline #6, a student's transition plan should include a variety of transition-related objectives and activities that tap into school and community resources. These might include: 1) obtaining part-time or summer employment; 2) receiving training and supports related to finding and maintaining employment; 3) participating in consumer and technical training; 4) obtaining a driver's license; 5) learning how to manage finances and live independently; 6) participating in community recreational activities; or 7) learning about postsecondary options, financial aid, and admissions requirements.

Some students and their families will need additional postschool supports that are provided by vocational rehabilitation, mental health and developmental disabilities agencies, state employment and training departments, and centers for independent living and advocacy. Depending on a family's preferences and needs, you might help family members to benefit from these resources by contacting the student's guidance counselor and/or special educator to obtain information, going with the family to visit a variety of agencies, and encouraging family members to attend resource fairs at your high school or local parent information center.

If your student's goal is to attend a postsecondary institution, the student, guidance counselor, and family will want to research the admission criteria and types and level of services available at the colleges, universities, and/or technical schools in which the student is interested. It is important for these students and families to understand the ways in which they will be supported at the postsecondary level, as colleges and universities provide accommodations under the auspices of Section 504 and the Americans with Disabilities Act, neither of which carries the same level of entitlement as special education. Try contacting local parent organizations to introduce parents to other families who have used postschool and community resources, and invite agency representatives to attend transition planning meetings as early as possible. Each of these activities will help students and families to learn about eligibility requirements, application procedures, contact people, and the nature of available school and community services and supports.

Build a Network of Support in Your Community

In the context of transition planning, a network refers to people who care about a student, live and/or work in the community, and are willing to contribute to support during and after high school. There are a number of reasons why it is important to build a strong network of community support around students with disabilities. Students who are connected to a network are more likely to access community experiences and opportunities available to them, to obtain employment and/or postsecondary education upon graduation, and to know both paid and unpaid people who will continue to support them in achieving their long-range goals once they have left high school. People in students' networks may also become friends who will help them develop other friendships and participate in leisure and recreational activities in the community.

You can help a student build a network of community support by asking community members who know the student and his family to attend the IEP and transition planning meetings, to help with brainstorming ideas for possible employment, postsecondary education, living, and recreational opportunities. You can also help build a student's network of support by involving community members in carrying out specific activities listed on the transition plan. You may want to encourage students to join local organizations or clubs of interest, fitness and outdoor groups, youth or advocacy groups, community service groups, or groups affiliated with places of worship. The workplace is an excellent location for you to facilitate natural connections between a student and one or more co-workers.

In these ways, you may teach students that they have a role to play in building community networks. You may develop this awareness further by teaching social, communication, and self-advocacy skills that will allow students to initiate interactions that may eventually lead to friendships and wider networks of support. It may be helpful to use prompting questions that help students identify their particular preferences and interests in relation to community groups and activities, such as: "What are some things you've done with your free time in the past that you'd like to continue doing? If you could pick anyone to spend free time with, who would it be?"

9 Review the Plan at Least Once a Year

The annual review of the IEP and transition plan provides your team members with a natural opportunity to give feedback on the student's progress in achieving annual transition goals and objectives, as well as to consider whether team members need to clarify or revise the goals they developed at the outset of transition planning. This review of the student's progress in relation to postschool goals also allows team members to adjust the plan for the coming year.

You should remind the student and family members to be sure that goals continue to be based on their needs, preferences, and interests. The IEP and transition planning process is a dynamic one, in which the student's goals may change direction or become more focused over time.

Team membership may change as the student's needs and preferences shift and become clearer. To deal with these changes, it is common for teams to invite representatives of vocational rehabilitation, adult services, and/or post-secondary institutions to transition planning meetings during the last two years of high school. During meetings, they can provide information to families, help answer questions about eligibility and application procedures, and get to know the student and family better.

You can help the annual review meeting become a time of celebration by inviting the student and other team members to tell stories of accomplishment during the past year. A team member can record these stories on flip chart paper or in a journal as part of a portfolio documenting the student's achievements.

Often, reviews of the IEP and transition plan reveal unanticipated positive results. One parent told us that the end-of-year review and celebration reminded him that "our daughter is probably capable of more that we might have expected, especially in the areas of employment and independent living." A student on another team commented, "After working for a year, I know that I really want to live on my own after graduation. So I need to learn how to cook, do my laundry, and pay my bills."

Remember, Transition Planning Benefits All Students

10

As a final note, we encourage you to think of ways in which you can employ the principles and practices associated with transition planning to benefit students both with and without disabilities. IDEA (2004) clearly stresses the importance and benefits of transition planning for students with disabilities. In addition, many secondary schools have recognized the importance of expanding opportunities for all students to connect their academic programs to community-based experiences that will help them to clarify and realize their postschool goals. For example, many schools have implemented programs to provide: 1) applied learning experiences and career portfolios; 2) service learning and community-service opportunities; and 3) employment opportunities such as apprenticeships, entrepreneurships, and internships.

In recent years, many secondary schools have encouraged students to take courses at their local colleges and universities as a way of complementing their high school plans of study. Usually, any student may participate in these programs and receive credit toward graduation.

You can help promote this emphasis on career and transition planning for all students by checking with your school's guidance department to find out what resources and program options are available in your school and community. Guidance counselors can play a critical role in helping all students make a successful transition to adult life, because they are usually responsible for helping students develop four-year plans of study and have direct access to information on postsecondary education, training opportunities, and career assessment opportunities.

In addition, guidance counselors can help students and parents to identify postsecondary institutions that have particularly strong support services and resources for students with disabilities. You may also wish to identify ways in which you can expand your own curriculum content and connect it to existing programs to help students attain their career goals. For example, one English teacher asks her students to identify careers they might like to explore that involve writing. Students conduct projects in the community that relate to various writing roles, such as journalism, screen writing, cartoon writing, creative writing, and technical writing. Educators in today's schools are beginning to realize that expanding curriculum and collaborating with the community leads to the development of a community that supports its schools and its school system.

Selected References

Furney, K.S., Carlson, N., Lisi, D., & Yuan, S. (1993). *Speak up for yourself and your future! A curriculum for building self-advocacy and self-determination skills.* Burlington: University of Vermont, Department of Education.

Giangreco, M.F., Cloninger, C.J., & Iverson, V.S. (1998). *Choosing outcomes and accommodations for children (COACH): A guide to educational planning for students with disabilities (2nd ed.).* Baltimore: Paul H. Brookes Publishing Co.

Individuals with Disabilities Education Improvement Act of 2004, PL 108-446, 20 U.S.C. §§ 1400 *et seq.*

Individuals with Disabilities Education Act Amendments of 1997, PL 105-17, 20 U.S.C. §§ 1400 *et seq.*

Pearpoint, J., Forest, M., & O'Brien, J. (1996). MAPs, Circle of Friends, and PATH: Powerful tools to help build caring communities. In S. Stainback & W. Stainback (Eds.), *Inclusion: A guide for educators* (pp. 67–86). Baltimore: Paul H. Brookes Publishing Co.

Pearpoint, J., Forest, M., & O'Brien, J. (1993). *PATH.* Toronto, Ontario, Canada: Inclusion Press.

Pierangelo, R., & Giuliani, G.A. (2004). *Transition services in special education: A practical approach.* Boston: Pearson Education.

Wehman, P. (2006). *Life beyond the classroom: Transition strategies for young people with disabilities (4th ed.).* Baltimore: Paul H. Brookes Publishing Co.

Wehmeyer, M.L., & Field, S. (2007). *Self-determination: Instructional and assessment strategies.* Thousand Oaks, CA: Corwin Press.

Personnel & Administration

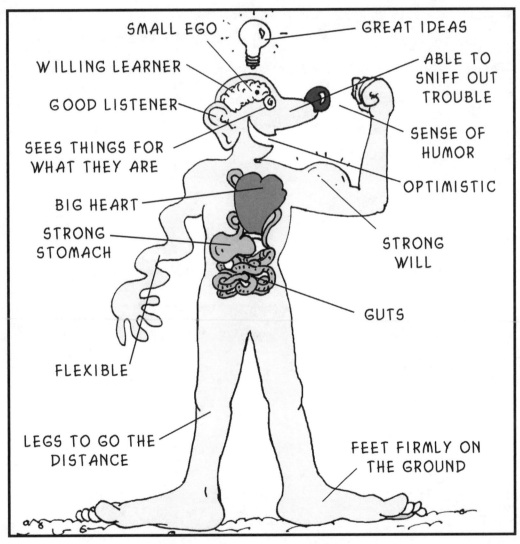

ANATOMY OF AN EFFECTIVE TEAM MEMBER

Quick-Guide #18

Getting the Most
out of Support Services

Susan W. Edelman, Michael F. Giangreco, Ruth E. Dennis,
Patricia A. Prelock, Marie MacLeod, and Marie Christine Potvin

Quick-Guides to Inclusion
Ideas for Educating Students with Disabilities, Second Edition
Michael F. Giangreco & Mary Beth Doyle

Editors

Dear Teacher,

When a student with disabilities becomes a member of your class, that student's success and yours as the teacher may require support from additional professional personnel who have specialized skills that complement the skills you bring to the job. The type and number of support personnel will vary and be individually determined based on the student's needs. Typically, these personnel include special educators, related service providers (e.g., physical therapist, occupational therapist, speech-language pathologist, psychologist, orientation and mobility specialist, audiologist, assistive technology specialist), and possibly other consultants or specialists whose involvement are required for the student to have access to, and benefit from, both their individualized educational program and the general education curriculum. All of the services to be provided should be described in the student's individualized education program (IEP).

Having a variety of personnel who are assigned to support a student and who have diverse, and to some extent, overlapping skill sets, doesn't ensure that the impact will be supportive of the student or you as the classroom teacher. The ten guidelines included in this Quick-Guide are offered as a framework for you and your team to consider so that support services are provided in ways that are truly helpful within the context of your classroom. Each guideline is followed by a brief description. At the end you will find a list of "Selected References" if you wish to explore more in-depth information on this topic. In the meantime, this Quick-Guide should facilitate your first steps in getting the most out of support services.

Good luck!

Susan, Michael, Ruth, Patty, Marie, and Marie Christine

GUIDELINES-AT-A-GLANCE

1. Be Aware of What Support Services Have to Offer

2. Approach Support Service Providers as Collaborators

3. Agree on Expectations and Goals for Students

4. Clarify Your Role as Teacher

5. Know the Types of Supports You Need and Want

6. Distinguish Between "Extra Hands" and Specialized Help

7. Help Support Service Providers Understand Your Classroom

8. Participate in Scheduling Support Services

9. Have a Process for Effective Communication

10. Evaluate the Effectiveness of Support Services

Be Aware of What Support Services Have to Offer

As a classroom teacher, you may have had previous experiences working with special education support personnel, or this could be a relatively new experience. In either case, it is important to become knowledgeable about what your team members have to contribute to the team, both professionally and personally. It is equally important for support personnel to learn about the professional and personal skills you bring to the table.

To become familiar with the professional skills of other team members, we suggest you become knowledgeable on two levels. First, it is important to understand the scope and roles of various disciplines, as well as how those roles differ from, and overlap with, other disciplines. For example, what do occupational therapists or orientation and mobility specialists do? How do the activities of these disciplines differ from, or overlap with, other disciplines such as physical therapy or special education? Your knowledge of other disciplines can be increased through face-to-face interactions and by sharing written information from your professional organizations or other sources. Second, we suggest that team members share their unique professional abilities. Within professional disciplines, there may be specialization through professional development or specific professional certification in a particular approach or area of expertise. For example, the speech-language pathologist on your team may have specialized skills in augmentative communication systems or computer applications, while the psychologist may have a background in positive behavior support approaches to deal with challenging behaviors. In choosing which of the specialized skills you would like to incorporate in your classroom, the team should consider the level of evidence behind these specialized skills and approaches.

On a more personal level, you might be surprised to find out how handy knowledge of interests, hobbies, sports, or community activities (e.g., gardening, woodworking, music, art, baseball) can be throughout the team process. Personal interests or skills can be hidden assets that, if known and applied, might enhance the capacity of the team. We suggest you share this information with your team as well. Becoming aware of both the professional and personal knowledge and talents of the various team members should provide a foundation for the team to more fully understand each other and work together.

Approach Support Service Providers as Collaborators

We can't expect every team member to have specialized skills in all areas—that's why we need to rely on each other. Working together as a team allows professionals to identify new skills they will need to obtain through training, technical assistance, or consultation from others with specialty skills.

Team members have been identified because they have important contributions to bring to the team. While we look to support service personnel to provide needed expertise, we may inadvertently establish unproductive hierarchies within the team if we always defer to specialists. Reliance on an "expert" model can create unrealistic expectations among team members and interfere with the very collaboration that is so essential to solving many of the complex challenges presented by students. Yes, many support service personnel may be more or less "experts" in their areas, but you, too, have unique knowledge and skills to bring to the team's efforts.

Traditional skills associated with particular disciplines and the actual skills of individual team members vary widely, so we cannot assume the nature of the expertise of any team member. We also cannot assume support service personnel have been trained to provide school-based services, given that there are many subspecialties within each discipline. For example, a physical therapist may have spent several years working with senior citizens or in a sports medicine clinic and may not necessarily possess the knowledge and skills needed to work with a wide range of children with disabilities in general education settings. A speech-language pathologist may have general knowledge and skills in the assessment and treatment of children with language disorders, but may not have expertise in augmentative communication for students who are essentially nonverbal and require a specific communication system.

Even when a professional's focus has been school-based services for children with disabilities, the same issues may exist. For example, a special educator who is trained and accustomed to working with students who have learning disabilities may be asked to support a student who has severe or multiple disabilities. These types of distinctions only reinforce the importance of sharing expertise to compensate for each other's gaps in knowledge and define our roles as collaborators. Through collaboration you can avoid the trap of simply dividing up roles into slots of expertise and deferring to one another.

Agree on Expectations and Goals for Students

3

Many general education teachers grapple with the question, "What am I expected to teach the student with disabilities who is part of my class?" When team members do not share the same expectations about what the student will learn or who should do the teaching, it can be a source of conflict. It is vital for the classroom teacher to play a substantive and ongoing role in the instruction of the student with disabilities.

The first step to getting the team on the same wavelength is to reach a consensus about the components of the student's educational program. This should include a small set of individualized priority learning outcomes (i.e., individualized education program [IEP] goals) and a set of additional learning outcomes that reflect access to the general curriculum in the classroom. General supports that are provided *for* the student should also be determined. Sometimes support service providers suggest having their own set of goals; this should raise a red flag! Separate goals lead to confusion, fragmentation, and disjointed services because team members are moving in different or individual directions rather than agreeing to head in the same direction. Having separate goals for each discipline is a recipe for disaster! In order to truly function as a team, the team members need to support and encourage the student's progress throughout their educational program by having shared student goals.

Once the team has agreed on a student's educational program components, it's not uncommon for some teachers to feel anxious about how they will address the student's individualized goals within class activities. Through activity-based experiences, students can pursue individualized goals at appropriate levels in varying curriculum areas. For example, during a Social Studies board game about world geography, the student with disabilities might be working on geography goals at a different level or might be pursuing learning outcomes from other curriculum areas (e.g., communication, social skills) via the geography activity. Remember, you are part of a team and are not expected to do this alone.

As a teacher, you are familiar with the requirements for grade-level content, assessments, and individual student progress reporting. The team needs this information to determine how, when, and who will assess student progress. Clear and shared expectations for both the student and support personnel will help your team function more smoothly.

Clarify Your Role as Teacher

As the classroom teacher, you have many responsibilities to all the students in your class, such as planning, implementing, monitoring, evaluating, and adjusting instruction. Doing these same things for your students who have disabilities is also part of your role. The basic principles of teaching and learning are the same, regardless of the labels assigned to children. Therefore, with the right kinds of support, a capable teacher can teach just about any student. Support may come in the form of specially trained personnel (e.g., a physical or speech-language pathologist) or from others such as peers, paraprofessionals, other school personnel, or volunteers.

The role of related services providers is to assist the student with disabilities in accessing instruction. For example, a physical therapist can assist you in appropriately positioning a student with physical disabilities to ensure participation in class activities and account for disability-related characteristics. Your role is to co-design the curriculum and instruction with the special educators. The related services providers are there to assist with their specialized knowledge and skills when necessary. As the instructional leader, it is your responsibility to make your support needs known to the team so the appropriate related services providers can be called upon for support and you can work together to assist your students with disabilities.

If you have a paraprofessional who is providing assistance, this support is most effective when the classroom and special education teacher maintain the responsibilities to design, implement, and evaluate curriculum and instruction. Paraprofessionals may assist you in this work, but they should not become the de-facto "teachers" for the students with disabilities. Several guiding questions might help you to clarify your role versus the paraprofessional's role. Do you:

- Plan instruction for the student with disabilities to about the same extent as other students?

- Spend as much time teaching the student with disabilities as other students?

- Spend time with the student with disabilities during non-instructional times?

- Play a primary role in evaluating the progress of the student with disabilities?

If your answers to these questions are "yes" then you are being the teacher for all of your students. If there are any "no" answers, ask your team to help you to balance your role as the teacher of all students in your class, with them as support personnel.

Know the Types of Supports You Need and Want

5

A mismatch between what teachers want from support personnel and what they get is a common problem. For example, you want someone to demonstrate a teaching method but instead you are handed an article to read, or you need certain materials and instead you are invited to a meeting. It is important to clarify for yourself and your team the types, content, and intensity of supports you need and want on an ongoing basis. Listed here are four basic types of supports that you may need at various times.

Resource support includes: 1) tangible materials (e.g., adapted equipment), 2) financial resources (e.g., funds for community-based learning for the student), 3) informational resources (e.g., professional literature), and 4) human resources (e.g., parent volunteers, peer tutors).

Moral support includes interactions that validate the worth of people's efforts, by sending the message, "You are headed in a positive direction—keep going." This includes active listening characterized by nonjudgmental acceptance of ideas and feelings. When moral support such as this is provided, enough trust exists between people so that perspectives can be shared without fear of put-downs, criticism, or breaches in confidentiality.

Technical support includes concrete strategies, methods, approaches, and ideas. This can be accomplished through in-service training, staff development activities, peer coaching, collaborative consultation, demonstration, modeling, or problem-solving sessions. Technical assistance results in the acquisition of new skills that can be implemented, adjusted, and re-implemented in a cyclical fashion as necessary to meet student and team member needs.

Evaluation support includes assistance in collecting and presenting information that allows the program and supports for a student with disabilities to be monitored and adjusted. It also provides ways to assess the impact of support services on students, families, and professionals through meaningful methods of data collection, analysis, and interpretation.

Being clear about the kind and amount of support you need, as well as what helps and what doesn't help, will facilitate the work of the whole team.

Distinguish Between "Extra Hands" and Specialized Help

6

When teachers need human resources, it is important to distinguish between the need for someone who has specialized skills and the need for someone who can provide an extra pair of helping hands—both can be important. Making this distinction clear will help ensure that resources are beneficial and efficient.

Sometimes teachers come to rely on support service personnel (e.g., special educators, speech-language pathologists, physical therapists) as an extra pair of helping hands and can feel let down when these support personnel schedule other activities and are not available. If teachers need extra hands, but not necessarily specialized services, we suggest first drawing on natural supports such as classmates, cross-age peer tutors, parent volunteers, or community members.

The next level of human resources may be to hire an instructional assistant for the classroom. Sometimes teachers really want and need the knowledge and skills of specialized support personnel to solve problems, suggest adaptations or accommodations, or demonstrate specific strategies. Teachers should be clear about the type of support that will most benefit the student's success in the classroom.

Consider the following scenarios as examples to help distinguish between the need for an extra pair of hands and the need for specialized support:

- The instructional assistant is absent, and the teacher needs someone to help run some teacher-planned activities. (helping hands)

- The teacher is having difficulty finding a writing implement that works well for a student with physical disabilities. (specialized support)

- The teacher has planned a field trip to the local science museum and needs assistance supervising the students. (helping hands)

Each time you find yourself needing human resources, ask yourself, "Do I need an extra pair of helping hands, or specialized support?"

Help Support Service Providers Understand Your Classroom

As the only professional staff member in your classroom all the time, no one is in a better position to know the flow of activities and classroom routines better than you—the teacher. Teachers have repeatedly told us that many of the recommendations they receive from support service personnel simply won't work in their general education classes because support service personnel are not sufficiently aware of the classroom context and dynamics (e.g., cooperative groups, class rules, routines, other students).

Even the most skillful consultant needs to apply her individual skills within the context of the classroom to be most effective. Although we hope that support service personnel will become increasingly aware of the importance of learning and understanding the classroom context and dynamics, this needs to be a primary concern of every teacher who hopes to receive meaningful support.

First, invite support personnel in to observe your classroom so that their recommendations can align with your classroom routines and expectations. Then generate a list that can be posted in your classroom or shared with team members regarding the types of contextual information you think are most critical for people to know. For example, a student approached a support service staff member to ask for the answer to a question on a class assignment. The support service provider thought she was being helpful when she answered the student's question. She didn't know that the teacher had established a protocol for students to first "look it up" and then "ask a classmate" before asking a teacher, who would then guide students to the information rather than simply telling them the answer. Although the support services provider's intentions were good, they were a mismatch in this context.

What information do you want support service personnel to be aware of in your classroom? Do you prefer that support staff jump right into activities with students or that they observe and join at a transition point that you designate? What class governance rules and routines should they be aware of? Do they know, for example, that every Friday afternoon you have a special science activity? When all team members have an understanding of your classroom, they can learn quickly how best to interact with you and the students in your class in ways that align with your established routines.

Participate in Scheduling Support Services

8

Teachers sometimes tell us that they feel they are at the mercy of the many support service providers' schedules. The result is that support service providers may show up in the classroom at inopportune times.

Sometimes the presence of support service personnel can become overwhelming or distracting when they arrive in groups, whether planned or unplanned. This potential disruption to the classroom can be avoided with collaborative team planning.

Although balancing the scheduling needs of many people is always a challenge, we suggest that teachers be proactive about: 1) the purpose of the support service provider's visit (e.g., to observe the student's participation in a large-group language arts activity and collaborate on problem-solving ideas for meaningful inclusion), 2) when it would be most helpful for support personnel to be in the classroom (e.g., particular times of day or days of the week), 3) when they want to sit down and meet with support service providers (e.g., during fourth period when the students are in physical education, during recess, or after school), 4) whether or not they want more than one support service person in the room at a time (e.g., overlapping support service personnel may or may not be beneficial or necessary), and 5) what actions and follow-up will take place as a result of the visit (e.g., development of an action plan or follow-up activities).

Of course, the solutions to these and other scheduling-related problems will undoubtedly be different across situations, requiring individualization and flexibility. Some classroom teachers prefer to have the student's special educator arrange and coordinate the visits of support service providers. Even if this is agreeable to the classroom teacher, all of the aforementioned points are still relevant to consider and act on. Being proactive about scheduling support services can ensure that services are used most efficiently and, we hope, that teachers will find the involvement of service providers increasingly helpful.

Have a Process for Effective Communication

9

The hallmark of collaborative teamwork is effective communication among team members. When team members interact with students and other team members on varying schedules, it is often a challenge to share accurate and adequate information with everyone in a timely way. Nothing can undermine your efforts, or the efforts of support personnel, quicker than misunderstandings that come from miscommunication or lack of communication.

Relationship experts all agree that communication is the key to most any interpersonal interactions. So, it is no surprise that a successful team has an established plan or process for effective communication.

When considering interpersonal communication skills and strategies for face-to-face interactions, we recommend team members establish norms, or agreed-upon standards, to guide communication. During formal meetings, norms can be reviewed and adjusted by the team as needed. They might include an effort to practice such skills as active listening, paraphrasing, using language or terms understood by all, and speaking one person at a time.

Norms for informal communication might address the expectation for confidentiality regarding the student and family. Positive working relationships can emerge from communication that is clear, complete, and cordial.

It is equally important to have a process or plan for how best to communicate when team members are not together. Support professionals often have differing schedules, and it is rare for the team to be all in the same place on a day-to-day basis. Decide with your team about best ways to share information about the student, about classroom activities, notes of progress or observations, and so on. Decide with your team if you will use e-mail, phone contacts, a logbook of notes, sub-group meeting minutes, or other strategies.

Keep in mind that all members of the team, including parents, should have equal access to information that affects their interactions with the student while maintaining confidentiality. Your team will work more effectively if you can establish a process to support communication that's clear, complete, accessible, and timely.

Evaluate the Effectiveness of Support Services

Because there are national shortages in many support services (e.g., speech-language pathology, physical therapy), parents and school personnel alike often feel fortunate to have a service available and listed on a student's IEP. We often, however, fail to evaluate whether the service is having the effects we originally intended. Sometimes it is unclear from the IEP just what the intended impact of support services is supposed to be. When this is unclear, support services can become parallel services rather than *related services* as defined by the Individuals with Disabilities Education Improvement Act of 2004 as "required to assist a student with disabilities to benefit from special education."

Related services must be both educationally relevant and necessary. This is different than asking, "Can a service help?" The answer to this question will almost always be "Yes." It is not the team's job to provide every conceivable service that might help, but rather to provide those services that are *necessary* for the student to receive an appropriately individualized education.

Once services are provided, we need to continually evaluate their impact. To adequately evaluate support services, we must know: 1) explicitly which parts of the educational program they are intended to support, and 2) the kinds of support approaches being used (e.g., making adaptations, training others, providing individual services, planning for collaboration).

To evaluate these aspects of support services, it is important to ask how the approaches of support personnel are related to the student's educational program and to what extent. Next, we need to ask whether support services have been effective in increasing the student's access to educational opportunities or have had a positive impact on student learning. For example, has the introduction of an augmentative device increased the student's opportunity to respond in morning group, or has the physical therapist's support to the physical education teacher facilitated the student's participation in the physical education class?

Finally, and most importantly, we must consider whether the student's life is better as a result of receiving support services. The team's responses to these and related evaluation questions will provide substantive information to assist with future decisions.

Selected References

Downing, J.E. (2002). Working cooperatively: The role of team members. In J.E. Downing (Ed.), *Including students with severe and multiple disabilities in typical classrooms: Practical strategies for teachers (2nd ed.).* (pp. 189–210). Baltimore: Paul H. Brookes Publishing Co.

Friend, M., & Cook, L. (2003) *Interactions: Collaboration skills for school professionals (4th ed.).* Boston: Allyn & Bacon.

Fleming, J.L., & Monda-Amaya, L.E. (2001). Process variables critical for team effectiveness: A delphi study of wrap around team members. *Remedial and Special Education, 22,* 158–171.

Giangreco, M.F. (2001). *Guidelines for making decisions about IEP services.* Montpelier, VT: Vermont Department of Education. Available at: http://www.uvm.edu/~cdci/iepservices/

Giangreco, M.F., Cloninger, C.J., & Iverson, V.S. (1998). *Choosing outcomes and accommodations for children: A guide to educational planning for students with disabilities (2nd ed.).* Baltimore: Paul H. Brookes Publishing Co.

Giangreco, M.F., Prelock, P.A., Reid, R.R., Dennis, R.E., & Edelman, S.W. (2000). Role of related service personnel in inclusive schools. In R.A. Villa & J.S. Thousand (Eds). *Restructuring for caring and effective education: Piecing the puzzle together (2nd ed.).* (pp. 360–388). Baltimore: Paul H. Brookes Publishing Co.

Giangreco, M.F. (2000). Related services research for students with low-incidence disabilities: Implications for speech-language pathologists in inclusive classrooms. *Language, Speech and Hearing Services in Schools, 31,* 230–239.

Hunt, P., Soto, G., Maier, J., & Doering, K. (2003). Collaborative teaming to support students at risk and students with severe disabilities in general education classrooms. *Exceptional Children, 69,* 315–332.

Mattson, B. (2001). *Related services (2nd ed.). NICHCY Digest.* Washington, DC. Available at: http://www.nichcy.org/pubs/newsdig/nd16txt.htm

Rainforth, B., & York-Barr, J. (1997). *Collaborative teams for students with severe disabilities: Integrating therapy and educational services (2nd ed.).* Baltimore: Paul H. Brookes Publishing Co.

Snell, M.E., & Janney, R. (2000). *Teachers' guide to inclusive practices: Collaborative teaming.* Baltimore: Paul H. Brookes Publishing Co.

Quick Guide #19

Creating Partnerships with Paraprofessionals

Mary Beth Doyle and Patricia A. Lee

Quick-Guides to Inclusion
Ideas for Educating Students with Disabilities, Second Edition

Michael F. Giangreco & Mary Beth Doyle

Editors

Dear Teacher,

    Sometimes when a student with disabilities is placed in your classroom, a paraprofessional is assigned to help you support that student as well as the rest of the students in the classroom. Most teachers are accustomed to working alone, so it can be quite a different experience sharing a classroom with another adult. One way to increase the likelihood of this being a good experience is to prepare in advance. Take the time to answer the following questions: In what ways can a paraprofessional assist me in meeting the needs of my students? Do I need a certain type of support for my students with disabilities? Is paraprofessional support the type of support that I need? What type of training or information do I need in order to use the paraprofessional's support in the most effective manner?

    The 10 guidelines included in this Quick-Guide are intended to enhance the partnership between classroom teachers and paraprofessionals, so that together you can meet the needs of students with all types of characteristics in the context of the general education classroom. Each guideline is followed by a brief explanation and example. A list of "Selected References" is included at the end if you are interested in more in-depth information. Enjoy this opportunity to get to know the paraprofessional who will be a member of your instructional team this school year.

Peace,
Mary Beth and Patty

GUIDELINES-AT-A-GLANCE

1. Welcome the Paraprofessional to Your Classroom

2. Establish the Paraprofessional as a Team Member

3. Clarify Roles and Responsibilities

4. Establish Shared Expectations

5. Ensure Guidance by Qualified Professionals

6. Facilitate Peer Interactions and Relationships

7. Establish Procedures for Unexpected Situations

8. Promote Student Responsibility

9. Establish Times and Ways to Communicate

10. Evaluate Effectiveness of Paraprofessional Supports

Welcome the Paraprofessional to Your Classroom

Think about how you would like to be welcomed to a new setting and do those simple, yet important, things for the paraprofessional. Prepare a place for her that reflects her adult status in the classroom (e.g., desk, mailbox, coffee cup). Avoid giving her a student-type desk or having her hang her coat on the hooks next to the students' hooks. Introduce her to others on the faculty and staff. Give her a tour around the school, highlighting those places where you and your students frequent, such as the faculty room, library, and art room. Demonstrate respect by asking the paraprofessional's opinion on classroom decisions (e.g., student arrangement, learning centers, student work displays).

Perhaps the most important thing you can do every day is to thank the paraprofessional for her effort and contributions. Tell her that you appreciate her ideas and support. Offer her very specific feedback related to teaching and learning. For example, if you have asked her to welcome the students as they enter the classroom, mention that you notice and appreciate that she makes eye contact with every student as she greets them with a friendly "hello" or that her pat on the shoulder was a kind gesture for a specific student who was having a difficult day. Providing feedback on specific behaviors increases the likelihood that the paraprofessional will continue to do them while building a professional atmosphere of respect and regard.

Through our experiences, we have learned that if these things do not occur, paraprofessionals may end up working in isolation within the classroom; often working exclusively with the student with disabilities. As a result, both the student and the paraprofessional become separated from the rest of the class even though they may share the same physical space of the general education classroom.

Plan very carefully how the paraprofessional is needed throughout the school day. Prepare a daily schedule for her that highlights her responsibilities. Vary those responsibilities to include material preparation, classroom support, and when appropriate, student support. Your preparation and guidance is an outward sign of respect and regard for the paraprofessional as a member of your classroom team. When paraprofessionals are welcomed, the foundation is laid for a productive partnership.

Establish the Paraprofessional as a Team Member

2

In most schools there are several types of teams (e.g., grade-level teams, subject area teams, student support teams). Each team consists of a variety of people (e.g., students, parents, paraprofessionals, teachers, related services personnel) and has different, though interrelated purposes. Start by identifying the teams on which the paraprofessional needs to be an active member. You can do this by asking questions such as, "What types of information might the paraprofessional contribute to this team?" "What will those contributions look and sound like during the meeting?" "Does the team need the paraprofessional's input at every meeting or based on specific agenda items?" Invite paraprofessionals accordingly, with a specific reason for their involvement in mind.

Once the paraprofessional is part of the team, there are several things that you can do to maximize the probability of substantive involvement. Prior to team meetings, make sure the paraprofessional knows the purpose of the meeting, has an agenda, and knows how to get items added to the agenda. Suggest ways to prepare for meetings in advance. As the meeting starts, explain to the other members that you and the paraprofessional work together to meet the needs of all of the students in the classroom. Invite the paraprofessional's opinions, observations, questions, and comments on relevant topics. Like other team members, the paraprofessional may have tasks to complete as a result of the meeting. Check to see that the tasks are in alignment with appropriate roles of a paraprofessional.

In situations where the importance of the paraprofessional is not established, there may be diminished motivation for the paraprofessional to contribute creative ideas, suggestions, and important feedback. The whole team suffers if they neglect this significant resource. As the teacher, demonstrate that the paraprofessional is a valued and respected team member; we hope others will follow suit.

It is also important to note that generally speaking, the classroom teacher and special educator should be working together with the paraprofessional on an ongoing basis. The teachers should be designing instruction and assigning tasks that align with individual roles (e.g., preparation of materials) on an ongoing basis. The paraprofessional can give the teachers ongoing input or feedback regarding those tasks, but are not responsible for generating them. This type of interaction is respectful of differential roles and increases the likelihood that the students are receiving the best specialized support possible.

Clarify Roles and Responsibilities

It is not uncommon for classroom teachers and paraprofessionals to experience initial confusion about roles and responsibilities—there are many ways to avoid this problem. Think about your own role as a classroom teacher and make a list of your responsibilities. Next, make a list of what you would like the paraprofessional to do during the day. Keep in mind that you are the teacher for all of the students, and that the role of the paraprofessional is to assist you. For example, you might ask the paraprofessional to assist with the implementation of instruction you planned, but you would not expect her to plan the instruction. You might ask that the paraprofessional set up learning centers, although you would select the activities and subject matter. You could ask her to welcome students, collect homework, collect notes from parents, and catalog them in your system. It is your responsibility to clarify what is and is not her responsibility based on your differing roles as teacher and assistant.

When there is a lack of clarity about the paraprofessional's roles and subsequent responsibilities, there can be a tendency to think of her as being exclusively responsible for the student with disabilities, or functioning as the primary teacher for the student with disabilities. Neither practice is appropriate. Paraprofessionals are not certified teachers and should not be expected to function as teachers. Rather, paraprofessionals are employed to assist qualified professionals in the delivery of educational services to students with and without disabilities. Be certain that you and the special educator take responsibility to co-plan instruction for your students with disabilities. Plan carefully how the paraprofessional can assist with the implementation of the instruction. Whenever you are uncertain about the responsibilities that have been assigned to the paraprofessional, apply the *would it be okay?* test. If, for example, the paraprofessional is providing the majority of the instruction to a student with disabilities, would it be okay for students without disabilities to receive the majority of their instruction from a paraprofessional? Or, would it be okay for the paraprofessional to maintain communication with the parents of students without disabilities? If not, then you need to reevaluate the role of the paraprofessional in the identified situations.

Finally, training and evaluation should be directly linked to the roles and responsibilities you have identified. Such an approach is respectful and supportive of your role as a classroom teacher, of the paraprofessional's role as an assistant, and ultimately of the roles of all of your students as learners.

4 | Establish Shared Expectations

As the classroom teacher, you have the "big picture" for your students' learning. You have plans for how you will implement the curriculum, instruction, and classroom management. It is important that the paraprofessional understands your expectations. Discuss with the paraprofessional what you hope students will accomplish in the various subjects. Invite the paraprofessional to contribute thoughts and ideas. Together, develop a set of shared expectations for student learning and classroom management.

Think about the way you manage your classroom. What level of activity are you comfortable with? How do you establish your classroom rules and expectations? What is your typical response to classroom conflicts? Share these thoughts and practices with the paraprofessional. Be explicit about which situations are you comfortable with having the paraprofessional use her own judgment to intervene with students, as opposed to situations that require checking in with you first—these situations may change as you work together more as a classroom team. Throughout the year, provide specific feedback to the paraprofessional regarding the implementation of your plans.

If the paraprofessional has been employed to assist primarily with one student, review the individualized educational program (IEP) and explain how student's IEP goals will be addressed within typical class activities with peers. Be explicit regarding how the teachers and paraprofessionals will work together to teach the student by demonstrating how to support the student. Demonstrations for the paraprofessional include providing very specific training regarding instructional and/or behavioral supports that are necessary to support students.

It is important that this training occur in the settings where the paraprofessional is supposed to use them. If, for example, a time delay procedure will be used during classroom instruction, then the special educator must be in the classroom modeling this procedure for the paraprofessional. After practice, the special educator would come back to observe and give feedback to the paraprofessional on the use of the same skill. When paraprofessionals are left on their own to figure out what students are learning and the teacher's preferred classroom management system, time may be wasted and team members may be working at cross purposes. In addition, students are more likely to get mixed messages that hamper educational progress. When expectations for student learning and classroom management are shared, there can be a sense of common purpose for adults and students, as well as clarity regarding what all of the students are learning and how the paraprofessional is expected to support that learning.

Ensure Guidance by Qualified Professionals

5

Always remember that, as the classroom teacher, *you* are the instructional leader for all of the students in your classroom. Even when a paraprofessional has been employed to assist one or more students with disabilities, it is your shared responsibility, with the special educator, to oversee the learning environment, including the activities of the paraprofessional.

Show the paraprofessional how to assist in specific instruction, as well as with the daily routine for all students. Remember, typically paraprofessionals are not certified teachers; that is why it is inappropriate for paraprofessionals to be given the responsibilities of designing and implementing instruction for students. While it is not unusual for these responsibilities fall to the paraprofessional by default, it is not advisable. Imagine for a moment that you are a parent of a child who experiences difficulty learning. Ask yourself, "Would it be okay for my child to be taught by a paraprofessional for the majority of his day, week, or year?" The same standard should be applied to each of the students in your classroom.

Too often paraprofessionals are left alone to figure out what they are supposed to do because teachers have not provided appropriate guidance. When activities are not designed and guided by certified staff, the paraprofessional's efforts can become fragmented and separate from the total learning environment. Classroom practice may be compromised, and school policies may be violated unintentionally because the paraprofessional is not part of the formal communication loops.

If you are trying to determine whether or not the paraprofessional is doing too much or taking on responsibilities that really belong to certified teachers, put yourself to the test. Take out a student's IEP, read the goals, and describe the student's current level of performance and level of engagement with each goal. If you do not know this information, it is likely that the paraprofessional has assumed the major instructional role on the team. You must respond by taking back your instructional responsibilities.

When certified staff design and guide the activities of paraprofessionals, all students receive a more coordinated and integrated education. Remember, you are the classroom teacher for all of your students, and the paraprofessional is there to assist you with this important work.

6

Facilitate Peer Interactions and Relationships

There is strong agreement that social relationships play important roles in all of our lives. Children begin socializing at a very young age, first within their own families, later with peers in childcare settings, and then in kindergarten. These early experiences offer a variety of opportunities for children to learn important skills, including how to: share, communicate, problem solve, self-advocate, and simply enjoy being with others. Adults have important roles to play in supporting the social development within the school context. In some situations, social facilitation is necessary. This is an area where paraprofessionals may benefit from specific training and feedback.

Often adults become barriers rather than facilitators. So while well intentioned, the outcomes do not necessarily match the original intent. Being a facilitator of social relationships requires that the paraprofessional is aware of natural opportunities that are available throughout the day for socialization (e.g., hallways, near the lockers, during small-group activities). Once opportunities have been identified, paraprofessionals can act as a *bridge* by identifying the point of similarity (e.g., lockers are near each other) and connecting students with each other.

Acting as a communication bridge is also important. When someone addresses the paraprofessional with a question or comment about the student with disabilities, it is advisable to redirect the person to speak directly with the student (e.g., "That's an interesting question; you should ask Paula"). This is important because direct communication is foundational to building friendships. Similarly, when parents ask the paraprofessional questions about curriculum and instruction, the parent should be redirected to the classroom teacher, because it affords the teacher the opportunity to be more engaged with the student with disabilities.

In addition, the classroom teacher or special educator might teach other students about the unique communication patterns, strengths, and needs in a manner that is status enhancing for the student with disabilities while increasing the likelihood of interactions occurring. Then the adults should step back and give students opportunities to engage with each other.

Finally, invite students into social spaces and step away. Give students the space and shared experiences that are required in order to build friendships without adults interrupting. Students have enormous capacity to be kind and generous with one another. In order to increase the likelihood of authentic friendships taking root, adults need to give students space.

Establish Procedures for Unexpected Situations

7

Schools are places of continual change. Schedules, absences, field trips, special events, visitors, assemblies, testing days, and a myriad of other irregularities make absolute consistency impossible. As a classroom teacher, you know the importance of flexibility and probably have strategies to deal with unexpected changes in daily routines. This may not be true for the paraprofessional. As you begin the school year, share with her a copy of the typical daily and weekly schedules. Be certain to provide her with the necessary training and support that she will need in order to facilitate many of the typical daily routines.

Discuss with the paraprofessional how you would like to handle unexpected changes in daily routines. Be as specific as possible. For example, what happens when the teacher, the paraprofessional, or other classroom personnel are absent? How do you proceed when visitors come to the room? How can the paraprofessional be helpful during these times? What are the paraprofessional's responsibilities when students are engaged in testing or field trips? Does the paraprofessional have responsibilities related to the implementation of teacher-developed instruction; if so, what does she do when instruction is not planned in advance? Develop a strategy (e.g., notes in your plan book, on her desk) where you can communicate changes as you become aware of them. Agree upon ways (e.g., time and places) for her to consult with you if she is uncertain about how to proceed.

When paraprofessionals are unaware of what to do in unanticipated situations, they are left in the position of having to guess. Though you cannot predict all of the situations that may occur, you can give guidance to the paraprofessional as to what things cause changes in the typical schedule and preferred ways of responding. This planning will give the paraprofessional a proactive way to contribute to the classroom.

8 Promote Student Responsibility

Students learn from taking risks; with that risk-taking, there are bound to be both successes and failures. It is crucial that students be allowed to experience both. You and the paraprofessional can create learning opportunities that are safe enough for those risks and supportive enough for real student growth to occur. Share your own stories with the paraprofessional about students you have assisted in becoming more independent and responsible for their own learning. Share examples of students who have learned from their mistakes. Invite the paraprofessional to do the same.

Convey that you are there to make the classroom a place where the students gain more independence and responsibility throughout the year. Stress the importance of monitoring how much assistance is given to students so they don't become unnecessarily dependent.

Encourage the paraprofessional to ask questions, like "What am I doing for the student that she can do for herself?" "What am I doing for the student that she could ask a peer for assistance instead?" "What does the student need to learn to do next to become more independent?" "When was the last time that the student was given the opportunity to make a mistake?" When the student does make a mistake, engage in a professional manner. Give support, provide feedback, and reteach if necessary. As a teacher, first diagnose the student's error and then explain to the paraprofessional why the student made the mistake. Communicate the relationship between the error, the student's misunderstanding, and problems with the teaching.

If you become concerned that the paraprofessional is spending too much time with the student with disabilities, ask yourself, "Am I spending enough time teaching this student myself?" "Are the special educator and I providing enough guidance and supervision to the paraprofessional?"

When student responsibility is not emphasized or clarified, it is easy for a paraprofessional to feel responsible for ensuring that the student with disabilities is experiencing success 100% of the time. The paraprofessional may rush to keep a student from making an error that actually would have resulted in new learning for the student. Be certain to provide the paraprofessional with feedback about this delicate balance between necessary and unhelpful supports. Emphasizing student responsibility and talking about how much to assist students are keys to success.

Establish Times and Ways to Communicate

9

In order to work effectively with paraprofessionals, it is important to communicate on an ongoing basis, using both formal and informal strategies. It has been our experience that frequently team members are so busy that communication is the first thing to be neglected. Ultimately this leads to more challenges as team members are uncertain about who is responsible to do what and when. In order to avoid the difficulties associated with poor communication, simply develop a system of communication that takes into account *what* you need to communicate about, as well as, *how* and *when* that will be done.

Generate a list of topics that you frequently need to communicate about (e.g., upcoming activities, daily lesson plans, development of student adaptations, preparation of instructional materials, contacts with parents). How do you currently communicate about these issues (e.g., verbal, written, not at all)? Is the strategy effective and efficient, or does it need modification?

As the classroom teacher, it is your responsibility to develop a simple strategy to ensure that communication takes place. You might develop a classroom calendar that highlights upcoming events, provide the paraprofessional with a daily schedule, provide access to your plan book, or write notes about student adaptations and place the notes in your plan book. Whatever strategy you decide to use, commit to using the strategy for several weeks and then reevaluate the effectiveness before deciding whether modifications are necessary.

Identify a time during the day or week when you can meet with the paraprofessional to touch base, plan, and discuss classroom and student-specific issues. It has been our experience that as few as 10 minutes a day can do wonders!

It is also important to be clear about who is responsible for communicating with the parents of students with and without disabilities, as well as ensuring confidentiality in all cases. Although the paraprofessional may play some role in communicating with families of students with disabilities, it is vital that you and the special educator offer at least the same type and extent of communication you typically offer to parents of your students who don't have disabilities, including educational progress, behavior concerns, celebration of accomplishments.

Evaluate Effectiveness of Paraprofessional Supports

10

Far too often, teachers evaluate a paraprofessional's performance at the end of the academic year without ever having provided any training or input during the year. Just as we do with students, evaluation should be linked to opportunities for instruction, practice, and feedback. Evaluating the effectiveness of paraprofessional supports is an important aspect of the instructional cycle.

The paraprofessional's roles and responsibilities are related to yours as the classroom teacher. Therefore, as you provide feedback to the paraprofessional, you will undoubtedly be evaluating yourself. By the very nature of the job, paraprofessionals must rely on you and other team members for direction, training, and feedback. Refer to the list of responsibilities that you generated by responding to the questions in Guideline #3. Use this list as the framework for providing the paraprofessional with specific feedback. For each role or responsibility, have the paraprofessional self-assess and identify areas in need of improvement. Compare the self-assessment with your own perspectives, and discuss whether additional modeling, training, or other supports are warranted. Use this as an opportunity to document the paraprofessional's strengths as well as areas in need of continues growth.

As you work with the paraprofessional to establish a professional development plan, ensure that you provide instruction that models the principles of effective teaching and learning. Specifically, identify a skill that needs to be taught. Teach the skill directly in the context where the paraprofessional will need to use it (e.g., the classroom). Provide opportunities for guided practice, then independent practice, and finally give direct feedback on the paraprofessional's use of the new skill. Implementing this type of training cycle will increase the paraprofessional's skills and strengthen the paraprofessional workforce in your school.

Without direct and substantive training and feedback, paraprofessionals do not receive the benefit of professional assistance in learning how to be effective assistants in the classroom. When paraprofessionals receive training and assistance and participate in their own evaluation process, it promotes a sense of well-being and effectiveness.

Selected References

Broer, S.M., Doyle, M.B., & Giangreco, M.F. (2005). Perspectives of students with intellectual disabilities about their experiences with paraprofessional support. *Exceptional Children, 71*, 415–430.

Causton-Theoharis, J.N., & Malmgren, K.W. (2005). Building bridges: Strategies to help paraprofessionals promote peer interactions. *Teaching Exceptional Children, 37*(6), 18–24.

Causton-Theoharis, J.N., & Malmgren, K.W. (2005). Increasing interactions between students with severe disabilities and their peers via paraprofessional training. *Exceptional Children, 71*, 431–444.

Devlin, P. (2005). Effect of continuous improvement training on student interaction and engagement. *Research and Practice for Persons with Severe Disabilities, 30*, 47–59.

Doyle, M.B. (2002). *The paraprofessional's guide to the inclusive classroom: Working as a team (2nd ed.).* Baltimore: Paul H. Brookes Publishing Co.

Etscheidt, S. (2005). Paraprofessional services for students with disabilities: A legal analysis of issues. *Research and Practice for Persons with Severe Disabilities, 30*, 60–80.

Giangreco, M.F., Broer, S.M., & Edelman, S.W. (2001). Teacher engagement with students with disabilities: Differences based on paraprofessional service delivery models. *Journal of the Association for Persons with Severe Handicaps, 26*, 75–86.

Giangreco, M.F., & Doyle, M.B. (2004). Directing paraprofessional work. In C. Kennedy & E. Horn (Eds.), *Including students with severe disabilities* (pp. 185–204). Needham Heights, MA: Allyn & Bacon.

Giangreco, M.F., Edelman, S.W., & Broer, S.M. (2003). Schoolwide planning to improve paraeducator supports. *Exceptional Children, 70*, 63–79.

Giangreco, M.F., Edelman, S.W., Broer, S.M., & Doyle, M.B. (2001). Paraprofessional support of students with disabilities: Literature from the past decade. *Exceptional Children, 68*, 45–63.

Quick-Guide #20

Administration
in Inclusive Schools

Richard Schattman, Ruth E. Dennis, and Donarae Cook

Quick-Guides to Inclusion
Ideas for Educating Students with Disabilities, Second Edition
Michael F. Giangreco & Mary Beth Doyle

Editors

Quick-Guides to Inclusion: Ideas for Educating Students with Disabilities (2nd ed.) © Michael F. Giangreco, 2007
Available through Paul H. Brookes Publishing Co., Baltimore, 1-800-638-3775

Dear School Leader,

Regardless of whether you have been providing education for students in inclusive settings for many years or whether this is a relatively new endeavor, you understand that schools are constantly changing. As you know, changes in federal policies and the increasing emphasis on higher standards for student performance present some challenges to both maintaining an inclusive model of education and further refining it. Closer to home, you are probably facing additional pressures arising from changes in state policies, the influence of special interest groups, financial constraints, and other community circumstances.

You realize that the changes needed to support inclusive education for all of your students have far-reaching implications for your whole school and community. The inclusion of students with the full range of special educational needs means so much more than merely the physical placement of these students within general education classrooms. Creating a quality inclusive school challenges us to take a comprehensive look at our core values and beliefs regarding diversity, the efficacy of our practices, and many aspects of our daily operation. You will need to re-examine many of the policies and practices that have been part of the traditional structure of your school to ensure that there is alignment between your school's inclusive mission and its actions.

This Quick-Guide is designed to support you as you consider ways to implement and advance an inclusive model of education for students with a wide range of characteristics. We realize that the incremental school reform you are undertaking never happens without some bumps in the road. Rest assured that many schools have traveled this bumpy road and emerged as better learning environments for all their students. We hope the ideas we share with you on the following pages lend support to your efforts as you create a school that cares for all of its community's children. While ultimate responsibility lies with a range of individuals, your leadership is critical for others to commit to the good work of inclusive education that lies ahead.

Good luck,
Richard, Ruth, and Donarae

GUIDELINES-AT-A-GLANCE

1. Develop a Shared Vision, Mission, and Beliefs

2. Create One Tent: A School for All Children

3. Share Leadership Responsibilities

4. Involve Parents

5. Start Early to Build an Inclusive Community

6. Create Increased Time to Collaborate

7. Link with Other Community Services

8. Create Inclusive Expectations for All Students

9. Use Performance Data to Enhance Education

10. Develop Your School as a Learning Organization

Develop a Shared Vision, Mission, and Beliefs

The vision, mission, and beliefs we have about educating students with disabilities are not separate or different from those we have about educating all students in our schools. Strategic planning is probably a process familiar to most of you in your role as an administrator. A strategic planning process can be useful as you integrate, implement, and assess your efforts to include all students. In fact, a sound strategic plan is a key factor differentiating schools that embrace inclusive education as an essential part of their approach from those that view it as a "program" or something that is done because others insist.

In order to be most effective, a strategic plan should reflect a broad consensus among constituents. Internal constituencies include teachers, support service staff, parents of attending children (both with and without disabilities), paraprofessionals, custodians, cafeteria workers, school board members, and administrators. External constituencies include extended family members, business leaders, civic leaders, and other interested community members.

Strategic plans begin with a shared vision. *Community Conversations* are a grassroots strategy for building a vision. These conversations address broad questions such as, "What is good for our children?" and "What is good for our community?" By facilitating conversations in the school and community, administrators are in a position to encourage constituents to contribute their perspectives. When many voices are heard, it is more likely that the emergent vision will address the needs of all students.

Mission and belief statements grow out of the community's vision. The mission reflects a realistic assessment of what influence and impact the school can have in promoting the community's vision. The mission clarifies the school's role in supporting the shared vision. Belief statements reflect what is important to your school community and serve as guiding principles that all can use as you make plans and assess your efforts.

As an administrator, you play a key role in assuring that a shared vision, mission, and beliefs are validated, discussed, and reflected in the policies and day-to-day practices of your school. They will guide your efforts to educate all students and build an inclusive school community.

Create One Tent:
A School for All Children

Although inclusive education has been discussed extensively for the past 25 years, quality examples are still not the norm in American public schools. Segregated practices persist, in part because many schools continue to operate a dual system of special and general education with organizational models and funding formulas that maintain their separation.

In contrast, One Tent implies that the community public school is for *all* students. While the concept of inclusion sounds benign, it is not. It is a notion that requires us to examine our personal beliefs about the meaning of education in a democratic society, our belief in the worth of the individual, and our practical operation of public schools.

Under One Tent, all students are provided access to the resources they need. All are accountable to the standards that have been adopted by the federal, state, and local schools, all are assessed according to common standards, and all are expected to live within the values and guidelines that have been established for student conduct. Students with special education needs receive accommodations and adaptations to the general education curriculum, structure, and activities as needed. High expectations for achievement and social development should not be confused with rigid standardization; One Tent does *not* mean, "one size fits all."

Under One Tent, special education and general education staff work collaboratively. A special education teacher might team teach with general educators to instruct students with and without disabilities. Special education staff work closely with general educators and interact with students both with and without disabilities. If you are a special education administrator, you will need to be knowledgeable about the school's culture and processes, and partner with the principal to support staff. Central office personnel have a role in providing technical assistance, seeking additional resources and funding, and coordinating services. If you are a school principal, you have the same responsibilities for both special and general education staff, including support of staff development and performance evaluations.

One Tent is a notion that is easy to agree with and somewhat more difficult to implement. Despite these changes, One Tent is an essential concept if inclusive education is to become a genuine practice.

3 Share Leadership Responsibilities

In inclusive schools, decisions that were once relegated to a few special educators are now a shared responsibility with parents, general educators, and principals. The diverse and complex needs of all students can only be addressed when leadership is distributed and shared among those who have a stake in the lives and educational outcomes of all students, and when team members learn and use effective collaborative team processes. As an administrator, you have a role in promoting and supporting shared leadership on at least three levels of teamwork.

First, at the individual student team level, the role of each of the team members is negotiated with other members, including parents. Administrators may support the work of the team by providing information, solving logistical problems, interpreting regulations and policies, or helping to coordinate plans with other school personnel.

Second, administrators play a role in formulating and supporting school-wide efforts such as task-force teams for specific school initiatives. These teams may address topics such as literacy, standards, curriculum, assessment, or technology. These task force teams articulate goals, formulate plans of action, identify needed resources, and make decisions that will influence the implementation of new practices that affect all children.

Finally, the administrator has a role as a member of a central administrative team, or design team. This team includes representatives all of the various contingency groups and is primarily charged with assuring that all of the activities of the school district align with its overall vision and mission. Through the work of this design team, administrators can be assured that initiatives that will shape the future are coordinated and reflective of fundamental values and beliefs.

Shared leadership requires that the roles of administrators evolve from director to encourager of leadership in others at the student team, school, and district levels. As others assume important leadership roles on these various levels, you are in a unique position to share information and resources that they may need and to help them assess their efforts on behalf of all students. Sharing leadership is different from delegating responsibility or authority; it involves nurturing and building capacity of individuals who are invested in ensuring positive outcomes for all students.

4

Involve Parents

nvolving parents is an essential practice in an inclusive school. The nature of that involvement varies depending on the extent to which families perceive that they are valued members of the school community.

To extend parental involvement to those who have previously been less involved requires expanding traditional parent involvement opportunities in ways that are flexible and sensitive to family needs. Administrators should communicate to parents that they are needed, wanted, and welcomed. Administrators must also ensure that the culture of the school, including staff and family interactions, are supportive of many types of parent involvement.

Parents know their own children best, have the greatest vested interest in their success, and bring valuable knowledge to their child's team. Since each family is unique, part of the school's responsibility is to provide them with the support they need to articulate their concerns and priorities for their child. As administrators, you might also become familiar with parent support networks and agencies in your area and develop a sound relationship with them. They can provide information and assistance to families who want to understand and participate more fully in their child's program. Just having parents at the table for meetings is not enough.

Families must also have a role in defining the school's overall vision and mission. All parents should be welcomed to contribute their perspectives and to learn from the views of others. Families who are involved at this level serve an important role as ambassadors of the school. Family members can often have more influence on community decisions than school personnel, and they can be valuable allies in your efforts toward inclusion.

As you and your school community chart the waters of change and innovation in programs and services, parents must participate if those changes are to become firmly established. Many parents have the time, interest, experience, and ability to contribute to major school initiatives. Their involvement brings new information and a broader range of perspectives, provides an opportunity for parents to work with the school on a proactive level, introduces parents to the school organization and teamwork processes, and encourages investment in initiatives that affect not only their child but all children.

Start Early to Build an Inclusive Community

5

An inclusive school system has a vested interest in ensuring high-quality early childhood programs so that children enter school with foundations to support early learning. To build an inclusive community, administrators must also ensure that their school system develops and implements educational programs that are ready to serve young children with a range of characteristics. Programs should be designed to include all families and ensure that the parents of young children are interested, knowledgeable, and involved in their child's education.

High-quality early childhood programs are critically important to schools and communities for several reasons. First, they are able to address and minimize developmental needs at a time when they first become evident. The early childhood curriculum is adaptable and can address a range of important social and preacademic skills. The challenge of including children in later school years is diminished when their needs are identified and addressed early.

Second, early intervention and preschool special education services attend to the skills required of teachers for the child's success in future environments, such as kindergarten. Transition activities for children and staff are important when planning to include children in the mainstream. Finally, inclusive early childhood programs have the opportunity to support families in advocating for their children's integrated educational program in positive and productive ways. Parents are prepared for transitions to school-age programs and feel more confident in their important role on their child's educational team.

Both schools and early childhood programs can be enhanced when there are deliberate efforts to locate early childhood services in physical proximity to, preferably within, the school itself. Proximity affords parents opportunities to meet and become familiar with other parents and with future teachers, for early childhood and school staff to share knowledge and other resources, for parents and children to explore future environments and routines (e.g., library, lunch in the cafeteria), and for children to become comfortable in their school before they enter kindergarten.

Starting early reflects a proactive culture within a school, and values planning, preparation, and forethought. These elements will enhance quality and care for young children and provide the foundation for building an inclusive school community.

6   Create Increased Time to Collaborate

Administrators have a responsibility to ensure that personnel have the resources they need to do their jobs effectively. One of the most critical resources in an inclusive school is time needed for teachers, parents, related service providers, paraprofessionals, and administrators to collaborate. We use the term *create* because we realize that finding time often seems as if you are asked to make something out of nothing.

In fact, there are a number of systemic changes that may be required if you are to create time for collaboration. The implementation of block scheduling, scheduling of common planning times, and the utilization of a variety of new class arrangements should be considered.

Classroom arrangements such as loops, multi-age, and multi-grade classes can provide class placement options that maximize the efficiency of collaboration by reducing the amount of annual team membership turnover. Teacher participation in the development of the school's master schedule is important to assure that they have the time needed to plan for all of the children. Team meeting time can be kept to a minimum by holding sub-team meetings, thus ensuring that only essential team members are involved to address specific issues.

Once time for planning becomes a part of the normal school day, teachers need to hone their meeting skills. As an administrator, you can ensure needed staff development focused on effective meetings strategies. Each meeting should be guided by an agenda that includes items important to each of the team members, including parents. Starting and stopping times should be adhered to, and a specific amount of time should be targeted for each agenda item. Accurate minutes ensure timely communication with members who may not be present. Effective meeting skills are often best taught through example and participation in a well facilitated meeting, with some time devoted to discussing the process itself.

As team members become more familiar with meeting processes, they can begin to share and assume roles. As team members acquire more collaborative skills, they often come to value the opportunity to work more closely with each other. Collaborative teamwork, supported by creative and efficient approaches to time utilization, is an essential aspect of an inclusive school climate.

7 Link with Other Community Services

It is essential that inclusive schools coordinate efforts with families and with other community organizations to address the needs of children. We know that many social and economic factors have a significant impact on the kind of supports parents need in order to care for their children. Schools are often expected to provide psychological nurturance, after-school programs, health and safety information, and moral guidance for children with and without disabilities. At the same time, schools are increasingly asked to account for student progress toward national and state academic standards.

Schools cannot operate in isolation if they are to address the range of needs of children and families. As a result, they must enter into collaborative partnerships. A variety of sources can provide informal and natural supports for families, such as places of worship, extended family, childcare providers, and big brother/sister programs. School personnel should be familiar with the resources available, so that they can provide information to families who may be interested.

Other more formal relationships can be forged with health and social service agencies, and often require administrative support or policy initiatives to ensure coordinated efforts on behalf of children. For example, agreements with agencies might involve a "coordinated service plan" for an individual student. This written agreement defines why a plan is needed, the desired outcomes, who is responsible for what, and timelines for specific activities. The center of any service plan is the family, with a focus on their goals and their dreams for their child's future.

Contracted services also provide a mechanism for schools and community groups to link. For example, the school may contract with its community mental health agency for intensive home-based services or with the health department for immunization clinics at school. Schools might also link with community agencies to provide training open to families, service providers, and school personnel, so that the community shares its resources. When schools form stronger links with other community services, school personnel, families, and community groups move away from a scarcity mind set and see a broader range of resources available for the support of their children.

Create Inclusive Expectations for All Students

8

In an inclusive school, every event and activity should reflect the assumption that all students belong and should have opportunities to participate. Opportunities for participation of students with disabilities should be consistent with opportunities available to peers without disabilities. Participation has been identified as a key factor affecting the long-term quality of life for persons with disabilities and should be a focus of our planning in schools. Participation should be evident in the core activities of a classroom, in co-curricular activities, extended activities in the community, and in special school events. For some students, participation may require individualized supports or adaptations.

Administrators devote much of their attention to supporting student instruction in the classroom. In order to address ways of making education meaningful for all students, we must extend our thinking to the co-curricular and extracurricular areas that account for much of the enrichment and extension of classroom learning. Rather than assume that assigning a paraprofessional to a student will satisfy a student's support needs, an administrator must look toward increasing the capacity of classroom teachers, coaches, club leaders, and peers as natural supports.

Behavior expectations for participation should also be addressed. Schools that have thoughtful, supportive, and clear expectations for student behavior should apply those standards fairly to all students while accounting for individual differences. Students who have challenging behaviors should be provided with appropriate supports so that they do not disrupt the learning of their classmates—this applies whether the student has a disability or not. Obviously, care must be taken to support students and teach, rather than punish and exclude, students who exhibit challenging behaviors.

As an administrator, you can help identify and provide resources for school personnel, including classroom management strategies, peer supports, cooperative groupings, or development of crisis intervention plans of action. Administrators play an important role in clarifying student expectations and providing resources to support the participation of all students in all school activities.

9 Use Performance Data to Enhance Education

Historically, schools have been asked to provide student performance data based on standardized tests. Some people view this as a reason to exclude students with disabilities, for fear they will lower score averages. As directed by both the Individuals with Disabilities Education Improvement Act of 2004 and No Child Left Behind, states have now instituted strict rules regarding the inclusion of children with special needs in statewide assessments.

Only when we are willing to have our assessments reflect the performance of *all* students will public education gain a comprehensive portrait of the strengths and needs of schools. Inclusive schools supplement standardized and standards-based performance assessments by using authentic assessment such as academic portfolios, reading inventories, and life skills portfolios. These assessments should be ongoing and diagnostic, providing teachers with day-to-day information about how their students are learning.

To collect performance data for all students, some accommodations in assessment strategies may be needed. These accommodations may make it more difficult to use data in the traditional ways, such as quantitative comparisons among schools. Instead, data that reflect accommodations for students with special needs can be used to describe changes within a school over time.

Administrators should use assessment data to improve educational practices. Results of assessments that include all students can encourage teachers to consider how they can best teach all children in their classrooms, and can be used to help teachers identify professional development goals. The inclusion of students with disabilities as part of comprehensive student assessment can also stimulate a broad range of general and special education initiatives that will benefit the entire school.

In an inclusive school, administrators are responsible for evaluating the performance of staff as well as students. The teacher evaluation process is an opportunity for classroom teachers to gain insights and support for their efforts to address diverse student needs in the classroom. The process for staff evaluation can be applied to other professional staff as well, including special educators and related service providers. Principals model their commitment to a truly inclusive system when they take responsibility for including all students in performance assessments and for utilizing staff evaluation processes that address their efforts toward a common goal.

Develop Your School as a Learning Organization

As an administrator, you realize that professionals must have a supportive network from which to derive motivation and energy in order to feel successful. In inclusive schools, the professional community is enlarged as a learning organization that includes school and community professionals across disciplines and their community of consumers. From this community, new ideas and approaches emerge. The learning organization assumes responsibility for planning professional development, and members often look to each other for new information or mentoring. In schools that are learning organizations, we see a number of important qualities.

First, they welcome critical review and input from a range of stakeholder groups, including teachers, administrators, parents, support staff, and other community members.

Second, they demonstrate a commitment to teamwork based on trust and a willingness to work interdependently with others toward shared goals. This willingness to embrace a team approach reduces professional isolation often experienced by those operating in more traditional professional arenas.

Third, they examine problems and seek support for solutions in creative ways. They are willing to take risks and implement innovative practices, knowing that they can learn from their mistakes as well as their successes. Fourth, they reflect on both the content and the process of their work together as a means of developing standards of professional practice that are more inclusive, more community based, and which improve morale among staff.

Finally, learning organizations attend to their need for renewal and celebration. Renewal occurs through participation in staff development as well as participation in activities of recognition. Staff meetings might be punctuated by ceremonies of recognition for a job well done or a shared victory. While teamwork is stressed, individual achievement is also recognized and celebrated.

It is essential for an inclusive school to value itself as a learning organization, with ongoing need for input and support at many levels. As an administrator, you too will need this input, support, and renewal to do the important work of building a dynamic and inclusive school community.

Selected References

Bateman, D., & Bateman, C.F. (2002). *What does a principal need to know about inclusion? Eric EC Digest #E635.* Arlington VA: ERIC Clearing House on Disabilities and Gifted Education. Retrieved July 20, 2006, from http://ericec.org/digests/e635.html

Giangreco, M.F. (2002). Foreword: Values, logical practices, and research: The three musketeers of effective education. In J.E. Downing (2002) *Including students with severe and multiple disabilities in typical classrooms: Practical strategies for teachers (2nd ed.).* (pp. ix–xiii). Baltimore: Paul H. Brookes Publishing Co.

ERIC/OSEP Special Project. (2002). *To light a beacon: What administrators can do to make schools successful for all students. ERIC/OSEP Topical Brief ED46607.* Arlington VA: ERIC Clearing House of Disabilities and Gifted Education. Retrieved on July 20, 2006, from http://ericec.org/osep/topical/Beacons.pdf

Hunt, P., Soto, G., Maier, J., & Doering, K. (2003). Collaborative teaming to support students at risk and students with severe disabilities in general education classrooms. *Exceptional Children, 69,* 315–332.

Moore, C., Gilbreath, D., & Maiuri, F. (1998). *Educating students with disabilities in general education classrooms: A summary of the research.* Eugene OR: Western Regional Resource Center, University of Oregon. Retrieved July 20, 2006, from http://eric.ed.gov/ERICDocs/data/ericdocs2/content_storage_01/0000000b/80/25/71/e3.pdf

Quenemoen, R., Thurlow, M., Moen, R., Thompson, S., & Morse, A.B. (2003). *Progress monitoring in an inclusive standards-based assessment and accountability system (Synthesis Report 53).* Minneapolis, MN: University of Minnesota, National Center on Educational Outcomes. Retrieved on July 20, 2006, from http://education.umn.edu/NCEO/OnlinePubs/Synthesis53.html

Sailor, W., & Roger, B. (2005). Rethinking inclusion: Schoolwide applications. *Phi Delta Kappan, 86,* 503–509.

Villa, R.A., & Thousand, J.S. (Eds.) (2005). *Creating an inclusive school (2nd ed.).* Alexandria, VA: Association for Supervision and Curriculum Development.

Quick-Guide Extras

HARVEY FOLLOWS THE COACH ON THE
PATH TOWARD INCLUSIONVILLE.

Assisting Students Who Use Wheelchairs

Guidelines for School Personnel

Michael F. Giangreco, Irene McEwen, Timothy Fox, and Deborah Lisi-Baker

Quick-Guides to Inclusion
Ideas for Educating Students with Disabilities, Second Edition

Michael F. Giangreco & Mary Beth Doyle

Editors

Quick-Guides to Inclusion: Ideas for Educating Students with Disabilities (2nd ed.) © Michael F. Giangreco, 2007
Available through Paul H. Brookes Publishing Co., Baltimore, 1-800-638-3775

Some students who use wheelchairs are quite capable of getting around with their own manual or power chair. Even when students are very good at using their wheelchairs, they will occasionally find themselves in situations where they need assistance. Other students may need more help, such as transferring in and out of their wheelchairs or moving from place to place. If you see a student struggling to overcome a barrier, such as trying to open a heavy door to enter a room, don't automatically assume that the student needs or wants your help. Your best bet is to do the same thing you would do if you saw any student you thought could use some help. First, ask if the student wants your assistance. If the answer is "Yes" then you can ask, "What kind of help would you like?" Most students who need this kind of occasional assistance can effectively communicate what they need and exactly what would be helpful.

Students who have limited language skills, lack a formal language system, or rely primarily on nonsymbolic forms of communication (e.g., facial expressions, vocalizations, pointing) may have difficulty communicating, especially with people who don't know them well. In these cases, if you really want to help, you have to be willing to look and listen. Students who have been in their wheelchairs for too long without a break, for example, may make certain sounds or move in ways that suggest they are uncomfortable. You have to interpret those nonsymbolic communications the best you can. You might guess the message is "I want to get out of this chair!" If the student smiles or gives a sigh with relief after getting out of the chair, you can feel reasonably sure you interpreted the communication correctly. Over time, and with information provided by people who know the student well, you can become increasingly skillful in interpreting a student's nonsymbolic communication. You can also create language boards or use computer programs to make it easier for a student to communicate wants and needs.

TRANSFERRING TO AND FROM A WHEELCHAIR

The following sections offer suggestions for assisting students with transferring to and from a wheelchair and with wheelchair mobility. Students who use wheelchairs rarely sit in them all day long. Students need to transfer to and from a toilet, the floor, other equipment, or furniture. These position changes are important to prevent fatigue, discomfort, skin breakdown, and muscle tightness, which can occur when students sit in one position for too long.

Changes in position are not only necessary for physical or health reasons. Changing positions can also be important to allow students with disabilities to participate in classroom activities. If the class moves from an activity where everyone is seated at desks to one where they are on the floor, for example, the student who uses a wheelchair should be supported to join classmates on the floor. The student may need a little or a lot of support to be comfortable and stable while he is out of his wheelchair. Supports can be as sophisticated as a specialized floor sitting device or as simple as a wall to lean against, a pillow, or a friend to sit next to. As a general rule, the supports provided should meet the student's need, but in a manner that allows the student to participate in the activity and fit into the group. In other words, use the most typical support that works before using something unnecessarily specialized.

A student's physical therapist or occupational therapist can recommend general guidelines for how often a student should change positions. Of course, therapists are not around all of the time, so it is most important to listen to the student and encourage the student to communicate needs for position changes. In general, however, if a student is comfortable, avoid removing a student from a well-fitted wheelchair for positioning in specialized equipment that provides less adequate support and limits opportunities for participation in school activities.

To help a student move to and from a wheelchair, you must learn how to make those transfers safely and comfortably for the student and for yourself. Before attempting to transfer a student, be sure to consult someone who knows the student well to learn how to help him or her. You might be able to check with the student, parent, teacher, physical therapist, or occupational therapist.

Most students can assist with one or more steps involved in a wheelchair transfer. Always expect students to assist as much as possible with every step of a transfer. Be sure to give students enough time to do what they are capable of doing. Specific steps in the transfer will vary depending on where the student is transferring. An assisted transfer to the floor, for example, will be different than a transfer to a couch.

Young children, because of their size, tend to be easier to transfer. Because young children are easier to lift, the tendency is to do too much for the student. If young students are not allowed to learn and practice the skills they need to use in transferring, as they grow older and heavier the task of transferring becomes more difficult. Every opportunity to practice transferring is an important opportunity for learning. With each transfer the student can be practicing the communication, social, and movement skills involved. Learning to transfer independently, or with as little assistance as possible, can allow students more independence in their daily lives and can open opportunities that may otherwise be limited.

Because of the inherent risks in transferring students to and from their wheelchairs, both to the student with a disability and the persons providing assistance, it is always advisable to err on the side of caution. For example, trying to transfer a student by yourself, when a two-person transfer makes more sense, can result in either the student or you being injured. A physical therapist can show you how to help a student transfer safely and minimize the risk of injury to the student and your own back.

TRANSFERRING FROM A WHEELCHAIR

The following steps offer a general sequence for transferring from a wheelchair. The specific steps can vary greatly from student to student, and the order may vary slightly.

1. Let the student know that it is time to transfer.

2. Always minimize the distance between transfer points. If the student is able, ask the student to move the wheelchair to the proper position for the transfer. If not, inform the student of your intention and move the chair into position yourself.

3. Once in position, have the student lock the brakes on the wheelchair. If necessary, lock the brakes yourself.

4. Remove equipment and supports that may get in the way. For example:

   - Remove the lap tray and any switches or other devices.

   - Loosen the foot straps and move the footrests to the side.

   - Remove the block (e.g., abductor block) from between the knees.

   - Remove any chest, shoulder, or head straps.

   - Remove or adjust one side support (e.g., arm rest) in some cases.

5. Ask the student to lean forward.

6. Unfasten the seat belt.

7. While still leaning forward from the trunk and hips, ask the student to slide forward in the chair and put his feet on the floor.

8. Ask the student to stand up—this may require your assistance. Most students, regardless of the severity of the disability, can bear some weight, particularly if the student has been expected to bear weight since a young age. The ability to support at least partial weight during standing is extremely important, and students need to practice whenever they transfer. Except in emergencies (which are rare), never lift a student who can support any of his own weight. For your own health and safety while assisting the student, be sure to maintain good body alignment (i.e., straight back, bending from the knees).

9. Assist the student to move to the other surface, as you have been shown, by a knowledgeable person (e.g., therapist, parent). Make sure the student is comfortably and safely positioned before moving away.

10. Release the brakes on the wheelchair and move it to an appropriate location until it is needed again.

TRANSFERRING TO A WHEELCHAIR

The following steps offer a general sequence for transferring *to* a wheelchair. The specific steps can vary greatly from student to student, and the order may vary slightly.

1. Let the student know that it is time to transfer.

2. Always minimize the distance between transfer points.

3. Make sure the brakes of the wheelchair are locked.

4. Make sure the wheelchair is free of any supportive equipment that might get in the way of a successful transfer (e.g., foot rests, blocks and straps, seat belt).

5. Assist the student in assuming a standing position next to the wheelchair, as you have been shown by a knowledgeable person (e.g., therapist, parent). Maintain proper body positions to minimize your own risk of back injury.

6. Assist the student to stand and then turn and sit on the edge of the seat.

7. Ask the student to lean forward and scoot as far back into the chair as possible. Many students need help to do this.

8. While the student is still leaning forward, make sure the student is all the way back in the chair and is centered (not closer to one side of the chair than the other); this is extremely important. If the student is not centered and all the way back in the wheelchair, the student's posture will be poor. This will lead to discomfort and fatigue, and may limit head control and hand use.

9. While the student is still leaning forward, *fasten the seat belt*. Just like in a car or airplane, the belt should be secured snug and low across the lap to keep the student positioned properly. This is especially important for students who have difficulty repositioning themselves in their wheelchairs. Students who are able to reposition themselves will make their own adjustments to the seat belt's tension.

10. Attach or fasten equipment and adjust the student's positioning supports. For example:

    • Adjust the footrests and position the student's feet.

    • Place and secure any blocks or supports (e.g., abductor block).

    • Attach and secure any chest, shoulder, and head supports.

    • Attach the lap tray and any switches or other devices.

11. Ask the student to release the brakes, and you are ready to go.

WHEELCHAIR MOBILITY

Many students can move their wheelchairs most of the time but may need help in some situations. Others need help most of the time, and some students need help all of the time. No matter how much help a student needs, always make sure students who are using their wheelchairs are wearing their seat belts and any other supports they might need to be comfortable and safe. Try to keep the following guidelines and ideas in mind.

Pushing a student's wheelchair without permission is like rudely shoving a student who can walk. Always ask permission to move students who can move their own wheelchairs. If you see a student you think needs assistance, you might ask, "Can I help you back up?" If a student can't move her own wheelchair, let her know that you are going to move her: "It's time to go to lunch now; are you ready?" Pause to allow the student a moment to get ready to go. Then, before moving her wheelchair, let her know your intentions by saying something like, "Here we go!"

Turning off a student's power wheelchair to prevent the student from moving about is inappropriate. It is like tying a student who walks in a stationary chair. If the student is being mobile in a way that is perceived as problematic, address the behavior as you would a similar situation with a student who can walk. Consider the intention of the student's behavior. Is the student trying to tell you the lesson is boring, he wants to escape the situation, or he is more interested in something else across the room? Once you figure this out, do something constructive to address the behavior.

Remember that a manual wheelchair is a mobility device—it is not an exercise device. If propelling a wheelchair is difficult for a student, don't ask the student to push the wheelchair simply for exercise or because you think it will be character building. Students who use wheelchairs should be able to get around as easily as their classmates who walk and run. A power wheelchair may be necessary. If a student with a manual wheelchair needs help to keep up with friends, try to teach a responsible friend to help, rather than having an adult help all the time. Clear this approach with the student and family, and make sure the student helper is oriented to safe and respectful ways to offer assistance to people who use wheelchairs.

Talk with students when you push their wheelchairs, just as you would if you were walking with a student who does not use a wheelchair. In some situations, where the space is wide, flat, and smooth enough (e.g., wide hallways), you can actually push a student's wheelchair while walking beside it, rather than from behind the chair. This is not possible in all situations. It is most likely to be an option when the person providing assistance is quite a bit larger than the person in the wheelchair, thus allowing the person to adequately control the wheelchair with one hand. Use your judgment, and only walk beside while pushing a student's wheelchair in situations where it normally is courteous to walk side by side. This would not be a good idea when the halls are crowded between classes at a high school, for example, but would be appropriate if the student using a wheelchair and a peer were running an errand while the halls are empty.

OTHER WHEELCHAIR MOBILITY TIPS

1. Push students in wheelchairs forward up ramps. Go down steep or long ramps backward, particularly if the student is not able to lean back. Imagine what might happen if you lost your grip on a student's wheelchair and he were headed down a long ramp, unable to stop himself—it's not a pleasant thought!

2. To help a student go **up a curb** (if no curb cut exists), first move the student in the wheelchair forward until the front (small) wheels are near the curb. Let the student know you plan to tip the chair back slightly to get up the curb. Then tip the wheelchair onto its back wheels by pushing down on the push handles while stepping down on one of the tip bars (near the ground, inside the wheels) with your foot. Push the chair forward and put the front wheels on the sidewalk (some students can push on the hand rims or power their chair to help). When the back wheels almost reach the curb, lift the chair by the push handles and roll the back wheels up onto the sidewalk (some students also can help during this step).

3. To help a student go **down a curb** (if no curb cut exists), first move the student in the wheelchair backward until the back wheels (the large ones) are near the edge of the curb. Let the student know you plan to tip the chair back slightly to get down the curb. Then move the wheelchair back by holding onto the push handles and supporting the wheelchair while rolling the back wheels down the curb (some students can help by holding the had rim to slow the descent). Roll the wheelchair back until the front wheels are near the edge of the curb. Still holding onto the push handles, slowly roll the front wheels down the curb. Turn around and you are on your way.

4. When curbs, stairs, or other barriers exist, consider joining together with people who have disabilities to advocate for changes (e.g., curb cuts, ramps, elevators) that allow universal access. Although you may have been prompted to think about these barriers because of a student you know who uses a wheelchair, these types of changes can allow better or easier access for many other people (e.g., a parent with an infant in a stroller, a delivery person with a heavy load, a person who is temporarily on crutches, or an elderly person who has difficulty with stairs).

5. Be aware that some students, particularly those with difficulty controlling their trunk and head, may need extra supports (e.g., head strap) when being moved over uneven surfaces, such as when participating in field sports during recess or physical education class.

6. When assisting students in their wheelchairs on the playground or ball fields, it is often advisable to tip the wheelchair slightly onto the large rear wheels. As in all cases, always let the student know what you plan to do before doing it. When running the bases in a softball game or running on a field while playing "Ultimate Frisbee," for example, the small wheels of a wheelchair often get caught in the ruts and uneven surfaces. This can cause the wheelchair to tip forward unexpectedly. This is a prime situation where having the seat belt fastened is critical—without it the student can easily be thrown from the wheelchair. So let the student experience the faster than normal speed of running the bases and playing in the field by tipping the chair on its rear wheels and maintaining a safe speed.

Make sure every member of the school team, including the student and the student's parents, is aware of these general guidelines. More importantly, make sure those providing assistance understand the individual needs and preferences of the student. It is helpful to document a student's mobility needs and preferences in writing or with photos to orient school personnel, classmates, and friends in the safe and respectful ways to offer assistance.

Quick-Guide Extra #2

Community-Based Instruction

John McDonnell and Jayne McGuire

Quick-Guides to Inclusion
Ideas for Educating Students with Disabilities, Second Edition

Michael F. Giangreco & Mary Beth Doyle

Editors

One of the most important things that schools do is to provide students the education, training, and experiences necessary to allow them to achieve their goals after graduation. The knowledge and skills that students learn in school go a long way toward helping them to be successful, but research suggests that many will struggle using what they learn in school in real-life situations and settings. Community-based instruction (CBI) is one strategy that teachers can use to link the school's curriculum to the actual demands of living and working in the community.

CBI is important because it gives students opportunities to practice the skills they learn in school in the environments where they are needed. Think about it; would you teach someone to play basketball just by doing dribbling and shooting drills? Of course, these skills are critical to playing the game well, but learning how to be a good basketball player requires that you get a chance play the game and get good coaching while you are doing it! CBI is based on the same logic. This Quick-Guide Extra will help you understand the *whys* and *hows* of CBI, so you can help your students get the most out of their education.

WHAT IS COMMUNITY-BASED INSTRUCTION?

CBI is more than simply providing "community experiences" to a student. It is systematic instruction that is intended to help students achieve the postschool outcomes and the specific goals and objectives described in their individualized education program (IEP). For example, CBI can be used to encourage a student's application and generalization of the knowledge and skills they learn in school in the community settings they use every day. If a student is enrolled in a general education keyboarding class, CBI might be used to promote the generalization of the computer skills learned in the class to a community-based job. Similarly, if a student is enrolled in a health and nutrition class, CBI could be used to help students apply the knowledge they gain in the class to making appropriate food choices at a restaurant during lunch with friends. Finally, CBI could be used to help a student learn how to use a communication device to interact with peers in community settings.

A second important focus for CBI is to help students learn to complete routines and activities that are or will be important to their participation in the community as adults. When CBI is used for this purpose, it should be anchored to the specific postschool outcomes described in the student's IEP. These outcomes might include getting a paid job prior to graduation, learning how to ride the bus or train, or being able to use an automatic teller machine (ATM). In these cases, the teacher should design CBI so that it not only results in reliable performance, but that the level of assistance and support required by the student is reduced to the minimum level necessary to maintain performance across time.

Whether CBI is designed to promote generalization of skills learned in school or to establish reliable performance of new activities, it should always be structured to maximize the participation of students in the social networks of the school and community. From the outset, CBI should be designed to establish the student's connection with the natural supports available from friends, peers, community members, and family. CBI should supplement rather supplant the help, assistance, and guidance that can be provided by these individuals.

WHEN SHOULD COMMUNITY-BASED INSTRUCTION BE PROVIDED?

The decision to provide CBI to students should be made by the IEP team. In general, CBI will become more important as students approach graduation and as the focus of their educational program shifts to their ultimate transition from school to community life. Although there are no hard and fast rules, it is generally recommended that CBI be a major part of most 19- to 22–year-old students' educational programs. CBI is an important tool in helping them obtain a satisfying job, live in their own home, and develop a rich social life. For younger students, CBI should be balanced with their participation in general education classes and the general education curriculum. CBI can be an important means to enhance the relevance of what students learn in general education classes.

HOW CAN I INCREASE THE EFFECTIVENESS OF COMMUNITY-BASED INSTRUCTION?

CBI is a useful way to teach students the skills they need for increased independence in the community. There are a number of ways that teachers can ensure that students are getting the most out of CBI.

Choose meaningful outcomes. CBI is an instructional strategy that is used to achieve specific learning outcomes for students. Increasingly, students, parents, and professionals are looking to the general education curriculum as the framework for defining what students should learn in school. In most states, the general education curriculum is organized around broad outcomes such as productivity and contribution, citizenship, and lifelong learning. The IEP team should ensure that CBI for student with disabilities is anchored as closely as possible to the learning outcomes expected for all students in the school.

By definition, meaningful educational outcomes are those that are important to students and their families. So, establishing the expected outcomes of CBI should reflect the values, preferences, and expectations of the student and his/her family. The overall goal is to use CBI in ways that will improve the immediate and future quality of life of students in the community. To accomplish this, CBI must be tailored to students' specific strengths and needs, reflect their age and their peer group, and build on the opportunities and resources that are available in the community that they live.

Tap into the general education curriculum whenever possible to provide CBI. Even with the increasing pressure of high-stakes testing in general education, most professionals and policymakers have embraced the importance of anchoring the curriculum to the demands of adulthood and citizenship. For example, in most high schools there are a number of courses that are directly linked to local, state, and national school-to-work initiatives. These courses are designed to help students select careers and help them learn the academic, work, and social skills necessary to succeed. In many cases, CBI is a key component of these programs and can provide the base for providing students with disabilities instruction on a number of important employment, personal management, and leisure activities.

Another option for CBI in the general education curriculum is service learning. Today, service learning is seen as more than just a way for students to give back to the community; it is a way for students to apply the knowledge and skills learned in school to real-life problems and needs. The characteristics of effective service learning programs include: 1) developing specific learning goals and objectives that are linked to the curriculum; 2) cooperative planning, implementation, and evaluation of the project by all students; and 3) flexibility in determining the roles and contributions of each student in achieving the project's goals. These elements of service learning make it an excellent option for achieving the mutual goals of inclusion and CBI for students.

Many school districts around the country are developing concurrent enrollment programs with local universities and colleges. These programs allow students to access university or college classes for credit while enrolled in their final years of high school (e.g., ages 18–21). These programs often include a specific list of courses in selected subject areas that are considered critical by the local school district for postsecondary education or career success. Increasingly however, many concurrent enrollment agreements are broader and allow students to take any course that may contribute to achieving their postschool goals. As such, concurrent enrollment programs provide a vast number of opportunities to provide CBI to students with disabilities. For example, if students enrolled in an aerobics class at the community college could receive instruction that would improve their health and increase leisure options, they also could be provided CBI on activities that would be necessary for them to participate in the class, ranging from riding the bus to purchasing a bottle of water in the restaurants in the student union.

Finally, general and special educators must collaborate to incorporate opportunities for CBI for all students in general education classes. A number of approaches have been used, ranging from the use of research teams that allow students to go into community settings to collect data on a specific problem (e.g., observations, interviews) and generate viable solutions to the use of community-based assessments in which students must demonstrate mastery of knowledge and skills learned in the class.

Some advocates have expressed concern that CBI may be incompatible with the intent of inclusive education, because it removes students from typical school settings. However, most 18–22 year old students without disabilities do not attend high schools; therefore, pursuing community-based options at that stage of a student's school career is more age-appropriate than remaining in the high school all day. The move in general education toward anchoring the curriculum to the demands of adulthood and citizenship creates new options for students with disabilities to receive CBI to varying and individually determined levels across the age span. The challenge to students, parents, and teacher is to use the available range of alternatives to ensure that students can achieve their postschool goals.

Link CBI to students' neighborhoods and communities. CBI is most effective when it is done in the neighborhoods and communities where students live. This approach to CBI has several advantages. First, it allows the skills that students are learning in school to have an immediate impact on their day-to-day quality of life, by increasing their access to the resources that are available to all community members. Second, it can help students and their families to develop an awareness of the community resources that can inform their decisions about postschool goals and the types of supports that students will need in adulthood. Third, focusing CBI on where students live creates the opportunity to build on the natural supports available from neighbors, business people, and other relevant community members. Finally, it makes it more realistic for parents and families to support students' participation in activities, and to provide the opportunities for skills to be practiced.

Use peer as mentors and for support. You can increase the effectiveness of CBI by involving same-age peers. This might include volunteers, peer tutors, or other community members such as co-workers at a job site who are of a similar age. There are several ways in which peer mentorship can enhance CBI. Peers can serve as role models who can set an example of appropriate communication and social behaviors in community settings, they can facilitate students' involvement in typical social networks, and they can provide assistance and support to the student in completing community activities. Peers can also be trained to provide direct instruction to students to complete important personal management and leisure activities. For some activities and in some settings, like going to an aerobics class at the community college, peers may be more socially acceptable instructors than paid staff from the school. CBI provided by peers may also be more motivating to students, because it creates opportunities for age-appropriate social interactions and the development of friendships.

Use effective teaching methods. CBI can be a time consuming and potentially staff-intensive teaching approach, so it only makes sense to use instructional strategies that will make the most of these investments. The research base on CBI is quite extensive (McDonnell, 2003; Rosenthal-Malek & Bloom, 1998). Here are some general recommendations that teachers should follow in designing CBI for students:

1. Sample the range of settings and environments that student will be expected to use day to day during instruction.

Frequently, we want students to complete activities and skills in a variety of settings and contexts. For example, we probably would want students to be able to use a variety of ATMs, not just the one located near school. Research suggests that the best way to promote generalization is to structure our teaching programs so that students are exposed to the natural variation that we will find in the community. So in teaching ATMs we would want to make sure that students were asked to use ATMs from all of the banks and credit unions most commonly found in their neighborhood and community.

2. Use response prompting and fading strategies that promote errorless learning during the initial phase of instruction.

Research suggests that we can increase the efficacy of our teaching if we provide assistance to students before they make errors and then systematically reduce our assistance across time. A number of strategies have been suggested for achieving this, including the system of most-to-least prompts, graduated guidance, and time delay.

3. Systematically correct errors when they do occur.

Accomplishing this requires that the incorrect response be interrupted as quickly as possible, providing clear feedback to the student that their response was incorrect, and then providing assistance to the student to complete the correct response before moving on.

4. Use natural reinforcers.

CBI should be designed to tap into the reinforcers that are typically available in the setting. For example, learning to use restaurants to purchase lunch has a number of "natural" reinforcers, like eating things we enjoy and socializing with friends. Teachers must look for these natural reinforcers and use them systematically to help the student learn activities faster.

5. Provide enough instruction to promote acquisition of the skills.

Unlike school-based instruction, the complexity of the skills being taught and the logistics of CBI (e.g., traveling from school to a community site and back) often limit the number of opportunities that students can be provided to practice skills during an instructional session. In addition, students' participation in general education classes may limit the amount of time available each week for CBI. Although there are no easy solutions to this problem, we generally recommend that teachers provide more instruction on fewer community-based activities, to ensure that students can receive the amount of instruction necessary to promote acquisition. For example, instead of providing instruction on three or four community-based activities once a week, provide instruction on one key activity several times per week. This is more easily accomplished if the IEP team prioritizes the goals that require CBI when students' IEPs are developed, so teachers know what to work on first.

6. Collect student performance data and use it.

The only way to know if students are moving toward their goals is to collect data and to review their progress regularly. The most effective way to do this is by collecting information about their performance before the lessons start (i.e., baseline), and then again on regular intervals during CBI. These data should be used to determine if the student is making adequate progress, and if not, used to identify problem areas and make systematic changes in the teaching methods.

7. Embed instruction on academic, communication, social, and self-determination skills within CBI.

CBI offers an ideal platform for embedding instruction on a range of skills that will help your students become more effective and independent participants in their communities. Academic skills, such as math, reading, social studies, history, and science can be embedded in CBI by identifying natural opportunities within activities for the student to apply them. For example, instruction on the effects of cholesterol on the body that students are learning in their health and nutrition class could easily be embedded within CBI in grocery stores, by having students read the information from the nutritional panel on the packages. Community activities also provide a number of chances to embed instruction on communication and social skills. Finally, instruction on self-determination skills, ranging from making choices to self-advocacy, can be embedded within CBI. You can make the most of CBI if you keep a keen eye open for opportunities to embed instruction on these important skills.

8. Promote student independence and autonomy.

CBI should be focused on helping students to move toward greater independence as they prepare for adulthood. In evaluating the effectiveness of CBI, we should not only look at whether students can complete the activity accurately or generalize skills across settings, but whether they can do things by themselves. Consequently, a primary goal of CBI is to foster the greatest possible level of student independence in the community. This requires that support from school staff and peer tutors is reduced to the lowest possible levels. Of course, there are always concerns about the potential for injury or harm as students become more independent in the community. But as Robert Perske reminded us many years ago, these dangers are inherent in all activities for all people (Perske, 1972). He argued that if we deny independence to students based on our fears, then we deny them the "dignity of risk" that we all enjoy as adults. CBI must be carefully designed to minimize these risks for students, but it also must enable them to become as independent as possible.

9. Build natural supports for long-term performance.

One of the fundamental benefits of CBI is the opportunity to build "bridges of support" in the community that your students will access after graduation. Natural supports, offered by peers, family, co-workers, or community members, have shown to be a great asset for students as they transition out of school and into adult roles. To establish natural supports, the IEP team must first determine when students will need support in specific community settings. Once this is done, the teacher can begin to identify individuals within the environment who are able and willing to provide support. The final step in this bridge-building process is to provide information, training, and support to the individuals who are willing to help. However, effective natural supports are based on reciprocal and mutually satisfying personal relationships between people. Make sure to help your students develop the skills and abilities to maintain these relationships as they transition from school into adulthood.

Selected References

McDonnell, J. (2003). Secondary programs. In J. McDonnell, M. L. Hardman, and A. P. McDonnell (Eds.), *An introduction to persons with moderate and severe disabilities* (pp. 307–330). Upper Saddle River, NJ: Allyn & Bacon.

Perske, R. (1972). The dignity of risk and the mentally retarded. *Mental Retardation, 10,* 24–27.

Rosenthal-Malek, A., & Bloom, A. (1998). Beyond acquisition: Teaching generalization for students with developmental disabilities. In A. Hilton & R. Ringlaben (Eds.), *Best and promising practices in developmental disabilities* (pp. 408–429). Austin, TX: PRO-ED.

Test, D.W., & Spooner, F. (1996). *Community-based instructional support.* Washington, DC: American Association on Mental Retardation.

Quick-Guide Extra #3

Simple Technology
to Encourage Participation

June E. Downing

Quick-Guides to Inclusion
Ideas for Educating Students with Disabilities, Second Edition

Michael F. Giangreco & Mary Beth Doyle

Editors

Simple technology is any tool that can support a student's access to and participation in school, home, or community activities. It can be something as simple as a rubber grabber to open jars or a recorded passage in a book that a student can activate with a switch. In general, such simple technology does not need to be expensive or difficult to use. With the help of your team members, you can identify or create an array of simple devices at minimal expense. Other commercially available technological aids can be purchased relatively inexpensively.

We all use simple technology to make our lives easier. Some people make use of wrist supports at their keyboard to ease typing. We use highlighters to draw our attention to certain words and phrases in books, and clips in books help us find our spot to begin reading again. Our homes and schools are filled with various gadgets that help make our lives easier.

PURPOSE OF SIMPLE TECHNOLOGY

In general, simple technology supports your students to: 1) physically access materials used in tasks (e.g., slant board to hold materials at a better angle), 2) make tasks easier to accomplish (e.g., page separators to ease page turning and special grips on pens, markers), 3) facilitate partial participation (e.g., a batting tee for hitting a stationary ball), and 4) make tasks more fun (e.g., a spinner to randomly select a student to read). Some students with disabilities may not be able to perform all steps in an activity unless you make specific accommodations or modifications. Simple technology allows greater participation and success in activities that otherwise would not be accessible to them. You don't want students just sitting there watching what others are doing. So using simple technology in the classroom can increase their active involvement. Of course each student is different, so what works will be determined by student's physical, sensory, and cognitive characteristics as well as the demands of the activity and the environment. Almost anything goes, so it's a good way to hone creative skills and try things out. Don't be afraid to try something and then modify as needed.

GENERAL CONSIDERATIONS FOR THE USE OF SIMPLE TECHNOLOGY

Almost anything can be developed and used as a form of assistive technology. Here are some general considerations.

Age appropriateness: Consider the chronological age of the student before applying the use of adapted technology. As much as possible, make every effort to avoid having the student appear more juvenile as the result of using the device. For example, attaching a Barney (the big purple dinosaur) key ring to a high school student's jacket to help him zip and unzip it might work, but won't do anything to enhance his image. A large ski lift ticket might work just as well and attract much less negative attention. A general rule is to consider whether other students you teach would feel comfortable using the adaptation or not.

Student preference: Whenever possible, it is important to seek students' input regarding whether or not they would like to use the offered technology. Students have individual preferences and may not like the accommodation, even if it would make the task easier to perform. For instance, some students may reject the use of a slant board or large handgrips because they don't see their classmates using them. The importance of looking like the peer group can easily outweigh enhanced access. Sometimes just the physical appearance (e.g., size, color) might not be appealing to a particular student, who may then reject it. Therefore, think of asking the student's preference and approval as part of the development of the device. Also, encourage other classmates to use the technology at times (even though not needed); this can help ease the discomfort of "standing out."

Beneficial to all students: To counter the potential challenge of making a particular student look different in a negative way, make it acceptable for all students to use the assistive technology. Several of your students may benefit from pencil/pen grips, extra large zipper grips, footstools to rest their feet on, and extra high intensity light on their work. They also can use and enjoy switch-activated devices (e.g., scissors, staplers, pencil sharpeners) even if they don't need to use such devices. If you encourage all students to use this equipment, it can serve as a model for the students who really do need it.

SIMPLE TECHNOLOGY TO ENHANCE PHYSICAL ACCESS

Several accommodations can be used across activities to make tasks physically easier to perform. For example, various handgrips can be attached to pencils, pens, paintbrushes, markers and other such implements. They can also be used with forks, knives, and spoons at mealtimes. Such grips can be commercially purchased or created for your student using pipe insulation, foam rubber, clay, play dough, or even a washcloth wrapped around an implement and held in place with duct tape. The purpose of such grips is to make it considerably easier for the student to grasp the item. Likewise, large zipper pulls can be added to jackets, backpacks, or anything that uses a zipper to allow for an easier grasp that a student can manage. These can be made or purchased commercially, and the student should be allowed to select what is preferred.

Often turning pages in a book or magazine can be very difficult for a student who has challenges with fine motor skills. Page separators or page fluffers (simple aids to separate pages) can be added to pages so that a student has a much easier time turning one page at a time. A page-fluffer can be made from a tongue depressor with foam rubber or Styrofoam or dried sponge glued on it with the tongue depressor sticking out from each page, drawing visual attention as well as allowing the student to use it to push the page over. For books that are made by the student, a permanent page-fluffer can be added to each page. For library books or texts that do not belong to the student, the tongue depressor (with the thick or thin piece of foam rubber) can be glued onto a small piece of cardboard or file folder and that piece in turn paper clipped to each page. You can use large plastic and colorful paper clips in place of the tongue depressors if preferred. Page fluffers can be kept in a plastic bag and given to a peer to quickly affix to each page of a book as needed. At times it may be possible to tear a magazine or something similar apart and replace each page in a large photograph album that allows viewing but provides a thicker page for the student to turn. A simple bookmark or sticky tab can be used on pages to help students find a particular page if fine motor skills are not an issue.

Due to a physical or visual impairment, a student may need work elevated for easier access. A slant board can be commercially purchased or created inexpensively through the use of a large notebook (at least 3-inch binder) to hold work at a better angle for a student. Office supply stores also sell simple devices that hold paper at a vertical angle for better viewing. Such devices can be adapted to meet the needs of particular students. Also, some books tend to close and not remain open. When a student is unable to keep the book from closing, it might be helpful to replace the binding with simple rings and hole-punch the pages to allow the book to lie flat. Actually, this makes it easier for everyone.

Stabilizing materials: If the problem is keeping materials on the desk (and not rolling off), a very simple accommodation to hold material still on a desk or tabletop is the use of non-skid material (e.g., rubberized placemat) or suction pads or cups. Such nonskid material can hold paper, bowls, plates, and math manipulatives in place. This is particularly advantageous when a student's physical disability causes her to push materials away in a reflexive manner. If a student has difficulty staying in a recommended position in a wheelchair or other adapted seating, using nonskid material for the student to sit on can prevent the student from slipping into an uncomfortable position.

A sticky adhesive putty (e.g., *HandiTak*®) or double-sided tape can be a great inexpensive resource to hold items in place for a student, or to allow that student to write by sequencing pictures on paper using a bit of adhesive (putty or tape) to hold them on the paper. While glue can always be used, it is messier, and sticky adhesives make it possible to move pictures and fix mistakes a lot easier. *HandiTak*® also works quite well with small items, so that if a student is creating a tactile illustration for a book or report, she can use *HandiTak*® to do so.

Operating equipment: Some students in your class may really enjoy helping you turn on various pieces of equipment, such as slide projectors, overhead projectors, cassette recorders, or fans. With the assistance of your special educator, very simple switch technology can be obtained to allow students with significant physical impairments to activate such equipment. The student can use a hand or elbow or head or foot to press a switch that can turn on the equipment for the rest of the class. A control unit through a company such as *Ablenet*™ (see "Selected Resources") can allow you to set the time that the device operates before turning off. This is desirable so that you can call on the student again to turn it back on. Switches also can be used to cut out words or pictures when they are paired with battery-operated scissors, or they can be used with an electric pencil sharpener when students need this piece of equipment.

SIMPLE TECHNOLOGY TO SUPPORT COMMUNICATION

While most students will use speech to express themselves, a few students with severe physical and/or cognitive disabilities may not use speech at all (or only minimally). Although at times you may be thinking of ways to get your students to be less talkative, your students who do not use speech need to be encouraged to communicate with you and their classmates. Be sure to confer with your special educator and speech-language pathologist to help provide your students with ways to communicate. You can make use of inexpensive technology, such as talking photo frames, to support your students' requests for a break, attention, or help. Adding pictures with a printed message to these types of communicative aids can help to clarify the message for everyone. When students are out on the playground, or where it is difficult to hold on to and handle devices, see if they would wear a wristband made of terrycloth that can hold a pictorial/written message that the student may want to make use of (e.g., "I'd like to talk with you." or "Want to play?"). Similar messages could be attached to a simple keychain and clipped to a belt loop to make it more portable for a student. Observe your students and see where you feel they need to be able to say something to you or their peers. Then share these occasions with the special educator and speech/language pathologist to get additional input.

Students typically love talking about their interests and what's happening at school. Without speech, this becomes quite difficult, and so some of your students may end up just listening to others. The same technology as mentioned above, in the form of talking photograph albums, can be used to give the students a way to share stories, ideas, and events with classmates. Ask parents and family members for photographs of things that the student likes to do or collect, as well as photographs of family members and pets. You can put these photographs in a talking photograph album with the comment and/or question clearly written, and ask a classmate or friend of the same gender to record the messages. Your student without a voice can then sit down with classmates and share personal interests and ask them related questions that help support friendly social interactions.

You can also use such simple voice-output devices, such as talking photo frames, to let your student who does not have speech comment on peers' work or ask to see what they are doing or request help as needed. With devices such as the *Step by Step communicator* from *Ablenet*™ (see "Selected Resources"), you can record different steps of an activity, such as conducting a science experiment, following a recipe, cleaning up, or speaking sequential lines in a play. The student not using speech will hit the sequencer each time a new step to the procedure or line in the play is needed. In this way, the student is a very critical part of the activity, regardless of not being able to use speech. Always make sure that the accompanying picture and written message are clear, to aid in your student's understanding and to support literacy. Of course, all students need to request breaks, especially when becoming frustrated or fatigued. If you make sure that your student has a way to request a break by using an appropriate device, you may see less types of behavior that you do not want to see.

SIMPLE TECHNOLOGY TO SUPPORT READING

Some students in your class may not be able to read in a conventional manner, or may be reading well below grade level. These students will need alternative ways to participate in oral readings and to benefit from reading instruction. Very simple technology in the form of a cassette recorder and adaptive switch can be used to give students a voice in oral reading situations. A predetermined section of the story or text can be recorded by a very capable reader, and when it comes time to read that passage, you can call on the student who will activate the switch. While this particular student is not actually reading, she will need to attend and respond appropriately when you call on her. By doing this, you demonstrate to all of your students that everyone is expected to participate in oral reading. If you have access to *Ablenet's*™ *Bookworm* (see "Selected Resources"), you can use this device to record each page of a short book and attach it so that the student is required to activate each page to hear it read. Your students who read well may really like to record each page for a student who does not read.

The *LeapPad*® books are one form of simple technology that allows students to access core curriculum that has been modified to make it simple and added voice output. *LeapPad*® is also highly interactive, and students in general seem to enjoy its use. Classic literature from elementary through high school has been adapted to go with the *LeapPad*® system that reads the adapted books, spells certain words, and asks questions of the reader. *LeapPad*® books deal with basic literacy skills (e.g., phonemic awareness), storybooks, classic literature, and also topics of the human body, geography, science, and many other subjects across the age range (K–12th grade). These books are fun, relatively inexpensive, and can support the learning of a wide range of students.

A *Language Master* (sometimes called an audio card reader) is another simple tool that you can use to teach students key words from texts or facts from stories. Recording on the individual cards is quite easy, and students like to do this. Add pictures to the cards as needed to help the student who does not read conventionally. You can record questions on these cards and have the student with disabilities use them to ask questions of their peers. You can be quite creative with this simple technology to address a number of different skill areas.

Sometimes what is needed is a quick way to help students focus on the pertinent information (e.g., new words, text to be read). Simple technology in the form of erasable highlighters, highlighting tape, highlighted lines or bold line on transparencies (to put over the printed page), or a "window" cut out of a solid sheet of paper can all be used to draw the student's attention to what is most critical to read. These are also temporary in nature, so that you don't create permanent change to any text or library book.

SIMPLE TECHNOLOGY FOR WRITING

Simple technology, such as various handgrips added to pens or pencils, can ease the challenge of writing for many students whether or not they have disabilities. Some of your students however, may be much more successful if allowed to write with a computer and keyboard or adapted keyboards such as *AlphaSmart*™ boards. You can add key guards (plastic protectors that prevent all the keys from being pressed) to the keyboard if the student tends to lean on the board. You also can use tape or cardboard and block off certain keys that do not need to be used by the student, thus simplifying the task. Consider adding slightly larger letters with sticky backing to the keyboard, to make it a little easier for some students to identify letters. For some students, a common labeler is a great way to add words to their work.

Some of your students may need a somewhat unconventional way in which to write. Some students may like the fun aspect of linking letters or words together on cubes. You can encourage some students to write by sequencing letters or words on magnets. Magnetic-backed paper can be purchased, or you can use magnetic ads that come to your home for free. Just cover these with paper and you can add letters, words, or pictures to them. You can also encourage students to use adapted scissors (described earlier) to cut out pictures and complete written sentences with them.

SIMPLE TECHNOLOGY FOR SPELLING

Spelling activities typically occur in the elementary grades, and it can be challenging to include students who do not yet understand about letters and letter/sound associations. A simple device that spins when activated (e.g., an *All-Turn-It*® spinner from *Ablenet*™) provides a positive and fun way for a student to participate in some spelling activities. You can call on this student to press a switch that will activate the spinner, which randomly selects letters you have written on an overlay. Once a letter is selected, you can call on different students to name the letter, provide the associated sound, and think of a word that starts with that letter. During this time, the student who selected the letter can be asked to identify which picture (of two or three) starts with that letter. In this way you help everyone learn, albeit at different levels. You can use this spinning device to randomly select pictures that represent the week's spelling lesson. You can call on one student to spell the selected word, while a paraprofessional, special educator, or speech-language pathologist can ask the student who activated the spinner to listen to the word and find the representative picture (again from two or three options). Since you can easily change the overlays that go on this spinning device, you can adapt it to meet the needs of a number of different subjects. For example, you can use it to ask questions in biology, earth science, English, or government (or present the answers and ask your students to come up with the questions).

It can be fun to use the format of a TV show, like Wheel of Fortune, for a spelling lesson. You can replicate a simplified version of the wheel that shows letters, the word consonant, and vowel. Students try to decipher their spelling words by spinning the wheel and buying a consonant, vowel, or a particular letter (depending on what is randomly selected). While your student with disabilities may not be able to spell the words, he can learn to identify individual letters and colors on the wheel, and he may participate more by being allowed to spin the wheel.

A *Language Master* or audio card reader (described earlier) can motivate some students to learn their spelling words. Pictures of the words can be glued onto the front of the card, and the student who is learning pictorial information can be asked to identify a particular spelling word by pointing to the appropriate card. A peer partner who is working on spelling can then spell the word identified by the picture. Both students can check to see if they are correct by running the card through the card reader for the auditory output. In this way, you can successfully pair students with quite different learning needs.

SIMPLE TECHNOLOGY TO SUPPORT PARTICIPATION FOR MATH

All students can use some of the same simple technologies described earlier to teach math skills and facilitate active participation. Students just learning to identify numbers can supply you with the numbers you can use to demonstrate a specific math problem (from simple multiplication and division to algebraic equations). You can put specific positive or negative numbers onto an *All-Turn-It*® spinner by *Ablenet*™ and ask the student with severe disabilities to give you a number as needed during your class demonstration. This student will activate a switch to turn the spinner and randomly select a number. While you are using this number in your demonstration, the paraprofessional or special educator can place this number with two or three other numbers and ask the student to find the desired number. This same random selection of numbers for you to use in your whole class demonstrations can be done with the use of a magnetic wand and numbers written on small pieces of paper that hold a paper clip. When you call on the student to give you a number to use, the student would "go fish" for a number. Whoever is assisting this student could then ask the student to match this number to one of three possible numbers or to the appropriate number of manipulative materials, so that this student is also engaged in learning math.

Some students really enjoy hearing auditory feedback for their efforts, and so using a voice output calculator that is somewhat enlarged for ease of use is recommended. You can ask the student to check his peers' work when requested to help them work cooperatively. One of your students on grade level would do the mental math, and then your student who is learning to identify or match numbers would be asked to find the particular numbers in the equation using the talking calculator. In this manner, you can support peer interactions and provide the necessary math challenge for both students.

The use of common items to make math more fun can also help the student who is learning basic math facts. Students can make use of large dice to count the dots and play adding or multiplying games (e.g., first student of three to reach a certain number). One student can pick up the dice, roll, and count the numbers, and the other students can do the math. You can make or buy enlarged playing cards and dominoes to provide easier visual access and physical handling, and teach various skills in math while also encouraging peers to interact and support one another. A simple adapted abacus with beads on a single wire can help support a student who needs to count and compare numbers tactilely. For example, during a basketball game, one student who is blind and nonambulatory keeps track of the score by moving two beads to either side of the abacus as directed by a peer.

SUMMARY

Simple technology exists all around us. Creative use of simple, everyday material can greatly facilitate the active participation of certain students in all curricular areas, while adding to the enjoyment of all students. In general, while anything can be used, it is important to remember to make it look as age-appropriate as possible (not too juvenile), keep it simple, and make sure that it does not make the student stick out more than need be. While the adaptation should definitely be individualized to meet the unique needs of a particular student, it's fine to use it with other students as well. The use of the technological aid should make it more interesting and possibly more fun for all students in the classroom. As a result, you can support the active participation and learning for all of your students. So just go ahead and be creative!

Selected Resources

Ablenet, Inc. at http://www.ablenetinc.com to find the *All-Turn-It®* spinner, battery-operated scissors, various switches, battery interrupters, and control units.

Assistive Technology, Inc. at http://www.assistivetech.com to obtain information on assistive technology issues and uses.

Don Johnston, Inc. at http://www.donjohnston.com to find specialized software programs and adapted books for different-age students.

Enabling devices at http://enablingdevices.com to find affordable assistive and learning devices, unique switches, and some communication devices.

Leapfrog at http://www.leapfrog.com to find adapted stories, novels, and the *LeapPad®* that provides voice-output for these adapted materials.

PCI catalogues at http://www.pcieducation.com to find adapted novels, language master, or audio card reader, and other adapted materials at various age levels.

RJCooper at http://www.rjcooper.com for suction pads, switches, keyboard covers, and other adaptive technology.

Tash, Inc. at http://www.tashinc.com/index.html to obtain a variety of different types of switches and other adapted aids.